A
Mountain Harvest
Cookbook

A Mountain Harvest Cookbook

ROBERTA SICKLER

Illustrated by Jeff Jones

DOUBLEDAY & COMPANY, INC.
Garden City, New York • 1985

Copyright © 1985 by Roberta Sickler

Library of Congress Cataloging in Publication Data

Sickler, Roberta.
  A mountain harvest cookbook.

  Includes index.
  1. Cookery (Natural foods)   I. Title.
TX741.S56   1985   641.5'637   82-45273
ISBN 0-385-18235-X

Printed in the United States of America

Designed by Judith Neuman

First Printing

Preface

Along the Esopus Creek banks, in the lap of the eastern ridges of the northern Catskill Mountains, ancient people established everyday life in peaceful rhythm with ever-changing seasons. A harbinger of spring, the sugar maple tree gave them sugar, the creek, its spangled trout. Meadows yielded spices and healing herbs. Corn came out of the mud in summer and cranberries in the fall, as the maple trees painted the forested hillsides in fiery colors.

These native Mohegan people lived in the shadow of an imposing wall of blue mountains that displayed an awesome seasonal spectacle. This was known as Onteora, Land in the Sky. The people saw the primeval bluffs, gnarled, overgrown, and venerable with age, as the home of the temperamental spirit father of the Mohegan, Manitou. From his lair in the blue shadow of thick hemlock forests, Manitou haunted the dark ravines with gnawing rains. He raged with hungry winds that billowed from the mountain shoulders, and ruled the forests with wolves and bobcats. The dark slopes, where wild mountain springs gushed from the rocks, were hidden under impenetrable entanglements of vines and branches. Deer, turkeys, fox, and bear were Manitou's gifts, scattered through the gloomy trees for the solemn and consecrated hunt. Winter for the native people brought hunting excursions to the mysterious Land in the Sky, a rationing of provisions, the warmth of the fire, and a time for reflection and retelling of ancient legends.

Many seasons passed this way . . . then one day English explorers made their way up the great river that caught the mountain streams. They named the river Hudson, and claimed, by declaration of the queen, millions of acres of this sacred land. Wealthy land barons then brought European peasant farmers, Dutch, Germans, then Welsh, Irish, and their black slaves to carve into the heart of the mountains, forge roads, and clear the land for farming and small industry. Axes fell; cabins and barns were raised, babies born. The successions of plantings and harvests in this grim wilderness were marked by celebrations, struggles, and deaths, and interwove the fibers of many folk traditions. There was generated a landscape of legends that left deep impressions on the regional identity. Dutch names mingled with Indian words. Hollows and creeks were called after their wild inhabitants or first human settlers. Catskill, dark home of wildcats and rushing streams, was the official name substituted for the old Dutch popular name, "Blew Mountains." Celtic song, craft, and mysticism found a comfortable home in the Catskills, as in other colonies throughout the Appalachian Range. These cultural practices were layered with superstitious Dutch folklore, the German Christmas, English gardening and architecture, and native Indian wisdom.

Woodstock began as an Indian hunting campsite clearing, cupped in the arms of adjoining mountain slopes. The clearing became a legendary crossroads for trappers, traders, travelers, and scouts from the new colonies. Up from the river along the banks of Sawkill Creek, pioneer tenant farmers forged a pathway into a road. Dutch-speaking families cleared the hillsides and built houses from stone pulled out of newly plowed soil. Surviving the Revolution as a frontier settlement, Woodstock developed its sawmills and glass factories along the creek, with tanneries and blue stone quarries up in the mountains. A natural outgrowth of abundant resources, these industries balanced the difficult agrarian economy and contributed to a new and growing nation.

But resources were eventually exhausted, and small forests reclaimed the abandoned clearings. People who remained near the village gleaned sustenance from their land and a sustained practice of artistry and craft. In time, with the advent of trains and passenger river boats, urban dwellers were drawn to visit the rare rustic beauty of the region. The age of the elegant mountain resort hotels was born, beginning a tradition of pilgrimage to this wilderness preserve. From crowded Eastern cities the mountains and their settlement clearings drew romantics, nature students, and wealthy vacationers, a legend in themselves. They sought refuge in woodland isolation, or in community with artists. Jews, Italians, and others, both rich and working-class from the urban immigrant population, influenced the flavor, expanded the arts, and deepened the mythic character of the region.

Many visitors stayed on in Woodstock to enjoy quiet isolation, with convenient proximity to the world of New York City. Writers, painters, and sculptors came to live in the grace of Overlook Mountain. Along the bluffs of Byrdcliff and Rock City, in the wooded Maverick hillside, people lived in rough barns and hand-built cottages. Through rugged winters, sharing the disciplines of aesthetic vision, the creatively active community soon developed a climate of universality, protective toward the eccentric, a nest for the imagination. Musicians came to add energy to every village event, prevailing with a sparkling night life. Out of a history of community support in difficult times, the performance of music for the benefit of many causes came into practice. The quiet settlement soon characterized emerging values, tastes, and trends of the mid-twentieth century. At the threshold of a new human epoch, Woodstock gave its name to a regional gathering of multitudes in the joyful three-day celebration of peace and music.

In the blossoming of its legend, Woodstock, still a small town, is a living paradox. Visionaries, painters, musicians, and crafts-people, comfortable in a community of fellows, struggle to pre-serve a quaint old village life, while streams of curious visitors bring a kaleidoscope of cosmopolitan impressions. A cultural crossroads of our time, Woodstock hosts a new generation, nes-tled in the mountainside, with vintage galleries, slick shops, solar houses, woodland recording studios, and mountain shrines. Sea-sonal culture-heroes and seasoned old-settlement descendants now call Woodstock home. As former visitors continue to return and settle in the Catskill region, they fulfill an ancient myth: the overwhelming power of Manitou and Onteora, Land in the Sky, will cause you to leave a part of yourself here, to which you must always return.

For those who reside in the Woodstock area, there is a shared love for the wilderness. In the unstable economy of today, people again turn to their gardens. There is security in greater economic independence, and a place for solitude and sanctuary among succulent vegetable plants and glorious flowers. The gardener touches the earth and plays a greater role in his or her own destiny. Harvesting, preserving, and eating of the foods grown here, the gardener is part of the old lore of the mountains.

A MOUNTAIN HARVEST COOKBOOK presents elements of real lives, gardens and children, snow and sky, craft and feasting, woven with shadows of the past into formulas for recipes. Within a seasonal setting, this collection is a sampler to praise the glory of the seasons and the wisdom of community. It is for those who would seek peace and the fruitful integration of family, work, and nature.

Acknowledgments

Thanks to the people who inspired unwritten ideas that contributed wealth to the spirit of this book.

JAN REDMANE: *Watercress and Beet Salad • Springtime Tofu-Noodle Medley • Linguine with Shellfish • Rhubarb Fool • Sesame Pancakes with Stir-fried Vegetables • Strawberry Romaine Salad • Port Plum Jam • Fresh Tomato and Eggplant Pizza • Tofu and Broccoli with Spicy Peanut Sauce • Braised Tofu with Eggplant and Chick-peas • Broiled Sole with Basil • Roasted Pepper Salad • Summer Salad Mandala • Walnut Cheese Crackers • Blackberry Lime Mousse • Savory Pumpkin Pastries • Mushroom-Hazelnut Soup • Buckwheat Cakes with Wild Mushrooms • Woodland Sauté • Pumpkin-Rum Pudding • Squash and Apple Soup • Eggplant Soup au Gratin • Scallop Bisque • Autumn Couscous • Broiled Salmon with Garden Garnish • Baked Vegetables Catalán • Aubergine Zinfonia • Parsnip Salad • Carrot Mayonnaise • Equinox Salad • Sesame-Anise Bread • Plum Tart • Chocolate-Raspberry Fantasia*

LEA ROSEN: *Creamy Green Asparagus Soup • Onion Cheese Pie with Spring Surprises • Asparagus Parmesan • Chinese Sour Soup • Spinach-Almond Lasagna • Catskill Enchiladas • Baked Bean and Apple Casserole • Apple Nut Strudel • Savory Borscht • Miso Vegetable Soup • Tofu Turkey • Sweet Potatoes Supreme • Beets in Orange Sauce • Maple Nut Cookies • Shepherd's Pie • Almond Chili • Tofu Cakes in Maple Sauce • Winter Vegetable Stir-fry*

CAROL ZALOOM: *Stuffed Grape Leaves • Mountain Creek Soup • Onion Miso Soufflé • Apple Orchard Stew • Parsley Confetti Noodles • Eggplant Sticks • Creamy Vegetable Pie • Tofu Stew with Dumplings • Savory Corn Bread Loaf • Dinner Omelet • Festive Lasagna • Moussaka • Stuffed Flounder Rolls with Mustard Sauce • Cabbage au Gratin • Tofu Gravy • Kitchen Garden Salad • Maple Rum Cake • Strawberry Snow*

SANDI ZINAMAN: *Pasta Primavera • Potatoes Stewed with Wine • Onion Rolls • Little Chocolate Cake • Pine Nut Cake with Pastry Cream • Pickled Snow Peas • Strawberry Rhubarb Jam • Peach Jam • Tomato Tart • Baked Bluefish Fillets with Cherry Tomato Sauce • Peach-Strawberry Mousse with Crème Fraîche • Raspberry Jam • Gazpacho • Pesto • Buttermilk Wheat Bread • Peach Hazelnut Cake • Wild Mushroom Sauce for Pasta • Dutch Apple Pancake • Eggplant Parmesan • Challah • Currant Bread • Saffron Wreath • Jam Tarts • Spicy Split-pea Soup • Onion Soup • Winter Tomato Sauce • Dark Herb Bread • Cracked-wheat Bread*

ADDITIONAL CONTRIBUTIONS

RITA BERMAN: *Pear Chutney* • *October Beet Salad* MERLE BORENSTEIN: *Marinated Broccoli in Tofu Sauce* • *Brussels Sprout and Walnut Salad* SUSAN CAREY: *Beet Preserves* • *Sautéed Puffballs* SHEILA CLARK: *Tofu Cheesecake* DIANE COLLIER: *Wedding Cake* ROCHELLE COOPER and PAN RESTAURANT, KINGSTON: *Cashew Carrot Soup* ENID HOFSTED: *Blueberry Coffee Cake* KATE KLUBER: *Canary Hill Burgers* BETTY MACDONALD: *Woodstock Dough* • *Hearty Potato Soup* ILKA SCOBIE: *Fried Trout* • *Baked Trout* • *Winter Cabbage* SANDEE SHAW: *Pear Ketchup* • *Vitality Burgers* • *Tofu Mayonnaise* BENITA CROW SHIRAH: *Skunk Hollow Pumpernickel* HELEN WEAVER: Woodstock's *Prizewinning Tofu–Sesame Paste Appetizer* • *Riverby Housewarming Salad* SUSUN WEED: *April Violet Salad* RUTH WELLS: *Scalloped Potatoes* WOODSTOCK HEALTH FOOD CENTER; JUDITH GLASEL and EVE JOICE: *Tempeh Spinach Dinner* • *Garden Tofu-Stuffed Tomatoes Woodstock: Recollection by Recipe,* by JEAN GAEDE: RUBY and LAUREN PETERS, *Frozen Trout*; BERT VAN KLEEK and RICHARD CRANE, *Hard Cider* WOODSTOCK SUNFLOWER DELI, DEBORAH MEYERS: *Mock Salmon* • *Chinese Vegetable Salad*

With special acknowledgment for their contributed expertise: Anita and Spider Barbour, Don Moore, Susun Weed, Sam Wenger.

Contents

NOTE: Wherever the name of a recipe is capitalized in the text, the recipe is included elsewhere in the book. Consult the Index for page numbers.

Introduction

In the decade following the legendary tent kitchens of open-air music festivals, there evolved a revitalized reverence for nature, expressed in a cuisine for the new age. People approached the bottom of the food chain for sustenance, and founded an ethic for consciously healthful cooking and eating. Fresh, clean, healthful garden produce became central to this ideal. The new alternative cuisine continues to develop, with the innovations of creative cooks and the influence of an international scope of cooking styles.

Out of the mountains and gardens of the Catskill-Woodstock region, there come a number of artist-cooks. Over the years community events, weddings, birthdays, outdoor concerts have dazzled with beautiful food offerings from expert and creative resident cooks. Coupling artistry with colorful lives, these people have developed their own family traditions and unique kitchen magic.

A MOUNTAIN HARVEST COOKBOOK is an excursion through some of these Woodstock area kitchens. From the creeks, meadows, and gardens, ingredients are gathered for a spectrum of originally interpreted classic recipes. Spicy appetizers, rich main dishes, warm breads, bright salads, and tasty, delicate desserts are a reflection of the searching, expressive, and diversified character of Woodstock people. A synthesis of influences from historic America, Europe, and the Orient, the recipes offer a complete cuisine, with nuts, grains, and dairy nutritionally balancing legumes and vegetables at the foundation. A small selection of seasonal fresh fish recipes provides a tempting choice for increasing numbers of basically vegetarian epicureans. Recipes are sprinkled with specialty foods, some exotic or in early acquaintance with the American palate. These, and all the ingredients in the recipes, are available almost everywhere in supermarkets or health food stores or specialty shops, as noted.

A MOUNTAIN HARVEST COOKBOOK glimpses the landscape and wildlife of the Catskill region through the progression of the four seasons. The natural year is born in the quiet pre-equinox days, when the sap rises in the trees, and day lilies are sprouting under the melting snow. In a flux between frost and clear white sunlight in capricious winds, spring days are nourished in the cadence of planting and foraging, with tart, wild greens, baby vegetables, and surpluses of eggs and milk from local farms.

Summer comes with blooming fields and gardens, and the invasion of many visitors to Woodstock. Festival is in the air; outdoor play and gardening share daily life under the sun. Sweet with fruits and flowers, the summer forage ripens to combine deliciously with early garden produce. The summer cuisine is a carousel of color and delightful crisp, bright flavors.

Autumn breathes over August days in the mountains until cool nights paint the landscape a circus of blazing color. The country table is spread with the ripe abundance of gardens and orchards, with the complements of wild flowering herbs and mushrooms. In the mood of the autumn spectacle, "All Hallow's Eve" is a high occasion in the Woodstock community, an outrageous night to enjoy unrestrained personal theater.

The approach of winter brings a sense of gloom, a reluctance for inevitable hardships that lay ahead. However, in some enchanted way the beauty of the holidays and quiet snowfalls induces a peace and pleasure belonging only to this season. There is comfort in the use of stocked foods from the garden, rich aromas of hearty soups and casseroles, and warming teas from the summer's dried herbs.

Following the cycle of the mountain garden, A MOUNTAIN HARVEST COOKBOOK guides the cook to a selection of recipes born of the season, to be savored with a taste of regional rural American life. Prepared and garnished to harmonize with the weather and seasonal activities, these recipes invite the feaster to the quiet, nurturing pleasures of nature's table. The imagination is welcomed in the substitution of available seasonal ingredients. Subtle embellishments inspired by a diversity of regions add to the ever-flowering celebration banquet set forth by A MOUNTAIN HARVEST COOKBOOK.

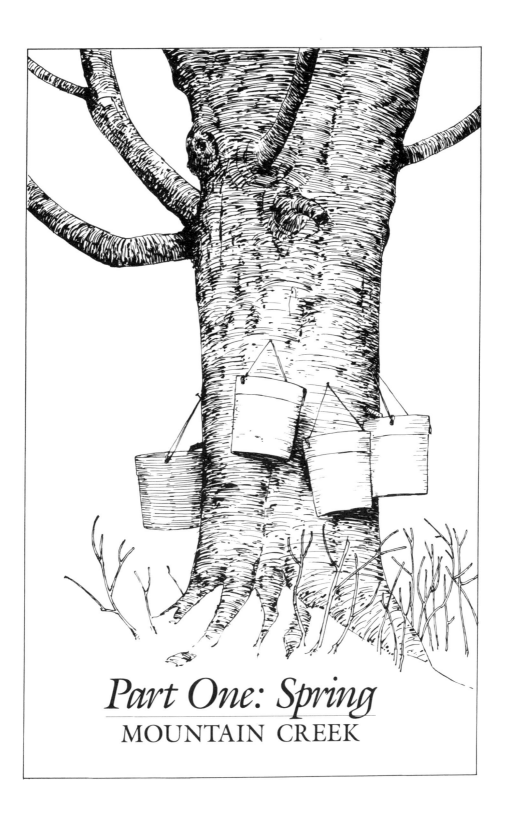

Part One: Spring
MOUNTAIN CREEK

Spring

Late February comes to Woodstock with a subtle breath of sweet air. Hearty greetings fill the street as familiar heads emerge from layers of wool and down to taste the promise of spring. Out of hibernation, from wood-heated mountainside cabins and studios, folks come with the smell of mud and fresh silvery sunlight. The sense of change in the air and the excitement of reunion inspires some to storytelling.

Along the News Shop counter gossip and tales of snowbound days flow over a hearty country breakfast and coffee. Spring is sought eagerly in talk of prospective gardens. Nature experts lend insights on the weather and progress of the spring thaw. A popular fantasy is revived, that some early spring, the community will be organized to tap the stately sugar maple trees that line the village streets in an old-time maple sugaring festival.

Up in the mountains, angry squalls defy the first hints of spring. A soft plump blizzard smothers roads and hollows. Through fat snowflakes in a glistening landscape, friends cross-country ski to call on neighbors.

A warm house, insulated with the quiet snow, welcomes vibrant conversation. Over mellow wine and homemade treats, there is hopeful speculation on the sap run and early return of the geese to Cooper Lake. The mountain view inspires the remembering of old Catskill folk legends.

The Sugar Maple Tree

Over abandoned farmland and uncut hardwood forests, lofty sugar maple trees raise great symmetrical oval crowns in a glowing invocation of spring. Warm breezes answer and loose themselves in a dance to herald the passing of winter.

Native Americans of the Northeast told that in the Beginning, Mother Earth gave forth a golden sweet syrup from within the maple tree that dripped on melting snows with the sun's first warming rays of spring. Woodland spirits disapproved, believing this treasure too great to bestow on humans. They showered the trees with their spirit water to thin the syrup to watery, clear sap. Now, the sweet mystery of maple lies veiled behind the great work required to obtain again the golden treasure Mother Earth first intended.

In Iroquois legend, a clever squaw first discovered maple syrup. One morning when going to fetch water, she found her birch-bark pail already full of a clear liquid. The liquid smelled clean and had a pleasant woody taste. To save herself a trip to the spring, the squaw cut up fresh-killed game, placed it in a clay pot, then covered it with the mysterious liquid. She hung the pot over her open fire to cook. It slowly simmered all day, and by evening yielded tender morsels of food under a thick, rich sauce.

Investigating the source of the wondrous cooking liquid, the Indians discovered that the husband's tomahawk had made a leaking gash in the tree where he had placed it the night before. Sap oozed from the gash to be caught in the bark pail that happened to stand directly below.

From then on Indians used maple syrup as a daily condiment. They cooked in the sap and even drank it directly from the tree as an energy-giving tonic. They sprinkled maple sugar over everything, and stored chunks as handy treats for fretting children.

Discovering that the sap ran in the last days of winter, the

Native Americans came to regard this season with joyous anticipation. Whole households tramped up to the woods through the snow for a jovial maple harvest celebration, the first important festival of the year. Early European settlers followed suit with wagons full of family and cooking vessels, marking the clearings with primitive winter shelters surrounding large open-pit fires. There must have been plenty of dancing to keep warm, and special, shared sweet moments with the first tasting of the dark elixir from the forest poured over pan-fried cakes with plenty of butter.

Long hours in the cold, snow, rain, and smoke, as the woodland spirits knew, serve to bring people in harmony with the same impulse in earth and sky that drew the first drops of sap out of the crotches and fissures of the trees, and onto the melting snows.

Up at the sugaring site, wood for the fires is stacked high in the late winter snow. Carefully chosen flat stones from a nearby dry wall, tapped into the right places, heal winter injuries in our homemade fireplace. A lashed slabwood three-sided shack is secured into place. A quick scouring readies the shallow evaporator pan and scavenged plastic buckets. We whittle and drill small sumac branches for spouts. Now, following the snowshoe path through the sugar bush, we tap the trees and hang the buckets.

In the still cold weeks of maple sugaring, one can sense the subtle beginnings of spring. Working each day to collect the liquid treasure from the trees, waiting in the warming rain as the sap boils, we watch the thaw and the arrival of robins, finches, larks, and bluebirds. Stoking the fires into the twilight, we hear the increasing intensity of mating chatter in the trees and the orchestration of swamp peepers. In a late night vigil, we watch evaporating sap billow into a great smoke cloud drifting up to the stars.

Tapping just one or two large sugar maple trees in your own yard revives the old American maple tradition, and may bring you as much as 1 or 2 gallons of premium-quality sweetener. Calculate obtaining about 1 gallon of syrup for every 30 to 40 gallons of sap collected, to determine scale of production. A family of four can be supplied with ample maple treats for a year by 1½ gallons of syrup.

Instead of making a gash, which may injure a tree, use an auger with a ½- to ¾-inch drill to carefully bore a hole into the tree's inner bark, allowing controlled drainage of sap. Drill 1 to 3 inches deep, depending on the size of the tree, cautiously avoiding the heart. Choose trees at least 12 inches in diameter, making multiple taps only in much larger trees. This kind of wound, if at least 6 inches away from last year's tap, or a newly drilled hole, will heal easily before the following season.

Spouts can be made from fresh-cut ¾-inch-thick sumac branches, about 4 to 6 inches long. Hollow out the soft core, and shave one end to a slight taper with a sharp knife. Insert the tapered end into the taphole and gently tap into a secure position with a wooden mallet, to channel the flow of sap from the tree into a bucket hung close beneath the spout. It is a good idea to improvise some sort of covering for the bucket, as protection from wet weather and to help keep out insects. Metal buckets with covers and spouts with hooks for a bucket handle may also be purchased at a local hardware store.

Native and Early American colonists, using open fires, dropped hot stones into their bark or clay pots to evaporate the sap they contained. We have the advantage of having large, broad basins, tubs, or shallow stainless steel pans available to hold sap and sustain direct heat for boiling. A simple slabwood, tar-papered lean-to will serve as an adequate "sugar shack." It will shelter the product from rain, and help conserve fuel and heat by enclosing the fire. You may choose an improvised outdoor fireplace with a tarpaulin raised over the area for weather protection; or you may want just to keep your large canning pot full of sap simmering on the wood stove all day. Sap should be collected and boiled at least every other day to avoid souring.

As the sap boils up, foam will rise to the top. This contains dirt and sediments that should be skimmed off for a cleaner, sweeter product. More sap may be added continuously, as the boiling sap evaporates, until it begins to get noticeably darker and sweeter. At that point, careful watching and frequent tasting are important to bring the syrup to the desired consistency. When completed, the syrup must be strained through several layers of cheesecloth, or a large milk strainer, available from feed and garden stores. The boiling hot syrup may then be sealed in hot sterilized canning jars for long-term storage. After opening, refrigeration will prevent spoilage.

As the sap runs to a bitter trickle, the last batch is poured off in the night and brought in to be jarred.

Dawn breaks, and we glance back to see a dramatic change in the sugar bush. Trees so full of promise a few weeks ago are blushing in the sunlight, their crowns bursting with red flowering buds.

Meadow Green: An Herbal Treasure

Behind the impenetrable Woodstock mountain wall, a legendary and powerful spirit-woman stirs to the gentle urging of spring. Early Catskill dwellers watched for her arousal out of the dreary rains of March when her commanding temper would engage the seasonal moods of the mountains.

As drifts of warm April air creep high and unchallenged into the hollows, the ancestor unleashes her imagination with melting snows. Snarling streams tear out of mountain springs to flood valleys. White waters uproot old trees, and move mountaintop boulders to newly carved creek banks.

Rocks settle and the rain ebbs into an ominous drizzle. The miracle of spring soothes the tired ragings and dank shadows become a serene and fertile mist.

Garnet sparkles out of the gray across the crowns of maple trees and begins the stitching of spring's exquisite mountain tapestry. In a gentle explosion, strands of chartreuse and lavender emerge, softly embroidering dark gullies of evergreen and patching the scars of old rock quarries. Wild cherry bursts lacy white from the corners of forest clearings. Blossoms shower over woods and fields. Out of the mist, crocus and daffodils appear along stone walls, radiant with color and the invigoration of winter. Clumps of oniongrass and watercress unfold in the woods and streams, preening and brightening in the moist breeze. Amid tiny blue butterflies and scattered ivory dogwood petals, tender shoots poke up toward sunlight. Green and rich in life-giving value, they are dazzling in their abundance, and free.

As lingering snow retreated into the last days of the sap run, Native Americans began to forage the woodlands, streams, and meadows of the Catskills. Here they found young greens, vital in healing power, to treat wounds and disease, and refreshing tender-bright additions to the daily stewpot. This gathering was central to the people's relationship with the earth. Many plants were imbued with powers of protection or charm and chosen to be woven into ritual and art.

Natives introduced these wild gifts of nature to the early European settlers. Many English, Dutch, and others brought a well-established herbal-remedy and -gardening tradition of their own. There soon evolved around Woodstock tales of people who were very knowledgeable in the use and growing habits of local plant life.

A devotion to herbal uses and a healing ministry in this wilderness setting was often regarded with suspicion, as an aberrant craft of witches. A few distinguished Woodstock individuals, however, ignored the regards of fearful people and tramped the hills collecting wild herbs. They bundled them home for storing. Roots, leaves, and flowers were dried or brewed into concoctions for the healing or nourishment of their families.

Now out of the wilderness, Woodstock carries on a tradition of herbal lore and practice. The area is a haven for alternate health services, where herbal uses are in common reference. Neighbors exchange root cuttings of comfrey and peppermint, while sharing a flora identification "weed walk" with an expert. Practiced people devoted to the land and its treasures, openly share medicinal and esoteric plant knowledge with eager neighbors.

Following a long, barren winter, residents of the stony Catskills search for fresh plant food and the greening of new life, as they welcome the spring. Among those sought in this eager quest are a few common wild plants that are both especially tasty and nutritious, and many of which have specialized healing attributes. Many of these plants can be found in most other regions of the country. All of them can be collected throughout the spring and into the early summer. Medicinal plants should be dried and stored for winter use. Pot green and culinary herbs can also be dried and added to winter soups.

Most herbs are dried by simply tying a bundle of plants together, then suspending the bundle upside down in a shady, dry, and airy place. Similarly, roots can be dried by bundling a few of the green tops, leaving the roots suspended in the air. Individual flowers such as day lilies or clover can be spread out over window screens that have been covered with fresh kitchen towels, then set up on racks or improvised blocks or suspended from wires attached to the pantry or porch ceiling. When herbs or flowers are dry to the touch, pack them immediately in clean, airtight jars to preserve their fragile properties, and store in a dark, dry and cool place.

BURDOCK *Stems and root*
Sauté stems; boil root and use as pot vegetable.

CATNIP *Leaves*
Brew for tea, especially liked by children. A sedative, it relieves colic and settles upset stomach.

COLTSFOOT *Leaves and flowers*
Brew fresh leaves and/or flowers, or smoke dried leaves to relieve chest congestion.

Coltsfoot

DAISY *Leaves*
Pick leaves from under the snow through early flowering for gourmet addition to salads. Dip fresh or dried leaves in boiling water, then lay on wounds, to sooth and help new tissue to grow.

DANDELION *Leaves, buds, flowers, root*
Use very young, tart leaves to spice up dinner salads or cream cheese sandwiches. Clean older, more bitter leaves, and pour boiling water over them. Drain and repeat. Drain again, and steam in the clinging moisture with a little butter and garlic. Toss dandelion buds or flowers in salads. Dip in batter and fry, or stir into other sautéed vegetables. Medicinal properties are concentrated in the perennial taproot. Boil young roots until tender for a delicious side dish. Dandelion provides special nutrients for the liver, stimulating and cleaning the entire digestive system. It is especially rich in calcium, iron, potassium, and Vitamin A. Dig up roots, leaving leaves intact to preserve the vital, healing milky juice.

Dandelion

DAY LILY   *Shoots, buds, flowers, and tubers*
Use tubers, spring shoots, buds, and flowers as food. All parts are delicious raw, lightly steamed or stir-fried. Dry buds and flowers to add to winter soups or stir-frys.

DOCK, CURLY   *Shoots, leaves, root*
OR YELLOW   *Tender shoots are especially succulent in salads. Use young leaves for salad or pot greens. The deep-growing, spindle-shaped yellow root is medicinally potent and rich in iron; it is a common ingredient in old herbal formulas. Dig up roots and shake off dirt. Clean gently, do not scrub. Pack fresh roots in olive oil and set in a sunny window to steep for six weeks. Use oil to heal sores and reduce swelling; good for hemorrhoid treatment.*

ELDER   *Flowers and berries*
Brew infusion of flowers for headache, skin washes, and children's fevers. Collect and crush berries for wine or jelly.

GRAPE   *Leaves and tendrils*
Blanch leaves and fill with grains and nuts. Brew with tendrils for tea. Use tendrils raw in salad.

HORSERADISH   *Leaves and root*
Leaves are cabbage-like in flavor, good in salad when very young, or in stews. Use freshly grated root in dressings and sauces. Blend to a paste with vinegar. Jar and store in refrigerator. Keeps indefinitely.

Jack-in-the-Pulpit

JACK-IN-THE-PULPIT	*Roots* *Dig roots and dry for one year. Cook as pot vegetable.*

| MINT | *Leaves*
Of the many varieties of mint, spearmint and peppermint appear most commonly. Delicious and refreshing as tea, brewed for hot or cold use. All mints are stimulating, and relieve digestive upsets such as gas pain or nausea. |

| MOREL MUSHROOM, COMMON | *Pitted, spongy dome varying from tan to gray, tightly attached to grayish stalk. This mushroom appears in spring, commonly in open, damp woodlands. Very desirable, choice mushroom; delicious prepared in cream sauce.* |

Morel Mushroom, Common

Mustard

| MUSTARD | *Leaves*
Common mustard, often called spring or winter cress, is a member of the large Brassica family, its seed a symbol of humility. Pick young, preflowering leaves for pot greens. Combine with sweeter greens, garlic, and butter, to mellow its bitter bite. Mix chopped raw leaves into a crispy spring salad to add zip. High in sulfur, the mustard family is the forerunner of modern antibiotics. Steep bitter, older leaves in boiling water. Use the infusion for an antiseptic cleanser. Gather seeds in late summer for a winter culinary spice. |

| NETTLE | *Leaves*
Brew for tea or use as pot herb. It is especially nourishing and tonic. Nettle tea reduces mucus. The plant also soothes and strengthens nerves. |

PLANTAIN   *Leaves*
Called "White Man's Foot" by the
Indians, plantain seed is easily spread
wherever people walk. Not to be confused
with the tropical plantain fruit, both
narrow- and broad-leaf plantain are
very good eaten raw or lightly steamed.
Flavor and texture are best in young
plants, but plantain can be eaten
throughout the season. "Nature's Band-
Aid," plantain leaves have a mild
ability to stop bleeding. Blanched or
pulverized leaves can be applied directly
to wounds to draw out infection and
effectively treat pain and itching. Good
for bee or nettle stings.

POKE   *Young shoots and leaves*
Use only young shoots. Delicious as a
spring salad staple. Do not eat older
plants, over 6 inches tall; they are
poisonous.

Poke

PURSLANE   *Leaves and stems*
Fresh leaves and stems are very tender,
sweet, and succulent. Excellent addition
to salads.

RASPBERRY   *Leaves*
Leaves may be brewed for pregnancy
tonic. A good pain reliever, it is
commonly used to ease childbirth.

RED CLOVER   *Flowers*
Brew flowers, dried or fresh, and drink
tea to improve energy. Also relieves chest
congestion, asthma, and bronchitis and
prevents infection.

Purslane

ROSEROOT   *Leaves and stems*
Leaves and stems are very sweet and succulent. Use all season as added flavor and texture for salads.

ST. JOHN'S WORT   *Leaves and stems*
Steep chopped plant in olive oil, and place in a sunny window for 6 weeks. Apply the infused oil to skin to prevent sunburn, or to treat burns and skin diseases. Soothing for tense muscles; a good massage oil.

SHEEP SORREL   *Leaves*
Pick leaves of young plant for use in salads or as a pot herb.

VIOLET   *Leaves and flowers*
The enchantingly fragile violet is eternally proclaimed as a symbol of romance and tenderness, with a flavor as sweet as its fragrance. Mentioned in the ancient Vedas, violets have been brewed and pulverized throughout history for treatment of headache and cancers. Properties of violet tend to draw out toxicity and disease. Juice the plant in a juicerator with carrots for a good daily tonic. Pull up the plant by its roots. Shake clean and rinse before drying. Use both fresh leaves and flowers in salads.

WATERCRESS   *Leaves and tops*
Use raw in salad or as soup garnish.

WHITE PINE   *New tips*
Brew new tips, and drink the tea to prevent hay fever, and to reduce mucous secretions.

WILD CHIVES	*Leaves*
Use raw, chopped in salad or for garnish on fish, soup, dressings, and sauces.

WILD LETTUCE	*Young leaves*
Use raw for salad when very young. Milky juices of the older plant are a narcotic pain killer.

WILD OREGANO	*Leaves*
Use raw in salad or as herb garnish or refreshing tea.

Wild Oregano

The Catskills' ancestral folk must have been partially dependent on wild plant life for survival, for where gardening is difficult, in scant, acrid soil, wild greens and herbs have flourished. Most herbs are rugged plants, preferring harsh soil and the cool weather of spring. Many now common and sometimes wild herbs are not indigenous to the continent, but were introduced by our forebears. Herb gardening, an ancient European practice, was brought with several favorite varieties to this general region of the country. Several wild plants held spiritual significance for Europeans, as they had for Native American foragers. The newcomers introduced the practice of garden arrangement for the purpose of elevating psychical or aesthetic effects. Early settlers commonly kept a small kitchen garden stocked with healing herbs and pot greens, convenient to that part of the house, and an ornamental, fragrant complement to the yard.

An old saying declared that a person who kept sage in his or her garden should never suffer illness. Many cultivated herbs have been brewed or pulverized to treat ailments, sage among the most potent and all-purpose. Basil, too, has been considered to possess great healing power. Parsley, very rich in Vitamin C and iron, could be one of the most nutritious foods in creation. Comfrey shares this distinction, both in its healing properties and in its nutritional value as a sweet pot herb. A tiny comfrey rootlet will, in a brief season, form a flourishing hub for any herb garden.

Comfrey is a perennial, sprouting with rhubarb in April. Varieties of blue-green mints soon emerge in ever-spreading thickets. Shiny blades of horseradish, gone wild, appear between clumps of violets and fiddleheads. In the thickening green meadow, a bush of feathery aromatic wormwood unfurls its mysteries in silvery dominion. In the garden, asparagus, the all-time favorite, is showing nubs of new shoots, a growth that can, when continually harvested, produce through midsummer. All these perennials offer culinary and medicinally useful choices.

The Garden Gate

The eloquence of May sings across the marshes in resonance with the dawn. Calls of blackbirds and thrushes come throbbing through the early mist. Swelling cattails and bursting lilacs rise with the sun. Cool breezes goffer the flowering tapestry, ruffling infinite shades of pastel.

Fresh jars of maple syrup gleam in the pantry. Bundles of drying wild plants adorn rafters and window frames. We look toward the quiet waiting garden. Following the thaw of a hard winter, the old soil will be enriched and soft, welcoming the disturbance of cultivating tools.

There is a saying in Woodstock, as old as the first settlers: When a wanderer asked, "Where are the Catskills?" the answer was, "You'll know them when you get to the place where there are two stones to every dirt." Removing stones is basic to farming in these mountains. Cultivated fields of discouraged old farms can still be discovered, bounded by the remains of ancient stone walls. Here flat rocks removed from the fields were piled, often with architectural precision, to survive the centuries: now hidden in new diminutive forests and inhabited with all manner of thriving creatures.

People here resort to much rearranging and piling of dirt to develop small family gardens along hillsides and rock quarries. Local soil is often fattened with a large ratio of well-cured manure, discarded from a local mushroom farm. This natural fertilizer can also be acquired from a local horse ranch, dairy, or chicken farm. Soil, well tilled and mixed with nature's fertilizers, can then be terraced with railroad ties or stones for gardening in highly productive, intensive plots, popular in the Woodstock mountain region.

There are several vegetable seeds that prefer cold weather for germinating. As soon as the ground can be worked, and before the heavy spring rains, we plant seed potatoes under light soil

and a thick pile of hay, peas along the fence, and nursery beds
of broccoli and red cabbage.

These plantings are soon followed by varieties of lettuce, and
other greens and root vegetables. With this schedule we are eating our own garden salad with savory herbs before June. The
practice of early planting also assures a hardy plant development
resistant to the deluge of pests to come with summer heat.

Willowy spiders and uncongenial wasps that come creeping
into the house with spring may be a nuisance inside; but in the
garden they are part of a hardworking, natural caretaker team.
We carefully collect these creatures along with any wandering
toad or lost ladybugs near the house, and move them to the
garden. Here they can feast on grubs, flea beetles, aphids, caterpillars, and other insect pests. Birdhouses along the fence will
attract purple martins and other insect-eating birds. An effective
springtime scarecrow for birds that steal seeds and peck at young
plants is a toy rubber snake, placed alongside newly planted fur-
rows.

As soon as the seeds and young plants are in the ground many
gardeners choose to mulch their garden. Covering the ground
around rows and between plants with thick layers of old hay or
straw will help suppress weed growth, hold in moisture, and
keep soil at a moderate temperature. Your own resources and
scale of gardening will determine the practicality of mulching.

As the lower layer of mulch-hay slowly rots, it feeds and builds
up the soil. Using hay mulch around ground fruiting plants such
as unstaked tomatoes, cucumbers, and vine squash helps protect
ripening fruits from ground decay. But some plants seem to
flourish with more human contact, as occurs when the gardener
is required to be in the earth with them, hoeing out the weeds
and aerating tender growing roots.

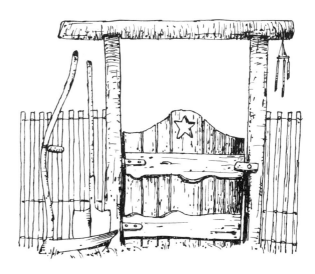

Spring Plantings

Out in the garden we lay rows and beds, marking them with string stretched between stick posts. Gathering for new nests, birds, points of pure color in the landscape, come to tug comically at loose string ends. Invisible toads hide between scattered rocks. Sunlight fills the sky and reflects off the hoe tip, shining deep into the bones.

Favorite seed varieties are chosen from a list of delicious and beautiful crops long tested and known to adapt in the Catskill region. Planted in well-drained soil, with the addition of manure and compost, and with frequent cultivation, these vegetables, herbs, and flowers will flourish.

SCHEDULE

Plant from March 20 to April 10

Additional plantings of lettuce and peas can be made throughout the season

Broccoli
Cabbage
Chard
Chervil
Dill
Garlic
Horseradish
Lettuce: *romaine, butterhead, looseleaf*
Onions

Parsley
Parsnips
Peas: *shell, snap, snow*
Perennials: *Asparagus, Rhubarb*
Potatoes
Radishes
Shallots
Spinach
Turnips

Plant from April 10 to May 1

Beets: *red ball, sugar*
Carrots: *medium, short*
Marigolds
Oregano

Perennial herbs: *Comfrey, Horseradish, Peppermint, Spearmint, Wormwood*
Thyme
Zinnias

Plant from May 1 to June 1

Beans: *bush, snap*

Shell Beans: *black, great northern, pinto, navy, red kidney, Swedish brown, lima*

Borage

Cantaloupe

Coriander (Cilantro)

Corn: *short-season small, midseason bicolor, late-season large*

Cucumbers

Dill

Lettuce

Nasturtium

Sage

Summer Squash: *zucchini, yellow*

Tarragon

Tomatoes, seedling transplants

Winter Squash: *buttercup, acorn, pumpkins*

Companion groupings encourage vigorous growth. Good companions in the pot are the same harmonious neighbors in the garden.

PASTORAL FEAST:
Spring Recipes & Menus

MEADOW SOUP
Serves 6

Here is a wild greens brew of very subtle quality, adapted from the colonial cookbook *The Compleat Housewife*, 1728.

3 quarts water
1 large, sweet onion
15–20 whole cloves
1 cup shelled pistachio nuts
6 egg yolks
¼ cup dry white wine
Juice of 1 lemon
6 tablespoons butter

3 cups chopped sheep sorrel
  leaves
1 quart chopped spinach
1 cup chopped yellow dock
  leaves
1 cup chopped plantain leaves
1 cup chopped fresh parsley

OPTIONAL GARNISH:
Thick slices of whole wheat or Crusty White Bread (*see Index*),
  toasted
Poached eggs or Minced chives or
Grated Parmesan cheese or Sour cream

Boil the water in a large, heavy kettle. Stud the onion with whole cloves, and drop into the boiling water. Finely mince or grind pistachio nuts, and add to the broth. Simmer gently for 15 to 20 minutes.

Beat egg yolks with wine and lemon juice. Add a small quantity of simmering broth to the egg and wine mixture, very slowly, to warm it up. Then pour the mixture into the simmering pot and continue to heat about 5 minutes.

Melt butter in a large skillet. Quickly sauté the cleaned and chopped greens in the butter over a medium high heat. Continue to stir about 2 minutes, until just tender. Stir the sautéed greens into the simmering soup and serve immediately.

The original recipe suggests serving Meadow Soup (referred to as "fasting broth") over thick slices of toasted bread, garnished with poached eggs. This is a comforting dish to warm up or wind down a busy day.

For a lighter, first-course soup, garnish instead with minced chives, a sprinkle of grated Parmesan cheese, or a dollop of sour cream. Serve with bread or rye crackers on the side, light cheese, and fruit.

SOUR CHERRY SOUP
Serves 4

Sour cherries from Hudson Valley orchards, or those that grow on an old backyard tree, have a very short season. Promptly captured for a serving of this delicacy, they make a memorable spring event.

1 pound sour cherries
1 quart boiling water
3 tablespoons honey
1 3-inch cinnamon stick

5 tablespoons dry red wine
2 tablespoons fresh lemon juice
4 tablespoons sour cream

FOR GARNISH: ½ cup blueberries (*optional*)

Cut each cherry in half, removing pits and stems. Place the cherries in boiling water with honey and cinnamon. Simmer until tender, about ½ hour.

Drain the cherries, reserving liquid. Remove half the cherries and set aside to add to the soup later. Through a sieve, press the remaining cherries back into the cooking liquid. Add wine and lemon juice. Simmer this smooth purée very gently for 7 minutes. Add the remaining cherries and chill.

Just before serving, beat sour cream into the soup. Spoon into small bowls and garnish each with a few blueberries.

MOUNTAIN CREEK SOUP
Serves 4 or 8

1 quart clear Vegetable Broth
Salt to taste
1 cup fresh lemon juice
3 eggs
2 cups sliced mushrooms (*optional*)

FOR GARNISH: ½ cup chopped fresh parsley

Combine liquids from any steamed or strained vegetables to obtain broth base for this soup. Salt the broth to suit your taste, and add the lemon juice.

Heat broth until very hot but not boiling. In a separate bowl, beat eggs well, and stir into broth while whisking briskly with a fork so that eggs are dispersed evenly and soup looks creamy. Sliced mushrooms can be added for taste and beauty. Serve immediately in individual bowls garnished with parsley. As an appetizer this will serve 8 people. With fresh baked bread and a salad it's an excellent summer meal and will serve 4.

CREAMY GREEN ASPARAGUS SOUP
Serves 6

Creamy green, smooth and warm, with young asparagus spears floating on top, this springtime dish is a filling reward after a hard day's work in the garden.

1½ pounds asparagus
1½ cups chopped onions
3 tablespoons safflower oil
¼ cup chopped fresh herbs (basil, oregano, marjoram)
3 tablespoons unsweetened butter
6 tablespoons flour (half whole wheat pastry flour and half
    unbleached white flour)
2 cups Vegetable Broth (*see Index*)
4 cups scalded milk, cooled
Tamari soy sauce to taste
Freshly ground black pepper

Clean asparagus and chop coarsely, setting aside approximately ¾ cup asparagus tips to add later.

Sauté onions in 1 tablespoon of the oil over low heat until soft.

Add fresh herbs and chopped asparagus to onions and cook slowly for 5 minutes.

When asparagus is just tender, add remaining oil, butter, and flour. Whisk into a roux, and allow to brown for a minute. Slowly whisk in the vegetable broth. Stir well until thickened. Set the soup aside to cool.

Meanwhile, lightly steam the asparagus tips. When soup is cool, purée in the blender. Combine the purée with the scalded milk in a large saucepan. Add tamari, a sprinkling of black pepper, and steamed asparagus tips. If necessary, heat the soup very gently, and serve immediately.

Serve Creamy Green Asparagus Soup with whole wheat breadsticks and a crunchy raw vegetable salad that includes sunflower seeds and a few raisins.

Any tasty green thing from the garden or forage can be used to make this delightful late spring or early summer soup.

STUFFED GRAPE LEAVES
Yield: 60—serves 6–10 as main dish

Spring feelings flow with the taste of young grape leaves, fragrant with the essence of pine.

60 small grape leaves
½ cup olive oil
½ cup minced fresh parsley
½ cup minced fresh mint
1 cup pine nuts or chopped walnuts
1 cup mashed tofu (6–7 ounces)
2 cloves garlic, chopped

4 scallions, finely chopped
Freshly ground black pepper
1 teaspoon cinnamon
1 teaspoon ground cumin
1 teaspoon paprika
Tamari soy sauce to taste
½ teaspoon salt
4 cups cooked brown rice

MARINADE:
¾ cup olive oil
Juice of 2 lemons

Preheat the oven to 350 degrees F. Select small, clean grape leaves, free of holes and caterpillars. Wash them, and place in a bowl. Cover with boiling water to soften.

In a large skillet, heat ½ cup olive oil. Add all the parsley, mint, nuts, mashed tofu, garlic, scallions, spices, seasonings, and tamari, and sauté gently for about 1 minute. Add cooked rice and mix.

Spread each grape leaf flat on work surface. Place about 1 to 2 tablespoons of the rice mixture on the veined side of each leaf. Roll the leaf up by first folding the sides over the stuffing, then rolling up to the point of the leaf. Layer the little rolled leaves in a medium baking pan, crisscrossing each layer.

Add water to cover. Cover the pan with foil. Steam in a moderate oven 30 to 40 minutes to heat through. Uncover and pour lemon-oil mixture over. Allow to cool.

This dish is very good served still warm or, better yet, allowed to marinate for 12 hours in the lemon-oil liquid, and served cold or rewarmed the next day.

Stuffed Grape Leaves are perfect finger food for party appetizers. They are also good for a main dish, allowing 6 to 10 per serving. Serve with a yogurt salad featuring cucumbers or fruit.

MAPLE CREPES
Yield: 12 crepes—serves 6

A soothing supper; a gourmet brunch.

MAPLE CUSTARD FILLING
3 eggs, well beaten
1⅔ cups milk
¼ cup maple syrup
Pinch of salt
Freshly grated nutmeg

3 apples, sliced
1 tablespoon lemon juice

1 recipe Crepes (*see recipe below*)

Prepare Maple Custard Filling: Preheat oven to 350 degrees F. Combine eggs, milk, maple syrup, and salt. Beat vigorously until well mixed. Pour into a 1-quart baking dish, sprinkle with nutmeg. Place the dish in a shallow pan filled with about 1½ inches of hot water. Bake for 1 hour. Custard is done when a cool kitchen knife is inserted and comes out clean. Place custard in refrigerator to cool.

Gently cook the sliced apples in a little water until tender. Add lemon and set aside. Prepare crepes.

Maple Custard Filling may be served as is for a simple dessert. Spoon into 4 or 5 individual dessert dishes, and top with the cooked sliced apples if desired.

CREPES
¼ cup unbleached white flour
¼ cup whole wheat pastry flour
½ teaspoon salt
2 eggs, well beaten
⅔ cup milk
1 tablespoon peanut or safflower oil

Sift together flour and salt. Combine eggs, milk, and oil; add flour mixture and beat until smooth. Preheat a 9-inch skillet or standard crepe pan. When a test drop of batter sizzles, lightly grease pan and pour approximately ¼ cup of batter into it. Immediately tip and rotate the pan to distribute the batter evenly and thinly all around the surface. Brown lightly 1 to 2 minutes. Then lift the edge of the crepe gently with spatula and turn to brown on the other side. Stack the crepes on a warm plate, until all are cooked and ready for filling.

TO ASSEMBLE CREPES:

Preheat oven to 300 degrees F. Place a row of cooked, drained apple slices down the center of each crepe. Add 2 to 3 tablespoons of custard, roll up the crepe, and set on a cookie sheet. When all the crepes are filled, place the cookie sheet in a warm oven for about 15 minutes, until the crepes are heated through. Serve immediately.

ONION MISO SOUFFLÉ
Serves 4

6 tablespoons miso
3 cups hot water
½ cup butter
2 onions, sliced in rings
12 slices whole wheat bread
2 cups grated cheese (Cheddar, mozzarella, or Muenster)
3 eggs, beaten
½ cup tamari soy sauce
½ cup grated Parmesan cheese

Mix miso into hot but not boiling water and set aside to cool.

Heat butter in a skillet and sauté onions until transparent. In a buttered 2-quart casserole, place 4 slices of bread. Cover with ⅓ the sautéed onions and 1 cup of grated cheese (Cheddar, mozzarella or Muenster). Repeat this with another layer of bread, onions and cheese. Finally top with a layer of bread and remaining onions.

Beat eggs and miso broth together. Add tamari and pour over the layers. Top with grated Parmesan cheese. Allow to set for ½ hour; meanwhile preheat oven to 350 degrees F. Bake for 1 hour. When done, it will puff up and be golden brown. Serve immediately.

SNOW PEA DELIGHT
Serves 4

3 tablespoons tamari soy
  sauce
2 tablespoons dry sherry
4 teaspoons cornstarch
¼ teaspoon honey
½ teaspoon peeled fresh
  gingerroot, grated
1½ pounds tofu, cut into
  ¼-inch slices
¼ cup peanut oil

½ pound mushrooms, sliced
2 medium onions, quartered
2 green peppers, cut in
  chunks
2 cups snow peas (stems
  removed)
4 cups hot steamed brown
  rice, cooked with 1
  teaspoon sesame oil

Combine tamari with next 4 ingredients in a deep bowl. Add sliced tofu; toss to coat the pieces, and set aside to marinate at least 15 minutes.

Heat oil in wok or Dutch oven. Add mushrooms, onions, and peppers together, and toss until vegetables are almost tender-crisp, about 4 minutes. Add snow peas; continue tossing until they are slightly wilted, about 1 minute. Remove vegetable mixture from the pan, and set aside.

Drain tofu, reserving marinade. Drop tofu pieces into remaining juices of the hot wok, and toss for about 1 minute. Add marinating liquid. Stir until thickened. Add the cooked vegetables, and stir until just heated through. Serve immediately with steamed brown rice, which has been cooked with a taste of sesame oil.

SPRINGTIME TOFU–NOODLE MEDLEY
Serves 4

6 ounces tofu, sliced into chunks

MARINADE:
2 tablespoons tamari soy sauce
1¼-inch slice peeled fresh gingerroot, mashed
2 tablespoons dry sherry or sake
1 teaspoon honey
4 tablespoons peanut oil
3 cloves garlic, minced
One ½-inch slice peeled fresh gingerroot, minced
4 scallions, finely sliced
½ pound mushrooms, sliced
2 carrots, julienned
½ pound asparagus, blanched
¼ pound fresh snow peas
10–12 cherry tomatoes
½ pound fresh spinach leaves

¼ cup tamari soy sauce
¼ cup dry sherry
½ cup water
1 tablespoon arrowroot
1 tablespoon sesame oil
½ pound buckwheat noodles, cooked
3 tablespoons ground toasted sesame seeds
Hot chili-seasoned oil (*optional*)

Prepare slices of tofu. Combine next 4 ingredients in a bowl, pour over tofu and marinate at least ½ hour.

Heat 2 tablespoons peanut oil in wok, toss in garlic, 1 teaspoon minced ginger, and then add scallions, mushrooms, and carrot slivers. Stir-fry 2 minutes.

Remove vegetables, set aside, and add marinated, drained tofu. Stir-fry until slightly browned. Add asparagus, snow peas, tomatoes, and spinach, tossing in remaining oil until spinach begins to wilt. Remove from wok and set aside.

Add 2 more tablespoons peanut oil, remaining minced gingerroot, and next 5 ingredients to wok, and stir quickly. As mixture begins to thicken, toss in cooked noodles and then add tofu and cooked vegetables and toss all together.

Check seasoning, remove to serving platter, then sprinkle ground toasted sesame seeds on top. Serve with chili oil, if desired, and radishes, and cucumbers with vinegar.

TEMPEH-SPINACH DINNER
Serves 4

This is a succulent, one-pot dinner—simple, quick, and substantial.

1 7-ounce tempeh cake
½ cup olive oil
4 ounces mushrooms, sliced
3 large scallions, chopped
4 cloves garlic, crushed

1 pound spinach, stemmed
  and coarsely chopped
1 cup grated sharp Cheddar
  cheese

Slice the cake of tempeh horizontally, into two thin sheets. Cut these two sheets into quarters, making eight 2 × 3-inch pieces.

Heat olive oil in a very large skillet with a cover. Place tempeh pieces into hot oil and brown on 1 side, over high heat, about 4 minutes. Turn tempeh. Drop in mushrooms, scallions, and garlic, smothering everything with spinach. Sprinkle cheese over top, and cover the pot. Reduce heat and cook until the spinach wilts, about 4 minutes. Serve hot with tamari soy sauce and tomato slices.

PASTA PRIMAVERA
Serves 4

This must be made with the freshest vegetables, straight from the garden.

2 small zucchini
1 cup broccoli flowerets, coarsely sliced
1 cup young, halved green beans
1 cup green peas
1 cup snow peas or sugar snaps
1 tablespoon butter and 1 tablespoon olive oil
2 cups sliced mushrooms
Salt
Pepper
Tamari soy sauce to taste
¼ cup chopped fresh parsley
4 tablespoons olive oil
3 cloves garlic, chopped
3 shallots, chopped
1 teaspoon chopped fresh or dried hot pepper
3 cups chopped tomatoes (preferably plum)
¼ cup chopped fresh basil
6 tablespoons butter
½ cup heavy cream
¾ cup grated Roman and/or Parmesan cheese
¼ cup toasted pine nuts
Chopped fresh parsley
Chopped fresh basil
Freshly ground black pepper
1 pound spaghettini or linguine, cooked *al dente*

Cook each of the vegetables till crisp-tender in a small amount of salted water. Drain thoroughly and combine in a large bowl.

Heat the butter and oil in a large skillet or Dutch oven. Add the mushrooms. Add salt, pepper, and tamari. Cook about 2 minutes over medium heat. Remove mushrooms from the skillet and add to the bowl of green vegetables, together with the parsley. Set skillet with cooking juices aside.

Heat 4 tablespoons olive oil in a small pot, add garlic, shallots, hot pepper, tomatoes, and cook about 5 minutes. Add basil, and salt and pepper to taste. Set aside.

In the large skillet with the mushroom juices, melt the 6 tablespoons butter. Add the cream and cheese, stirring till smooth. Add the vegetables and mushrooms, and tomatoes. Mix well. When hot, add pine nuts, and sprinkle with parsley, basil, and pepper, and serve over a platter of hot spaghettini or linguine.

LINGUINE WITH SHELLFISH
Serves 4

1 dozen mussels, scrubbed and debearded
½ cup water
½ cup dry white wine
Pinch of dried thyme
Pinch of dried oregano
1 tablespoon chopped fresh parsley
8–10 cloves garlic, minced
1½ cups butter
1½ dozen fresh clams, in shells
18 medium-sized shrimp, shelled, cleaned, deveined
1 pound linguine
3 tablespoons chopped fresh Italian parsley

Put cleaned mussels in a pot with ½ cup water, ½ cup white wine, thyme, oregano, and the 1 tablespoon chopped parsley. Bring to a boil and simmer until mussels open, discarding any that do not open. Strain and reserve mussel liquor. Keep warm.

Sauté half the minced garlic in ½ cup butter. Add fresh clams. Add water to cover. Bring to a boil and simmer until clams open. Do not overcook. Discard any unopened clams.

Sauté rest of garlic in remainder of the butter, add shrimp and sauté about 3 minutes until pink. Drain butter and juices from shrimp into clam pot. Set shrimp aside; keep warm.

Cook linguine in boiling salted water according to package directions. When cooked, strain, then take small amount of hot broth from clams and toss with linguine.

Place linguine on a large serving platter and arrange clams and mussels around dish. Combine strained mussel liquor, clam juices, and parsley. Bring to boiling point. Arrange shrimp on top of pasta and pour sauce over the seafood and linguine. Serve.

ONION CHEESE PIE WITH SPRING SURPRISES
Serves 6

A bright yellow sun, speckled with nutmeg and filled with spring surprises.

PIE DOUGH:
½ cup whole wheat pastry flour
½ cup unbleached white flour
⅛ teaspoon sea salt
6 tablespoons unsweetened butter
2–3 tablespoons ice water

FILLING:
1½ cups chopped onions
3 tablespoons butter
2 cups washed, chopped greens, from forage or garden
½ pound mushrooms, sliced
4 eggs
½ cup milk
1 cup heavy cream
½ pound Gruyère cheese, grated
Freshly grated nutmeg
Freshly ground black pepper

FOR GARNISH: Violets

Mix flours and salt in bowl. Cut in the butter, using a pastry cutter, until mixture has uniform, coarse texture. Sprinkle ice water over it, 1 tablespoon at a time, and toss lightly until dough forms a ball. Chill 1 hour.

Roll dough on floured board to ⅛-inch thickness and place into 9-inch pie dish. Prick bottom with fork at 1-inch intervals. Line with aluminum foil, and fill with dried beans. Return to refrigerator for another ½ hour.

Preheat oven to 425 degrees F. and begin to prepare filling. Sauté onions in butter until soft. Steam wet greens in a dry pan, covered, for a minute, then drain. Add greens and mushrooms to onions and let cool.

Bake piecrust in oven for 10 minutes. Remove piecrust and lower oven temperature to 350 degrees F. Beat eggs and add milk, cream, grated cheese, some nutmeg, and black pepper.

Spread vegetables on partially baked pie shell and pour milk-egg mixture on top. Grate fresh nutmeg on top. Bake at 350 degrees F. for 40 minutes, or until center of pie appears set. Test by inserting a knife into center. When it comes out clean, pie is done.

Garnish with violets and serve with vegetable salad.

SAWKILL TROUT

March and April waters issue from mountain springs, bringing spawning trout and eager fishermen to the region. Sports people, enchanted by rushing water sounds, stand hip-deep in the frothing creeks. Compelled by the spell of spring and the anticipation of a culinary delicacy for dinner, both locals and tourists share in this engaging play with nature.

Catskill trout are usually small fish, and after cleaning and trimming, they should be cooked whole. Remove heads and gills, rinse in cold water, and trout are ready to be fried, baked, or poached.

FRIED TROUT
Serves 6

Fried fresh water trout is a simple, old-fashioned favorite.

6 trout, each about 10 inches long   Salt and white pepper
1 cup cornmeal   Butter and oil for frying
2 teaspoons paprika

FOR GARNISH: Chopped fresh parsley

Clean and trim trout. Combine cornmeal with paprika, salt, and pepper. Coat all sides of each fish with the seasoned cornmeal.

Heat butter and oil in a heavy frying pan. Fry fish in the hot oil, gently, until golden brown, about 4 minutes on each side. Serve garnished with parsley.

BAKED TROUT
1 trout for each serving

FOR EACH 10–12-INCH TROUT:
¼ cup chopped onions   ¼ cup dry white wine
1 tablespoon butter   ¼ cup unbleached white flour
½ teaspoon minced garlic   Freshly ground black pepper
Juice of ½ lemon

Preheat oven to 425 degrees F. Sauté chopped onions in butter until tender. Add a little minced garlic, and lemon juice, and dry white wine to form a basting sauce.

Dredge cleaned and trimmed fish in unbleached white flour. Place in a lightly oiled shallow baking pan with the lemon juice-wine mixture. Sprinkle with freshly grated black pepper. Bake in the hot oven about 12 minutes, or until tender. Baste several times with the sauce as the fish bakes.

POACHED TROUT
1 trout for each serving

FOR EACH 10–12-INCH TROUT:
1 cup water
1 tablespoon vinegar
2 bay leaves

Combine water, vinegar, and bay leaves in a fish poacher or other wide, shallow pot. Bring to a rolling boil. Add cleaned, trimmed trout and simmer 2 minutes on each side. Fish is cooked when meat easily separates from bone. Remove fish from liquid and serve immediately.

During trout season, set aside whatever can be managed to be frozen for winter use. *Woodstock: Recollection by Recipe* has a special suggestion for this:

FROZEN TROUT
"Take fresh-caught trout and clean, leaving heads, but removing gills. Insert the trout in a plastic bag, and fill with clean, cold water. Expel the air from the bag and secure the neck. Put it in a bread pan (or milk carton). Put pan, bag, fish and water in the freezer. After the water is frozen, the pan can be removed. The trout never lose their beautiful color. They stay as fresh as the day they were caught for many months. When ready to use, remove the frozen brick of trout and defrost."

WILD GREEN SAUTÉ
Serves 4

Crisp and bright, tart new greens await the rich and warm taming of butter and garlic, a stimulating treat to set before a winter-weary palate.

2½–3 quarts dock (leaves and shoots), plantain and young comfrey (leaves)
2 to 3 large horseradish leaves
1 quart dandelion and mustard leaves

3 tablespoons butter
2 tablespoons safflower oil
1 tablespoon minced garlic
2 tablespoons lemon juice

Wash greens carefully, drain, and chop quite fine. Heat butter and oil together in a large heavy skillet. Drop in all chopped greens, still damp from washing. Toss in the butter and oil until the greens are wilted, about 4 minutes. Add minced garlic and toss until all is just tender. Sprinkle with lemon juice and serve hot.

POTATOES STEWED WITH WINE
Serves 6

6 large baking potatoes
2 large onions
4 cloves garlic
⅛ cup olive oil
⅛ cup butter
1 cup Vegetable Broth (*see Index*) or water
1 cup dry red wine
About 2 tablespoons chopped fresh herbs (such as dill or
    thyme or tarragon)
¼ cup chopped fresh parsley (save some for garnish)
Chopped fresh chives (if available)
Salt and pepper
Tamari soy sauce to taste

Peel and dice potatoes, onions, and garlic.

Heat oil and butter in a large skillet with a cover or in a Dutch oven. Sauté garlic and onion slowly until onion is soft and slightly golden. Add potatoes and stir until coated with butter.

Add broth, wine, herbs, salt, pepper, and tamari to taste. Let simmer gently for 45 minutes or so. The potatoes will absorb the liquid and break apart when ready to serve.

Sprinkle with reserved chopped parsley, some chives if available, and a few grinds of pepper and serve.

This is wonderful and soothing with good dark bread and butter, a salad, perhaps some cheese and apples, and the same wine that went into the pot.

ASPARAGUS PARMESAN
Serves 4 as main dish, 8 as side dish

2 pounds fresh asparagus
½ cup butter
5 cloves garlic
1 pound mozzarella cheese, shredded or diced small
½ cup grated Parmesan cheese

Preheat oven to 350 degrees F. Wash asparagus and trim white ends off. Place in a 12 × 8 × 2-inch baking dish.

Melt butter in small pan. Mash garlic and add to butter. Pour over asparagus.

Cover asparagus with both cheeses evenly. Cover pan tightly with aluminum foil.

Bake for 30 minutes. Then remove foil and bake until cheese browns lightly, about 5 minutes.

MOUNTAIN HERB SALAD
Serves 4

This is a salad to celebrate the first offerings
of spring with lively flavor,
fresh from under the snow.

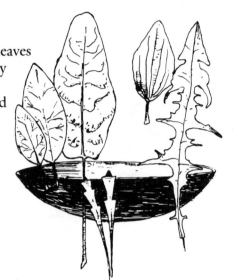

1 loosely packed quart plantain, violet, and daisy leaves
2 cups combined chopped roseroot leaves, comfrey
   and dock shoots and leaves
1 handful combined coarsely chopped mustard and
   young dandelion leaves
6 tablespoons olive oil
¼ cup wine vinegar
2 tablespoons prepared mustard
1 teaspoon honey
Sprinkle of coarse salt
Freshly ground black pepper
2 tablespoons minced catnip leaves
¼ cup finely chopped fresh chives

Rinse, drain, and pile the greens into a large salad bowl.
Combine the oil, vinegar, mustard, honey, salt, and pepper in
a jar. Shake vigorously. Drop the minced catnip and chopped
chives into the dressing and stir or shake again. Pour the dressing
over the greens. Toss the salad and serve immediately.

WATERCRESS AND BEET SALAD
Serves 4–6

Beet seeds, planted very early, can yield small, tender magenta
roots in time to color a crispy spring watercress salad.

1½ tablespoons wine vinegar
1½ tablespoons cider vinegar
4 tablespoons olive oil
Salt and freshly ground black pepper
2 cloves garlic, minced
2 tablespoons Dijon mustard
½ teaspoon honey
1 pound cooked beets, julienned
2 bunches watercress, stems removed
2 scallions, finely minced
2 tablespoons finely chopped fresh basil

Blend vinegars, oil, salt, pepper, garlic, mustard, and honey.
Add julienned beets to dressing. Toss well and chill for 1 hour.

After 1 hour, toss beets and dressing with watercress, minced scallions, and fresh basil.

Adjust seasoning and serve.

MAPLE AMBROSIA
Serves 4

¼ cup maple syrup
3 egg yolks
1 tablespoon lemon juice
¼ cup grated coconut
1 slice (½ inch thick) fresh pineapple
1 banana, sliced
2 tender ripe pears, cored and diced
½ pint heavy cream

Preheat oven to 425 degrees F. In a small heavy saucepot, heat maple syrup to boiling. Set aside until moderately warm. Beat egg yolks and add to syrup. Return the mixture to the stove and cook 1 minute over high heat, stirring constantly. Remove from heat and add lemon juice. Set the sauce in the refrigerator while preparing the fruit.

Place coconut on a flat baking tray and set in hot oven for 1 to 3 minutes, until delicately browned. Chop pineapple slice into small pieces. Place in a mixing bowl. Add sliced banana and diced pears. Sprinkle with the toasted coconut.

Whip the cream and fold into the chilled maple syrup sauce. Pour the maple cream over the fruit mixture, turn gently into a special serving bowl, and serve immediately.

APRIL VIOLET SALAD
Serves 4

4 oranges
½ cup yogurt
¼ cup violet flowers

FOR GARNISH:
Maple syrup

Peel and thickly slice oranges. Arrange on individual salad plates on a platter, overlapping rows. Spoon yogurt over the top, and sprinkle with violet flowers. Garnish with a few drops of maple syrup.

WATERCRESS AND PEAR SALAD
Serves 4

5–6 cups stemmed watercress pieces
2 firm ripe pears
2 tablespoons olive oil
2 teaspoons maple syrup
3 teaspoons fresh lemon juice

Place watercress in a salad bowl. Stem and core the pears and cut into large chunks.

Combine oil, syrup, and lemon in a cup. Stir briskly to combine well. Pour over the watercress and pears, toss, and serve immediately.

MAPLE GRANOLA SUPREME
Serves 8–10

Maple Granola Supreme is perfect for a quick breakfast on a sunny front porch, or a fortifying snack to carry on the hiking trail.

1¼ cups chopped walnuts
¾ cup chopped peanuts
½ cup chopped almonds
½ cup sunflower seeds
1 cup flaked or grated coconut
½ cup wheat germ
3 cups rolled oats
¾ teaspoon sea salt
1 cup finely chopped raisins
¾ cup safflower oil
½ cup maple syrup
1 teaspoon vanilla

FOR GARNISH:
Blueberries
Strawberries
Banana slices
Yogurt or light cream

Preheat oven to 350 degrees F. Combine all dry ingredients in a large bowl. Mix oil, syrup, and vanilla, and pour over all stirring to distribute evenly. Spread the mix about ¼ inch thick on large ungreased cookie sheets. Bake for 12 to 15 minutes. Stir the granola once during baking with a spatula, then spread out and continue baking until light golden brown and chunky. Cool and store in coffee cans with tight-fitting lids. Maple granola will keep indefinitely in the cupboard.

Serve Maple Granola Supreme in individual bowls rimmed with blueberries, strawberries, or banana slices, crowned with a dome of yogurt or served with cream.

HUSH PUPPIES
2½ dozen

2 cups stone-ground yellow
   cornmeal
1½ teaspoons baking powder
¾ teaspoon salt
½ cup minced wild chives
   or scallions

3 tablespoons melted
   butter or safflower
   oil
2 eggs, separated
¾ cup milk
Oil for frying

FOR GARNISH: Maple syrup

In a mixing bowl, combine cornmeal with baking powder and salt. Mix well, and stir in the chives.

In a separate bowl, mix butter or oil, egg yolks, and milk. Stir the liquid mixture into the cornmeal.

Whip the egg whites until soft peaks form. Just before frying, fold the egg whites into the batter.

Heat ¼ to ½ inch of oil in a heavy skillet over high heat. When a drop of batter sputters and browns the moment it touches the oil, it is hot enough for frying. Reduce heat to medium high. Drop quantities of batter into the hot oil from the side of a large serving spoon, forming little tapered cakes about 2½ inches long and ½ inch thick. Fry quickly until golden brown and crispy. Turn and fry the other side. Remove and drain. Serve immediately while piping hot, with maple syrup and fruit.

YOGURT WAFFLES
Serves 4

1½ cups whole wheat pastry
   flour
½ cup unbleached white
   flour
1 teaspoon baking powder
½ teaspoon salt

2 eggs, separated
1 cup yogurt
1 cup milk
4 tablespoons safflower
   oil or melted butter

FOR GARNISH: Butter, Maple Syrup

Oil waffle iron well. Heat iron about 8 minutes, or until a test drop of batter sizzles. Combine dry ingredients.

Beat egg yolks in another bowl. Add yogurt, milk, and oil. Mix well. Whip egg whites to soft peaks.

When iron is hot, pour liquid ingredients into flour mixture. Mix gently until well incorporated, but do not beat. Fold in whipped egg whites. Spoon batter onto hot waffle iron and bake until golden. Serve directly from the waffle iron with plenty of butter and maple syrup.

BUTTERMILK PANCAKES
Serves 4

½ cup buckwheat flour
¾ cup whole wheat flour
¾ cup unbleached white flour
1½ teaspoons baking powder
1 egg
2 cups buttermilk
3 tablespoons melted butter
1 tablespoon hot water
¾ teaspoon baking soda

FOR GARNISH:
Butter
Maple syrup

Combine flours, and stir in baking powder, until well mixed. In a separate bowl, beat egg and mix with buttermilk and melted butter. Place hot water in a cup, and add soda, stirring to dissolve.

Heat griddle or large frying pan on high heat. Just before cooking, add soda water to liquid mixture, then stir liquids into dry ingredients. Mix gently, do not beat. Pour batter onto hot dry griddle to form cakes about 4½ to 5 inches in diameter. Keep the heat medium high. Cakes should brown quickly, but not scorch. When bubbles form and then burst, they are ready to be turned. Brown on the other side and serve immediately. For a light, tender texture, avoid turning the cakes more than once. Serve with butter and maple syrup.

EASTER BREAD
Yield: 40 slices

Celebrate Easter morning or a spring wedding with a golden festive bread, rich with the abundance of new life on the farm.

2 tablespoons dry yeast
½ cup warm water
1½ cups heavy cream,
  scalded and cooled
4–4½ cups unbleached white
  flour
5 egg yolks
¾ cup honey
1 cup butter, melted and
  cooled

1½ teaspoons salt

2 teaspoons freshly ground
   cardamom

2 teaspoons grated lemon
   peel

2 tablespoons grated orange
   peel

1 cup golden raisins

1 cup chopped blanched
   almonds

1 cup milk, scalded and
   cooled

2 cups rye flour

2 cups whole wheat pastry
   flour

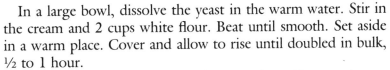

GLAZE: 1 egg, beaten

In a large bowl, dissolve the yeast in the warm water. Stir in the cream and 2 cups white flour. Beat until smooth. Set aside in a warm place. Cover and allow to rise until doubled in bulk, ½ to 1 hour.

Stir in the egg yolks, honey, butter, salt, cardamom, lemon and orange peels, raisins, and almonds, and beat until thoroughly combined. Stir in milk and rye flour until well combined. Add the whole wheat flour, enough to make a stiff, malleable dough. Sprinkle about ½ cup of white flour on the kneading board or table. Turn the dough out onto the floured surface and knead until smooth, at least 10 minutes, adding more white flour if necessary. Oil a large, clean bowl and place the kneaded dough in it. Turn the dough to coat the surface lightly with oil, and set aside in a warm place, covered with a towel. Allow to rise until doubled in bulk, about 1 hour.

Punch dough down, knead into a smooth ball. Oil a straight-sided, 4-quart enameled pail; or, if not available, use two 2-pound coffee cans. Put the dough, smooth side up, into the pail; or divide in half and put into the cans. Cover dough with towel and allow to rise about 20–30 minutes, until dough is nearly doubled in bulk.

Meanwhile, preheat oven to 350 degrees F. Baste top of dough with beaten egg. Bake for about 1½ hours for a 4-quart container, or 1 hour for the two 2-quart containers. Before removing from the oven, test by inserting a long straw or skewer. The loaf is done when skewer comes out clean. Brush the top of the loaf or loaves with melted butter while still hot. Allow to cool in the pail for about 20 minutes before turning out.

To serve the bread, cut into four equal sections, then slice. Serve with fresh sweet butter or Brie.

ONION ROLLS
Yield: 48 rolls

DOUGH:
1 tablespoon dry yeast
1 cup warm water
1 tablespoon honey
2 large eggs
1½ teaspoons salt
1¼ cups light vegetable oil
2 cups whole wheat flour
2–3 cups unbleached white flour

FILLING:
1 cup finely minced onion
1 teaspoon salt
1 tablespoon poppy seeds
1 tablespoon caraway seeds or dillseed or dillweed
¾ cup bread crumbs
¼ cup oil

GLAZE: 1 beaten egg

Dissolve yeast in water with the honey and allow to bubble up. Stir eggs, salt, and oil into yeast mixture and enough whole wheat and white flour to form a stiff dough.

Knead until smooth and elastic, on a well-floured surface; adding more white flour as needed. This takes from 7 to 10 minutes. Place dough in an oiled bowl and cover with a damp cloth. Let rise in a warm place until doubled in bulk—about 1 hour.

Punch down and knead briefly on a floured surface. Let rest.

Prepare filling by mixing all ingredients together.

With a floured rolling pin, roll out dough on a floured surface into a rectangle about 18 × 24 inches. Cut dough into 6 × 3-inch pieces.

Spoon about 1 heaping teaspoon filling onto center third of each dough piece, reserving a bit to sprinkle on top of formed rolls. Then fold one side over the filling and second side over that. Gently pinch ends to close. Place rolls, seam side down, on oiled cookie sheets and flatten them out until they are 5 inches long—then cut in half.

Brush rolls with eggwash and sprinkle with remaining onion mixture. Let rise until almost doubled, about 35 to 45 minutes. Meanwhile, preheat oven to 400 degrees F.

Bake the rolls for 15 to 20 minutes until golden. Remove to racks to cool.

They freeze very well.

MAPLE MOUSSE
Serves 4

A very special old-fashioned treat was Maple Mousse, made in a bucket of ice.

3 eggs, separated
1 cup maple syrup
1 pint heavy cream, whipped

Beat egg yolks until light, adding maple syrup gradually. Place in the top of a double boiler over boiling water and cook until thick.

After the syrup cools, fold in stiffly beaten egg whites and whipped cream. Pour into a 1-quart mold. Pack in a bucket of ice and salt: 4 parts ice to 1 part salt. Let stand 4 hours. Turn out to serve on a chilled platter.

MAPLE JACK

Maple sugar or syrup was the only sweetening condiment found on the dining tables of Early American kitchens of the Northeast. These American settlers used maple syrup all year round for baking, candy treats, and sweetening teas, just as the Indians did. Whenever there was a fresh snowfall over the woodlands, old-time maple harvesters made this quick candy treat.

Place a quantity of maple syrup in a heavy cooking pot over a medium heat. Bring to a boil and lower heat until syrup is lightly simmering.

Meanwhile collect fresh, clean snow in a wide pan and bring it to kitchen, or site of simmering syrup. After the syrup has boiled down somewhat, pour a few drops onto the fresh snow. If the hot syrup soaks into the snow, then more simmering is required. Continue testing until a few drops collect in a little pool and set up on the cold snow. The maple syrup should be slightly transparent and of a soft taffy consistency. At this stage, pour puddles of hot maple syrup measuring about 1 tablespoon each, onto the cold snow. Wait a few moments until cool enough to remove with the fingers. Children enjoy making Maple Jack, and are especially fascinated by the strange-shaped, smooth impressions left in the snow when the warm candy is removed.

RHUBARB LATTICE PIE
Yield: one 9-inch pie

FILLING:
3 cups diced rhubarb
2 eggs, beaten
½ cup plus 2 tablespoons light honey
1 tablespoon white wine
1 tablespoon flour

PASTRY:
¾ cup whole wheat pastry flour
¾ cup unbleached white flour
6 tablespoons butter
Ice water

6 large strawberries, sliced
2 tablespoons butter

Preheat oven to 425 degrees F.

Combine rhubarb, eggs, honey, wine, and flour in a mixing bowl and set aside.

In another mixing bowl, combine flours. Cut in butter until about the size of peas. Add ice water, a little at a time, stirring dry over wet until mixture just begins to hold together. Remove the dough to a flour-dusted surface and press together gently. Divide dough into two equal portions. On the lightly floured surface roll out one half the dough into a circle about ⅛ inch thick and 1 inch larger in diameter than the top of a 9-inch pie plate. Set the dough into the plate, leaving edge extending until lattice top is in place.

Roll out remaining dough to ⅛ inch thickness. With a sharp knife, cut into strips about ¾ inch wide. Fill the pie shell with the rhubarb mixture. Garnish with strawberry slices, and top with dots of butter.

Form a lattice with strips of dough over top: Place first strip across center of the pie. Place second strip over the first, going in the opposite direction, at right angles, forming a cross. Place the next two strips on either side of the first, then the following two on either side of the second. Continue in this way, keeping all strips about ⅜ inch apart and as uniform and parallel as possible, until all strips are used up.

Trim edges of dough, fold bottom edge over top, and press gently together. Place pie in the preheated oven for 15 minutes. Reduce heat to 375 degrees F. and continue baking for 25 minutes, until golden. Allow to cool about 30 minutes before serving.

LITTLE CHOCOLATE CAKE
Serves 6

This is a very rich, tiny cake intended for very small servings.

3 ounces chocolate (2 ounces Tobler bittersweet and 1 ounce
   Baker's unsweetened)
1–2 tablespoons coffee or water, for melting chocolate
4 tablespoons butter, cut up small
1 heaping tablespoon flour
¼ cup sugar
2 eggs, separated
Pinch of salt
1 tablespoon sugar
1 recipe Chocolate Icing (*see recipe below*)

FOR GARNISH: Whipped cream

Preheat oven to 350 degrees F. Butter a springform pan 6 inches in diameter and 1½ inches deep, and dust with flour.

Break up chocolate and melt in coffee very slowly over low heat. Add butter, flour, ¼ cup sugar, and egg yolks, stirring well after each addition.

Beat egg whites with salt until they hold a soft shape. Add 1 tablespoon sugar. Beat a bit more, and then fold a large spoonful of the whites into the chocolate mixture. Fold in remaining whites and turn into the pan.

Bake 30 minutes. Let cool in pan and remove sides only when cake is cool and firm. Cool on a rack and prepare icing. (See recipe below.) When icing is ready, pour over top of cooled cake, spreading a bit down the sides.

Serve in small pieces with a dab of whipped cream.

CHOCOLATE ICING:
2 ounces chocolate (1 ounce Baker's unsweetened and 1 ounce
   Tobler bittersweet)
2 tablespoons water
1 tablespoon sugar
1 tablespoon sweet butter, at room temperature
½ teaspoon vanilla
Pinch of cinnamon

Melt chocolate together with water and sugar. Add butter, vanilla, and cinnamon. Stirring occasionally, cook over low heat until it thickens. Allow to cool at least 30 minutes before pouring over cake.

CREAM PUFFS
Yield: 1 dozen large

Chickens come out to stroll in the wet grass, pecking sprouts and grubs, as spring encourages a high production of eggs. Plenty of eggs means the luxury of creamy egg pastry.

PASTRY:
½ cup unbleached white flour
½ cup whole wheat pastry flour
½ cup butter
1 cup boiling water
4 eggs

1 recipe Cream Filling (*see recipe below*)
1 recipe Honey Chocolate Frosting (*optional; see recipe below*)

Preheat oven to 425 degrees F. Sift flours together and set aside.

Combine butter and boiling water in a saucepan; keep over low heat until butter is melted. Add flour mixture all at once and stir vigorously over low heat until mixture forms a ball and leaves the sides of the pan. Remove from heat and cool mixture 5 minutes.

Add unbeaten eggs, one at a time, beating thoroughly after each addition. Continue beating until a thick dough is formed.

Drop by heaping tablespoonfuls onto a greased baking sheet, about 2 inches apart. Cover with a large shallow roasting pan or aluminum foil tent to create steam around the pastry, encouraging them to puff to greater volume.

Bake in the hot oven for about 30 minutes, or until beads of moisture no longer appear on the pastry surfaces. Do not open the oven door during early part of baking. Remove to racks to cool.

When cool, slit the side of each puff and fill with Cream Filling or honey-sweetened whipped cream (about 2 cups). For a luxurious touch, paint the tops with a bit of Honey Chocolate Frosting.

CREAM FILLING:
Yield: 2¾–3 cups
⅔ cup honey
5 tablespoons flour
¼ teaspoon salt
1¾ cups milk
2 eggs, lightly beaten
1 teaspoon vanilla
½ cup heavy cream, whipped (*optional*)

Combine honey, flour, and salt in top of double boiler, stir in milk gradually. Cook over boiling water until thickened, stirring occasionally.

Stir a little of the hot mixture into beaten eggs. Then slowly stir the warmed eggs into hot mixture. Cook over hot, not boiling, water for 2 minutes, stirring constantly.

Chill; add vanilla. For a richer filling, whipped cream can be added at this point.

HONEY CHOCOLATE FROSTING:
Yield: about ⅔ cup
½ cup cocoa
⅓ cup honey
3 tablespoons (about) very hot water
2 tablespoons butter
1 teaspoon vanilla

Mix cocoa and honey to make a smooth paste. Stir in hot water very slowly to thin the paste to desired consistency, keeping the texture very smooth. Over low heat, stir in butter until it melts. Add vanilla. Cool and crown the filled puffs.

RHUBARB FOOL
Serves 6

Thick cream, a token of spring freshening, joins cool red rhubarb in "Fool," a quaint country pudding.

1 pound rhubarb, trimmed
3 tablespoons orange honey or other light honey
½ cup port wine
Grated rind of one lemon
2 cups heavy cream

Preheat oven to 350 degrees F. Cut rhubarb into 1-inch pieces. Combine rhubarb, honey, port, and lemon rind in baking dish. Cover and bake until tender, about 30 minutes.

Cool. Refrigerate until well chilled.

Place rhubarb in blender or food processor and blend until smooth. Beat cream, with extra honey to sweeten, until stiff.

Spoon a thin layer of rhubarb purée across bottom of each of 6 glasses; then add a 1-inch layer of whipped cream. Continue layering rhubarb and cream, ending with cream. Push a knife down the side of each glass and every ¾ inch, bring it up again quickly to form feathers.

Refrigerate, and serve chilled.

PINE NUT CAKE WITH PASTRY CREAM
Serves 6

CAKE BATTER:
2 eggs
⅓ cup sugar
½ teaspoon baking soda
1½ cups unbleached white flour
¼ cup (½ stick) butter, melted
½ teaspoon lemon extract

PASTRY CREAM:
2 egg yolks
¼ cup sugar
1 teaspoon vanilla
1 teaspoon lemon extract
¼ cup flour
½ cup hot milk
¼ cup pine nuts, for garnish

To make cake batter, break 2 eggs into a bowl. Sift ⅓ cup sugar, baking soda, and 1½ cups flour together and add to eggs. Add butter and ½ teaspoon lemon extract. Blend ingredients well and refrigerate for at least an hour.

To make Pastry Cream, beat egg yolks and sugar until light-colored and fairly thick. Add extracts and flour and blend thoroughly. Scrape into a small pot over low heat. Add hot milk very slowly, beating with a whisk until well thickened. Let cool— about ½ hour.

Preheat oven to 375 degrees F. and butter a quiche pan with a removable rim—7 inches is a good size.

Put half the batter into the tin and smooth it. Pour cooled pastry cream over it, leaving a small margin around the rim. Top the cream with remaining batter in large dollops (it will cover fully as it bakes). Sprinkle with nuts, place on a cookie sheet, and put in oven. Bake for 30 minutes until golden brown. Cool before serving.

SPRING HERBAL BATH

To revitalize skin after a dry, indoor winter under many layers of clothing, sink into a hot bath treated with this infusion.

TAKE A LARGE HANDFUL OF THE LEAVES OF EACH:
Comfrey
Nettle
Dandelion
Daisy

Place herbs in a large pot and cover with about 4 quarts of boiling water. Allow to steep about 20 minutes.
Strain, heat, and add to hot bath water.

Spring Menus

FEAST OF MAPLE
*Sour Cherry Soup
*Hush Puppies
Butter and Maple Syrup
*Wild Greens Sauté
*Watercress and Pear Salad

EQUINOX SUPPER
*Meadow Soup
Feta Cheese
Rye Crackers
*Baked or Fried Trout
*Potatoes Stewed with Wine
*Mountain Herb Salad
*Pine Nut Cake with Pastry Cream
Wild Herb Tea

RETURNING ROBIN
*Mountain Creek Soup
*Onion Cheese Pie with Spring Surprises
*Watercress and Beet Salad
May Wine
*Little Chocolate Cake
Fresh Pears

WHITE DAFFODIL BRUNCH
*Easter Bread
Brie
*April Violet Salad
*Maple Crepes
Steamed Asparagus
White Grapes in Sour Cream
Chilled White Grape Juice

BANQUET OF ROSES
*Creamy Green Asparagus Soup
*Stuffed Grape Leaves
Burgundy Wine
*Linguine with Shellfish
Young Garden Greens,
Tossed with Rose Petals,
Lemon Juice, and Honey
*Cream Puffs

* Recipe included in Spring section.

Part Two: Summer
PATHS OF FLOWERS

Summer

Warm days and vivid attractions blossom with June over the northern Catskills. Woodstock resumes an air of festival, with suddenly crowded village streets. A parade of humanity, splashed with shocking colors, in T-shirts and billowing skirts, passes in steady procession through the flea market and along Tinker Street. Glittering shops present locally crafted pottery, toys, and jewelry, with Victorian dollhouses, designer fashions, rare books, and antique hats.

Tourists stream out of buses to mingle with local poets and carpenters on the Village Green. Here, along the benches and in the grass, musicians arrange rehearsals for special summer events, while seasonal building work is hustled over paper-bag lunches. Friends and strangers rendezvous amid the play of children and dogs, often serenaded by the guitar or flute of a lone street musician.

Flashing in the midday sun, red fire trucks and brass bands rally in Tinker Street to celebrate the Fourth of July. Small-town tradition is elaborated by street side firemen's skits, games, booths, and music, attended by visitors from far and near. In the highlights of midsummer, the Library Fair comes down from Woodstock's old days. Thousands join to celebrate village life styles for the benefit of library and community. Children with painted faces dance through the giant rummage tent and around the astrologer's booth. Revelers costumed in extra frills and their rummage best are captured by the roving photographer. The afternoon fills with games, pets, popcorn, and exhilarant music from local bands, while thousands of old books are traded.

Beyond the village, soft contours of Woodstock's Overlook Mountain lie richly festooned, mantled with sunlight. The emerald splendor of blooming hardwoods calls visiting artists and hikers to explore and picnic along the mountain slopes. Hidden under arcades of grapes and woodbine, mossy tufts spread over soft pine needles on the sun-dappled forest floor. Galleries of fern beds and the rock walls of ancient Indian caves define lavish woodland chambers, flushed with the fragrance of blooming mountain laurel.

In the heights of Woodstock Mountain, amid flowers and burgundy robes, summer guests attend resplendent ceremonies with Tibetan lamas at the lofty Buddhist monastery. Across the resonant contemplation, other pilgrims follow a footpath through the woods to the old Gothic-style chapel hidden in the shade of tall oaks and beech trees. Travelers hear the story of the eccentric wood-carving priest, who in his mid-nineties still welcomed barefooted flower-children, wealthy elite, or devout celebrities of all creeds to share the ritual and sanctuary there. As in the days before history, an ancient and revered Presence in the mountain over Woodstock is still a celebrated source of inspiration.

Out of lofty mountain rocks, the clear, foaming Sawkill Creek cascades into a secret icy pool, known only to local undaunted bathers. Murmuring along cedar-lined ridges, mountain streams fill the Tannery Brook below, to cool the thriving village.

Landscape and color-field painting echo the beauty of the village setting in summer galleries. In the Maverick woodland, the afternoon is cool, for a small audience listening to a string quartet. Israeli salad at Joshua's Café and summer drama at the Playhouse are the pleasures of dusk. Electric jazz rhythms warm the Woodstock evening from the Espresso. Sounds and electricity crescendo with supreme rock guitars and a fiery late-night dance at the Joyous Lake. At the break of dawn, Woodstock is a quiet, sleepy town again.

Blueberry Hill

Midsummer meadows grow lush with dewberries and butter-cups, blueberries, yarrow, and purple loosestrife. Dragonflies and fat bees skim the ground ivy and climb with pasture roses among the trees. The earth lies hushed as moist heat lures heavy clouds. Soon, the afternoon skies burst into thundering spectacle, re-freshing the day and energizing the soil and flowers.

Summer ripens with drooping sunflower heads and branches heavy with fruit. Blackberries drip from green clearings dotted with blossoming red clover. Black-eyed Susans and Queen Anne's lace sway elegantly in the meadow under a haze of pollen. Fields grow amethyst with loosestrife, as red-winged blackbirds play in the feathery spires of goldenrod. Faint burnished tones in the thick forest cloak foretell the autumn.

The heat of summer quells in the mountain's cooling July nights. A scabrous burring of the first timid katydid etches the darkness. By August, the pulsing drone of a katydid chant deep-ens to possess every direction of the night, warning that there is six weeks until frost.

The August forager creeps through blackberry thorns and thickets of nettle and poison ivy. Under an archway of twisted grape runners, fruiting elder branches and blackberry canes are woven together with bits of dried grasses and animal hair. A fragile wren's nest cradles newly hatched fragments of life, lying with their broken eggshells among the thorns. There are many discoveries in the wild after midsummer, including an abundance of culinary enrichments.

BLACKBERRIES — *Pick luscious berries for slump, cobblers, and jam. Freeze extra for winter desserts. Cut back fruiting canes after harvest for more production next year.*

Blackberries

BLUEBERRIES — *Gather berries promptly when their brief season arrives. Eat fresh with breakfast; make jelly, or freeze the rest. Drop frozen berries into muffin and pancake batters.*

Chickory

CHICKORY — *Put fresh, bright blue flowers in salad for sparkling flavor. Believed to open spiritual consciousness.*

CRABAPPLES — *Cook with low-pectin fruits to enrich texture for preserves or fruit butter.*

EVENING PRIMROSE — *Gather young, preflowering roots for stews or sautés. Use fresh yellow flowers in salad. Brew flowering tops for arthritis relief. Bundle and dry plants in a dark place.*

Evening Primrose

SUMAC (SQUAWBUSH) — *Steep red flowers for refreshing lemony tea, good hot or cold. Boil down flower infusion with maple syrup. Store and use to treat coughs. (Caution: Use red flowers only: greenish-white flowers are from poison sumac.)*

Sumac (Squawbush)

TANSY — *Collect and bundle the long stems. Hang in a dark place to dry. The yellow button flowers retain their color for winter bouquets, Christmas packages, and tonic herbal tea blends.*

WILD CARROT — *Collect tender roots before plants flower. Use for salads or steam and butter. Gather flowering tops and seeds to fragrantly garnish salads.*

Wild Carrot

The Scarecrow

As the solstice dawns, day eclipses night in a pinnacle of summer's triumph. Delayed darkness, a miracle of midsummer, recalls ancient people in a virgin landscape who burned fires into the shortest night to appease the sun, now descending back toward darkness and, ultimately, barren winter.

Throughout July's smoldering haze, the vegetable garden beams exuberance, a flourishing sanctuary where earth communes with humans. Out of the body of our planet, nutrients crystallize into new life forms, encouraged by the sun and rain and the gardener's gentle hand. Jungles of summer are fruiting with twisted shiny squashes, clusters of peas, pungent scallions and dill, and knobs of delicate new potatoes under the soil. Amid visual and epicurean treasures, we are aware participants in the great power of creation.

Corn is a majestic garden plant, tall and tressed, graceful and noble as a human. It is the symbol of American farming and cuisine. Even in Native American agriculture, the spiritual element of corn was emphasized. The tale of *Hiawatha* portrays a Native American guardian ritual for the corn. On a midsummer night, Minnehaha, Laughing Water, disrobed in the flowering corn and walked with the spirits of health and abundance, to trace a magic circle of protection around the crop.

Corn is a heavy feeder, its bearing an indicator for the general health of the garden. Anywhere soil has been naturally enriched and loosened, corn grows fast and bright green. Midsummer side dressings of manure tea or compost to young topping plants will help produce generous ears.

Growing strong in rich, well-nourished soil, all vegetable plants have greatest resistance to disease and pests. The few pests that are attracted to the garden can be controlled in periodic early morning raids and inspections. Dusky moist air finds cabbage loopers feeding openly, and squash beetles buzzing inside open blossoms. Bugs or infested flowers can be removed and destroyed.

With every July rainfall, huge weeds mysteriously regenerate. Rows must be turned and weeds pulled from close around the plants. Peas welcome extra water and cultivation to encourage production well into midsummer. To keep fattening tomatoes from ground rot and mice nibblers, lift newly fruiting vines to a simple framework constructed between rows. Burgeoning pumpkin runners should be guided away from smaller plants, which tendrils will uproot, and into their growing spaces. Raise a network of brush over lettuce beds to filter hot sunshine and protect from bolting.

With all plants from the spring established, there is time to give personal expression to a life-size scarecrow. Stuff buttoned old clothes with straw to form a body. Add a recently worn outer garment (hat, shirt, or shawl), which can be changed periodically to keep a fresh repellent human odor. Prop the new family member high on a pole with fluttering tin plates hung where the hands should be. The scarecrow's presence will abide the season, a statuesque warning to neighborhood critters.

Midsummer Planting

Early summer is the time for making new nursery beds for cabbage family plants to mature for the fall and winter. Shaded rows between tall corn make good late lettuce beds, where cooler soil will allow germination. Looking toward an overflowing October pantry, fill the empty, harvested garden spaces with new beds of root vegetables and hardy greens.

JUNE 15	JULY 1	AUGUST 1
Beets	Beets	Beets
Broccoli	Bok Choy	Chard
Cabbage	Broccoli	Kale
Carrots	Carrots	Lettuce
Cauliflower	Chard	Radishes
Corn	Chinese Cabbage	Spinach
Dill	Dill	Strawberries
Eggplant Seedlings	Kale	Turnips
Lettuce	Lettuce	
Snap Beans	Peas	
	Snap Beans	
	Spinach	
	Turnips	

Kitchen Cornucopia

Many garden vegetables produce a final burgeoning yield by midsummer. Several of these, with their companions thriving in the wild, should be collected and stored for winter use before the final summer planting.

All garden products must be picked at their peak of ripeness. Vegetables must be cleaned quickly in cold water, and canned, frozen, or eaten immediately to keep up with garden production and capture the garden essence. Experience suggests that most of the midsummer harvest is best suited for freezing. Tender asparagus, snap beans, broccoli, cauliflower, all peas, shelled, snap, or snow, spinach, herbs, and other greens, retain their color, texture, and flavor well in freezing. The faster the freezing, the better the results. Use small, airtight packages, spread out in the freezer for maximum circulation of the cold. Extra yields of certain vegetables make special treats for the pantry. Pickle green snap beans or snow peas with garlic and fresh sprigs of dill. Can young beets whole with additions of sugar beets for added sweetness. Beets stay bright magenta, firm, and sweet in the canning process or when pickled with vinegar, cloves, and orange peel. For best results, always select the youngest, healthiest vegetables for any processing. Consult the latest canning jar manufacturers' catalogues for up-to-date, precise instructions for safe and successful canning and freezing.

As locusts drone through dreamy afternoons, windows are propped open and the spell of dusky summer air is ever present. There is less to distinguish the outside from inside. Footsteps track garden leaves and dirt across the country kitchen floor. Great clusters of drying herbs and flowers obscure the rafters, as jewel-colored preserves and bouquets of marigolds line up on the table. Counter top and sink are cluttered with baskets and buckets overflowing with giant leaves of chard, bouquets of basil and dill, piles of corn, zucchini, peppers, and tomatoes.

Summer culminates in a lavish bounty. This is the pinnacle of the gardening year and country dining. Food directly from the earth is brought to the table in simple preparation. Reverent handling of garden treasures is most appealing to hot weather appetites. Raw vegetable mosaics dressed with variations of herbal and flower essences or lightly stir-fried with tofu and nuts are central to daily cuisine. Cantaloupe and raspberry salads are substantial combined with nuts, seeds, and dried fruit bits, dressed with crushed berries and honey.

Surplus from these summer repasts must be expediently stored away in useful and healthful ways for winter months ahead. Tomatoes often produce in unrelenting quantities. Many tomatoes as well as other produce can be squeezed into batches of rich sauce for pasta and other dishes. These sauces freeze well. The simplest way to deal with an abundance of tomatoes is to can them. This requires peeling and packing into sterilized jars with a water bath process.

Early and late corn may be producing simultaneously in the northeastern August garden. Large quantities can be steamed and served for a substantial meal, with butter and beans, or dark bread. Corn roasting in an open outdoor fire is memorable summer feasting. Remove the silk, leaving husks intact, and place in the coals. Corn is also delicious husked, wrapped in foil with butter, chopped parsley and cilantro, and a touch of garlic, then roasted. Always turn the ears frequently. Corn biscuits, dumplings, or pancakes are delicious for breakfast or supper. Raw corn salad with peppers and scallions is a spicy summer lunch. Extra corn should be taken very fresh from the stalk to the kitchen for canning or freezing. Pressure canning requires long processing at high temperatures. However, deep corn flavor and minerals are preserved. A delightful aroma wafts from jars freshly opened for winter chili or a corn casserole. Some people prefer freezing corn for better color and more delicate taste. There are varieties especially recommended by seed companies for each preserving method.

Peppers should be left in the garden until frost. Use them sparingly and allow a few to ripen to bright red, when a spicy sweet taste change occurs. Any surplus of peppers can be frozen in slivers. A few of the frozen slivers add much flavor to salad dressings and vegetable slaws. Traditionally, peppers have been pickled with sugar and spices, or put up in oil and garlic.

Overproduction of zucchini and other summer squash can be a problem, as they do not retain integrity in canning or freezing. They might be sliced and dried for flavorful additions to winter stews. However, without special drying equipment this process of food storage is not practical in a moist summer climate with minimal hours of direct sunlight. After eating zucchini in its many disguises—stuffed with seasoned bread crumbs, breaded, fried, and baked with cheese and tomato sauce, or lightly stir-fried with other vegetables—flaky zucchini tea breads can be baked, and frozen for winter breakfasts and luncheons. They remain quite oven-fresh, if wrapped well and frozen quickly.

A favorite way to store tomatoes, peppers, zucchini, and eggplant, is to make ratatouille. The concept of ratatouille comes to us from the French Mediterranean. It is basically the sensual and delicious combination of these vegetables with olive oil, onion, and garlic. There are many versions of this dish, with variations in proportions, addition of herbs, and length of cooking. An excellent ratatouille can be made by first peeling and simmering tomatoes with red wine, parsley, and light seasoning, into a rich sauce. The eggplant is sliced and browned; and equal quantities of peppers, zucchini, and onion slices are sautéed in an ample amount of olive oil, with garlic and basil. The tomato sauce is combined liberally with all the vegetables, and the dish is ready for serving stuffed in omelets, or as an accompaniment for steamed rice or baked fish. Ratatouille freezes well. It can be prepared in a large batch, then packed away in quantities convenient for fast and fancy winter meals.

With late summer comes the abundance of fruits in the northeast. Some strawberries, blueberries, and blackcaps are still producing past midseason. Peaches, watermelons, cantaloupes, and red raspberries are turning plump and rosy in Catskill backyards and orchards by August. To capitalize on this abundance, there are many kitchen treasures to prepare with fruit and a minimal amount of sugar or honey. Jams, preserves, and chutneys are joys to the family, especially children, good for lunches, treats, and gifts in leaner days to come.

One old-time practice was putting up jars of brandied fruit. Soft summer fruits in large chunks or halves were layered in wide-mouth jars with a choice of any type of brandy, and honey or maple syrup dribbled over the layers. Fruits stayed preserved in the brandy; often the jar was reopened throughout the season, with cherries, berries, peaches, etc., being added as they ripened. In antique jars, shiny and decked with ribbons, brandied fruit makes beautiful and gracious presents at Christmastime.

GARDEN DELIGHT:

Summer Recipes & Menus

WOODSTOCK'S PRIZEWINNING TOFU–SESAME PASTE APPETIZER
Serves 4

This recipe was inspired by a Japanese dish served at the Little Bear in Woodstock. The sauce is delicious on noodles or spaghetti, and the result is traditionally served cold.

1½–2 tablespoons tahini (sesame seed paste)	1 teaspoon white or rice wine vinegar, or to taste
1 tablespoon tamari soy sauce	1 clove garlic, crushed
1 tablespoon sesame oil	¼ teaspoon grated peeled, fresh gingerroot
1 tablespoon safflower oil	⅛ teaspoon cayenne pepper
1 teaspoon honey, or to taste	1 pound tofu

FOR GARNISH: Chopped scallions

In a small wooden bowl, place first 4 ingredients. Add honey and vinegar, adjusting amount according to taste. Add garlic and gingerroot. Then add cayenne carefully, a little at a time. The sauce should be spicy but not painfully hot. When you feel the seasoning is correct, put a plate over the bowl and let the sauce sit 2 or 3 hours. Cut tofu into bite-size cubes, place in wide serving bowl, pour sauce over, and garnish with chopped scallions. Chill and serve.

BAKED FARMER CHEESE
Serves 4

Baked Farmer Cheese is a luncheon or buffet delight, fresh and warm as a summer afternoon. This recipe comes from the farm, where the family cow has just freshened and there is a never-ending surplus of milk for making fresh cheese, ready to enjoy without aging.

1 pound farmer or fresh homemade cheese	⅓ cup chopped dates
⅓ cup chopped walnuts	1 teaspoon honey

Preheat oven to 350 degrees F. Combine all ingredients in a mixing bowl, and mix well. Press mixture into a small baking dish, 5 inches square, or equivalent. Bake about 20 minutes until the cheese seems "set" and faintly golden on top.

Chill the Baked Farmer Cheese, and serve with fresh fruit, light crackers, or bread.

SNAP BEAN PÂTÉ
Yield: 4 cups

⅔ cup sunflower seeds
⅓ cup walnuts
1 large onion, chopped
2 tablespoons oil

1 quart snap beans
2 teaspoons tamari soy sauce
Freshly ground black pepper to taste

FOR GARNISH: Few sprigs, fresh parsley

Combine seeds and nuts, and dry-roast in a heavy skillet for 2 to 3 minutes, stirring constantly as they lightly brown. Set aside.

Fry onions in oil until slightly browned.

Steam snap beans until just tender, but still green.

Combine all prepared ingredients with tamari and a little black pepper in food processor, and process until paste is formed.

Place the pâté in refrigerator and chill.

Serve in a bowl, garnished with parsley.

Snap Bean Pâté is very good with rye crackers, or any bread, especially Zucchini Walnut Bread (*see Index*) and thick slices of tomato.

CHINESE SOUR SOUP
Serves 4–6

A dish influenced by the Orient to awaken the eye, the palate, and the soul to summer.

1 ounce dried tree ear mushrooms*
Boiling water
6 cups Vegetable Broth (*see Index*)
½ cup fresh, closed day lily buds
   (Dried day lilies can be used; soak in hot water for
   ½ hour, drain, measure.)
½ cup drained canned straw mushrooms
¼ cup cider vinegar
2½–3 tablespoons tamari soy sauce
2 tablespoons dry sherry
12 ounces tofu, cut in strips
Freshly ground black pepper
2 tablespoons arrowroot, dissolved in ⅓ cup water
2 eggs, well beaten
2 teaspoons sesame oil

* Dried tree ear mushrooms can be found in many health food shops and shops that specialize in oriental delicacies.

FOR GARNISH:
3–4 scallions, chopped
Several fresh opened day lilies

Soak dried mushrooms in boiling water for about 20 minutes.

To the vegetable broth, add the drained tree ear mushrooms, lily buds, canned straw mushrooms, vinegar, tamari, and sherry. Gently drop in the tofu strips. Grind in a few sprinkles of black pepper and marinate for 1 hour.

Slowly bring the soup to a boil. Add the arrowroot water and stir gently until thickened. Allow to simmer for several minutes. Remove from heat and slowly whisk in eggs. Add sesame oil. Garnish with scallions and day lily blossoms.

Serve Chinese Sour Soup at once with whole wheat crackers and a raw vegetable platter with creamy garlic dip.

STRAWBERRY SOUP
Serves 4

From June's strawberry fields come jewels to crown many tasty wonders.

2 cups sliced strawberries
1½ cups canned peach nectar or 1 cup fresh peach pulp
    pureed with ½ cup water
2 cups water
2 cups apple juice
⅛ teaspoon nutmeg, freshly grated
⅛ teaspoon salt
1 tablespoon fresh lemon juice
½ cup Chablis or May wine

FOR GARNISH:
½ pint heavy cream, whipped

Place strawberries in heavy enameled pot with the peach nectar and water. Cover the pot and cook mixture over low heat until strawberries lose their color, and become soft, about 15 minutes.

Drain strawberries in a large strainer placed over a bowl to collect liquid. Press the berries through the strainer back into the liquid. Add apple juice, nutmeg, and salt.

Heat the soup, stirring constantly for 3 minutes to set flavors. Chill thoroughly.

Just before serving add fresh lemon juice and the white wine. Spoon into individual bowls, and garnish each with a puff of whipped cream.

GAZPACHO
Serves 4

Straight from the soil and sunshine, this wonderful garden dish tastes of late summer with the color and mood of autumn.

2 cups chopped ripe tomatoes
¾ cup chopped seeded
  cucumbers
¾ cup chopped onions,
  preferably red
½ cup chopped green peppers
2 cloves garlic

½ small hot pepper
2 tablespoons olive oil
2 tablespoons wine vinegar
2 cups cold water
1 tablespoon chopped fresh
  basil
Salt and pepper

FOR GARNISH:
Chopped parsley, or cucumbers, or green peppers, or onions,
  or tomatoes
Croutons

Place all ingredients in container of a food processor or electric blender and process until just mixed, allowing the mixture to have some texture. Pour into a large bowl and check seasonings. Chill at least 2 hours and serve garnished with a choice of chopped vegetables and croutons on the side.

CORN CHOWDER
Serves 6

Old-time homestead cooks used surplus corn in every imaginable way. A favorite treat for late summer cool nights was a supper of Corn Chowder, served with hot biscuits and fresh sliced tomatoes.

4 cups boiling water
2 heaping cups diced potatoes
1 small onion, diced
1 cup grated carrot
1 teaspoon sea salt
½ teaspoon freshly ground
  black pepper

4 cups (8 ears) fresh corn
  kernels
2–3 teaspoons minced fresh
  red hot pepper
½ pint heavy cream

Bring water to boil in a large Dutch oven or other heavy pot. Drop in potatoes, onions, carrot, and salt. Simmer until potatoes are tender, about 15 minutes.

Remove broth and cooked vegetables to blender, about a third at a time. Blend until smooth purée forms, adding more water if necessary. Return the purée to the large pot.

Add pepper and corn kernels. Heat soup to simmering point, and gently simmer for about 1 minute. Add minced hot pepper and cream. Adjust seasoning, adding more salt if desired; stir. Serve immediately while still hot.

TOFU AND BROCCOLI WITH SPICY PEANUT SAUCE
Serves 4–6

½ cup dry red wine
½ cup vinegar
¼ teaspoon dried red pepper flakes
¼ cup water
¼ cup heavy cream
5 scallions, thinly sliced
1 teaspoon honey
2 tablespoons tamari soy sauce
1 (½-inch) slice gingerroot, peeled and minced
4 cloves garlic, finely chopped
2 small green chilies, finely chopped
Freshly ground black pepper
3 tablespoons (about) peanut oil
1 pound tofu, thinly sliced
1 head broccoli (about 1½ pounds)
½ pound mushrooms, sliced
4 tablespoons chunky peanut butter

Combine wine, vinegar, and red pepper flakes in a 2-quart pot and bring to a boil over medium high heat. Boil until reduced to ¼ cup, 12 to 15 minutes. Stir in water, cream, 2 tablespoons scallions, honey, tamari, 1 teaspoon minced ginger, 1 teaspoon minced garlic, chilies, black pepper, and bring back to a boil. Cook, stirring constantly, until sauce is thickened. Set aside.

In a wok, heat 2 tablespoons of the peanut oil. Cook tofu slices until lightly browned. Remove tofu to a warmed covered dish and set wok aside.

Cut broccoli into small flowerets, and thinly slice stalks. Lightly steam prepared broccoli, leaving still quite crisp.

Add about another tablespoon of oil to the wok. Stir-fry remaining scallions, ginger, and garlic together. Add mushrooms; continue tossing the mixture until they are tender. Finally, add drained broccoli, tossing in the hot oil 1 minute.

Return sauce to a low heat. Whisk in peanut butter, 1 tablespoon at a time, whisking until smooth. Adjust seasoning.

Arrange stir-fried vegetables on a warmed platter. Place tofu slices on top and pour peanut sauce over the tofu. Serve with steamed brown rice.

BRAISED TOFU WITH EGGPLANT AND CHICK-PEAS
Serves 4–6

2 medium eggplants (about
1 pound each) halved
  lengthwise, peeled and
  sliced
1 tablespoon salt
½ cup vegetable oil
1 pound tofu, cut in
  2 × 1-inch chunks
2 medium onions, thinly
  sliced
3 large cloves garlic, minced
1 teaspoon ground cumin

4 large tomatoes, peeled,
  seeded, and chopped
1½ cups cooked chick-peas
3 tablespoons lemon juice
¼ teaspoon freshly ground
  black pepper
Salt to taste
1 tablespoon chopped fresh
  mint
½ cup torn spinach leaves
2 tablespoons finely chopped
  fresh parsley

Toss eggplant with salt in medium bowl. Drain under a weight,
in a colander. Let sit 30 minutes, then squeeze and dry.

Heat oil in large pan over medium heat. Cook eggplant slices
in batches until all are brown and tender. Keep warm. Wipe out
pan and return to heat.

Add a little more oil to pan. Sauté tofu chunks about 2 minutes on each side and remove. Keep warm. Sauté onions until
transparent, about 6 minutes. Stir in garlic and cumin and cook
1 minute. Add tomatoes, chick-peas, lemon juice, black pepper,
salt, and mint. Simmer 5 minutes. Return tofu to pan. Simmer
10 minutes. Return eggplant to pan and add spinach and chopped
parsley. Cook further, 5 to 10 minutes. Serve immediately with
either hot whole wheat pita bread or brown rice.

FRESH TOMATO AND EGGPLANT PIZZA
Serves 6–8

CRUST:
1 tablespoon active dry yeast
⅓ cup warm water
1 tablespoon honey
1 tablespoon olive oil
2½ cups stone-ground whole wheat bread flour
½ teaspoon salt
½ cup warm milk
1–3 tablespoons water, as needed

Cornmeal for sprinkling over pan

Sprinkle yeast over warm water and honey. Let stand 5 minutes until yeast dissolves. Add oil, whole wheat flour, salt and

milk and blend thoroughly. Form dough into a ball, adding extra water if needed to make firm and elastic, not sticky.

Knead 10 minutes on a lightly floured surface. Transfer ball of dough to an oiled bowl and turn several times so entire surface is oiled. Cover with a damp cloth and let rise in a warm place until doubled in bulk, about 1 hour.

Prepare tomato sauce while dough is rising:

TOMATO SAUCE:

Yield: 2½ cups

3 tablespoons olive oil
1 onion, finely chopped
2 cloves garlic, minced
1 pound tomatoes, peeled, seeded, and finely diced
1 6-ounce can tomato paste
1½ teaspoons dried basil or 1 tablespoon chopped fresh basil
1 tablespoon dried oregano or 2 tablespoons fresh oregano
1 teaspoon honey
1 teaspoon salt
Freshly ground black pepper
1 bay leaf
¼ teaspoon crushed red pepper

In a large saucepan, heat oil over medium high heat. Add onions and cook until soft and transparent. Add garlic, diced tomatoes, tomato paste, basil, oregano, honey, salt and pepper, bay leaf, and red pepper. Simmer, covered, 1 hour. Remove bay leaf. Unused portion of sauce can be frozen.

PIZZA TOPPING:

1 eggplant (1½–2 pounds), halved lengthwise, then thinly sliced
2 teaspoons salt
2 tablespoons oil, or as needed
1 clove garlic, minced
1 cup Tomato Sauce
1½ pounds shredded mozzarella cheese
1 onion, thinly sliced
2 tomatoes, finely diced
1 tablespoon chopped fresh basil
1 teaspoon salt
Freshly ground black pepper
1 tablespoon chopped fresh oregano or 1 teaspoon dried
Olive oil

Sprinkle eggplant slices with salt and toss well. Set in a colander with heavy plate over top to press out juices. Let stand 30 minutes. Squeeze and pat dry with paper towel.

Heat oil in a large skillet. Add garlic and eggplant. Cook till eggplant is browned on both sides.

TO ASSEMBLE:

Preheat oven to 475 degrees F. Punch dough down, knead briefly, shape into a ball, and let rest 5 minutes.

Oil a round pizza baking sheet at least 15 inches in diameter.

Roll dough (or pinch and pull) into a large circle, about ¼ inch thick. Sprinkle baking sheet with cornmeal. Place dough on the baking sheet and pinch up edges for rim. *(continued)*

Spread tomato sauce evenly over the crust. Sprinkle half the shredded mozzarella over the tomato sauce. Arrange eggplant over mozzarella, then onion rings, then finely diced tomatoes and basil. Sprinkle with salt and pepper and top with the rest of the cheese. Sprinkle with oregano and dribble a little olive oil over the top.

Bake 25 minutes, or until crust is browned and cheese is bubbly. Serve hot.

SPINACH-ALMOND LASAGNA
Serves 6

1½ tablespoons olive oil
4 medium cloves garlic, minced
¼ cup chopped sweet fresh herbs (parsley and basil)
½ cup almonds
¼ pound Romano or Parmesan cheese, shredded
1 cup ricotta cheese
1 cup cottage cheese

2 eggs, beaten
1½ cups chopped, cleaned spinach
3 cups Tomato Sauce (*see Index*)
1 pound lasagna noodles, cooked according to package directions
½–¾ pound mozzarella cheese, shredded

Preheat oven to 375 degrees F. Heat oil and gently sauté garlic and herbs. Set aside.

Roast almonds in a dry hot pan until browned, shaking pan occasionally to keep the almonds turning. Grind the roasted almonds in a food processor, and combine with 3 tablespoons grated Romano or Parmesan cheese.

Combine the remaining Romano or Parmesan, the ricotta, cottage cheese, and eggs in a mixing bowl. Mix in the sautéed herbs, almonds, and spinach.

Oil a shallow baking pan (10 × 14 inches) Spread about 1 cup of Tomato Sauce on the bottom. Place a layer of noodles over the sauce. Spread ⅓ of the spinach-almond-cheese mixture over the noodles. Sprinkle with ⅓ of the shredded mozzarella and cover with Tomato Sauce. Make 2 more layers in the same way, ending with sauce on top.

Bake the lasagna, covered with foil, for about 15 minutes. Remove cover and continue baking for another 15 minutes, until the top is lightly browned and bubbly.

Remove from oven and let the lasagna mellow a few minutes before serving. Serve warm with a fresh, green, leafy salad.

TOMATO TART
Serves 4

PASTRY:
¾ cup unbleached white flour
Pinch of salt
4 tablespoons unsalted butter, in small pieces
2 tablespoons (about) water

FILLING:
1 large onion, thinly sliced
2 tablespoons butter
2 teaspoons (about) fresh crushed thyme leaves
Salt and pepper to taste
3 large eggs
¼ cup heavy cream
¼ cup milk
Dash of tamari soy sauce
Dash of tabasco
3 tablespoons chopped fresh parsley

3 tablespoons chopped fresh basil (or fresh dill, or chives, or small amount of dried oregano)
6 tablespoons grated Romano cheese
1 tablespoon Dijon mustard
¼ cup grated smoked mozzarella cheese (or Cheddar or Swiss)
1½ to 2 pounds firm, ripe tomatoes, peeled and sliced ¼ inch thick

To make pastry, mix flour and salt; add butter and blend with a pastry cutter until mixture resembles cornmeal in texture. Add water as needed to form dough into a ball. Wrap in wax paper and chill for at least 1 hour.

On floured surface, roll out dough and fit it into an 8-inch quiche pan. Chill for another ½ hour, at least.

Preheat oven to 425 degrees F. Prick dough in a few places with a fork. Place pan on a cookie sheet. Line dough with aluminum foil and fill with dried beans. Bake 15 minutes. Remove foil and beans. Reduce heat to 400 degrees F., and bake 5 to 10 more minutes, or until dough takes on a light golden color. Remove pastry from oven to cool while preparing the filling.

To prepare filling, smother onions in butter in a covered frying pan over a low heat until soft and yellowing. Add thyme, salt, and pepper.

In a mixing bowl, beat together the eggs, cream, milk, seasonings, herbs, and 3 tablespoons Romano cheese.

Spread the mustard thinly over bottom of cooled pastry; then spread onions and smoked mozzarella. Lay tomato slices in concentric rings over the cheese. Pour on the egg mixture; sprinkle with remaining Romano.

Bake the tomato tart at 400 degrees F. for 30 to 40 minutes, until firm and golden. Test by inserting a knife into center. Serve hot or cold.

SESAME PANCAKES WITH STIR-FRIED VEGETABLES
Serves 4–6

SESAME PANCAKES:
2 cups unbleached flour
¾ cup (about) boiling water
¼ cup sesame oil

FILLING:
5 tablespoons peanut oil
3 eggs
½ teaspoon salt
1 ⅜-inch slice of fresh
   gingerroot, peeled and
   finely chopped
4 scallions, finely chopped on
   the diagonal
½ pound tofu, cut into slivers
½ cup fresh day lily buds,
   finely sliced on the
   diagonal, or ½ cup shelled
   peas

½ cup finely sliced
   mushrooms
½ cup finely cut bamboo
   shoots
½ cup finely sliced cabbage
2 tablespoons tamari soy
   sauce
2 tablespoons rice wine or
   dry sherry
2 tablespoons water
1 teaspoon sesame oil
¼ teaspoon pepper
1 teaspoon arrowroot

FOR GARNISH:
½ cup hoisin sauce*
½ cup sliced scallions

Place the flour in a bowl, making a well in the center. Carefully add the boiling water, stirring quickly, and 1 teaspoon sesame oil. On a floured board knead dough until smooth, about 5 minutes, adding more flour if necessary. Return dough to bowl and cover. Let rest for 20 minutes.

Turn dough out onto a floured surface. Knead a little, then roll into a sausage shape. Cut in about 18 pieces. Roll each piece between your hands to make a smooth ball. Flatten 1 ball, brush the top with some sesame oil, then join with another ball. Flatten with your hands. With a rolling pin roll out the flattened balls into a circle about 5 inches in diameter.

Heat a pan on the stove, brush with sesame oil. Add 1 of the double pancakes, cook about ½ minute, turn and cook other side, to lightly brown. Don't overcook. Pull apart into 2 separate pancakes. Keep warm (or they may be frozen and reheated by steaming). Continue to make the rest of the pancakes in the same manner.

---

* Hoisin sauce is a rich, spicy-sweet bean paste. A popular Chinese condiment, it is available in many specialty or oriental food shops, and occasionally in the supermarket's oriental section.

To prepare filling, heat 2 tablespoons peanut oil in wok over moderate heat. Add beaten eggs and ¼ teaspoon salt, scramble lightly and set aside.

Add remaining peanut oil to pan. Heat and add ginger and slivers of scallion. Stir-fry 30 seconds. Add slivers of tofu, and toss in hot oil. Add sliced day lily buds, mushrooms, and bamboo shoots. Stir-fry 30 seconds. Add cabbage. Stir-fry another 30 seconds.

Combine tamari, wine, water, oil, remaining ¼ teaspoon salt, pepper, and arrowroot. Pour over vegetables, add scrambled eggs, and toss well together. Check seasonings. Place mixture on a heated platter.

Present vegetable filling with the Sesame Pancakes and with hoisin and slivered scallions on the side so that those at the table can serve themselves. The hoisin is spread over a pancake and topped with the vegetable mixture and scallions; the pancake is then rolled up ready to be eaten.

CANARY HILL BURGERS
Yield: 8 large burgers

2 cups dried chick-peas
1 slice whole wheat bread, crumbled
1 tablespoon unbleached white flour
½ teaspoon baking soda
3–4 cloves garlic, minced
1 small onion, grated
2 tablespoons minced fresh dill

2 tablespoons minced fresh parsley
½ teaspoon ground cumin
3 tablespoons minced sweet red pepper
¾ teaspoon salt
Freshly ground black pepper
2 eggs
Oil for frying
Pita bread

Cook chick-peas in enough water to cover (about 2 hours). When they are tender, drain, reserving cooking liquid.

Coarsely grind cooked chick-peas in food grinder or processor. Measure the reserved cooking liquid, adding water if necessary to make ⅓ cup. Add to the ground chick-peas together with all other remaining ingredients except 1 egg, oil, and pita bread.

Form the mixture into large patties. Heat oil in a large, heavy skillet. Beat the remaining egg, and brush some on the patties just before frying. When the oil is hot, fry the patties until golden on each side. Drain on absorbent paper.

Golden Canary Hill Burgers are very colorful and delicious. Stuff the hot burgers into warm pita bread and garnish with Catskill Chili Sauce or Tahini Sauce (see Index). Serve with an array of Middle Eastern salads, black Greek olives, and hot Tuscan peppers.

CATSKILL ENCHILADAS
Serves 4–6

Here is an original enchilada bake that features fresh Catskill-grown corn. Canned corn can be substituted for a hearty winter dinner.

ENCHILADA SAUCE:
about 2 cups

1 pound tomatoes
3 tablespoons diced green chili pepper
1 tablespoon olive oil
2–3 cloves garlic, minced
½–1 teaspoon cayenne pepper

1 tablespoon ground cumin
½ cup finely chopped onion
½ cup finely chopped green pepper
3 tablespoons butter
3 tablespoons unbleached white flour

Drop tomatoes into boiling water for one minute. Drain and peel. Chop tomatoes and measure out 2 cups. Whirl in blender with chili pepper until smooth.

Heat olive oil in pan and add garlic, spices, and onion, cooking gently until onion is transparent. Add pepper and cook another 2 to 3 minutes. Add tomato–chili pepper mixture, and simmer for 30 minutes.

In heavy-bottomed pan, melt butter and stir in flour. Slowly add tomato mixture, stirring continuously until the sauce begins to thicken. Cook sauce over low heat for 20 minutes more, until very thick and rich.

This sauce may be made well in advance and freezes well.

ENCHILADAS:

1 recipe Enchilada Sauce
10 corn tortillas
2½–3 cups shredded Monterey Jack cheese
½ cup fresh corn kernels (about 1 ear)

½ cup chopped pitted black olives
¼ cup chopped fresh parsley
¼ cup chopped fresh cilantro
¼ cup diced scallions

Prepare Enchilada Sauce and keep hot.

Preheat oven to 350 degrees F. Heat a skillet over moderate heat and quickly roast tortillas on both sides, until browned.

Arrange remaining ingredients in separate dishes. Dip side of tortilla to be filled in the hot sauce. Sprinkle a uniform quantity of each ingredient over each prepared tortilla in order given, reserving about ¾ cup cheese. Roll the tortilla and place seam side down in oiled baking pan, 10 inches by 14 inches. (The enchiladas may be frozen at this point for later use. Just add sauce before heating.)

Cover the tortillas with remaining sauce, sprinkle with remaining cheese, and bake 15 to 20 minutes, until browned and bubbly.

Serve with fresh green garden salad and mellow red wine garnished with chilled peach chunks.

SCALLOPED POTATOES
Serves 4–6

This dish is an old-fashioned American classic. Here it is embellished with other vegetables and baked in nut cream instead of the traditional milk.

5 medium-large potatoes
5 tablespoons peanut or cashew butter
2 cloves garlic, chopped
¼ teaspoon paprika
2 tablespoons cornmeal
1 teaspoon salt
2 cups sliced onions
1 cup sliced mushrooms
¾ cup peas
¾ cup fresh corn kernels (about 2 ears)
½ cup chopped fresh parsley

Preheat oven to 350 degrees F. Slice the potatoes thinly. Place in a cooking pot, and cover with cold water. Simmer until the potatoes are just tender, about 15 minutes. Drain, reserving liquid, and set aside.

Place nut butter in a blender with garlic, paprika, cornmeal, and salt. Measure out potato cooking liquid, and supplement with extra hot water if necessary to make 4 cups. Pour the hot water over the ingredients in the blender, and process until smooth.

Oil a 2-quart casserole, and cover the bottom with about a third of the potatoes. Sprinkle with about a third of the sliced onions and mushrooms, peas, corn, and parsley. Pour a third of the nut-butter mixture over the vegetables, and repeat with an arrangement of 2 more layers. Bake the casserole for about 30 minutes, until bubbly and slightly browned on top.

NOTE:
This is a delicious, hearty casserole for winter, which can be made with your own frozen peas and canned corn.

CURRIED SUMMER SEMOLINA
Serves 6

The addition of curry lends a delightful flavor to semolina. There are as many ways of making curry as there are of making a bouillabaisse, but the essential ingredients are mustard seed, turmeric, cumin, black pepper, and cinnamon.

3 tablespoons peanut oil
1 tablespoon yellow mustard seed
1 medium onion, chopped
1 large carrot, diced
½ bunch broccoli, (about ¾ pound) flowerets divided; stalk
  sliced
1 cup diced summer squash
1 cup peas
1½ tablespoons turmeric
1½ teaspoons ground cumin
⅛ teaspoon cayenne pepper
3 teaspoons cinnamon
½ teaspoon cardamom
½ teaspoon coriander
⅓ teaspoon freshly ground black pepper
7 cups boiling water
½ cup currants
1½ teaspoons salt
1¾ cups semolina
3½ tablespoons sweet butter

FOR GARNISH:
1 pint sour cream combined with 1 pint yogurt

Heat oil in a large heavy pot. Add mustard seed and heat until they begin to pop. Add onions, carrots, and broccoli. Sauté gently for about 1½ minutes. Add squash and peas and stir into the mixture for about 1 minute.

Add spices to the vegetable mixture. Toss to mix and continue to sauté for about 1 minute. Add boiling water, currants and salt. Raise heat until the water returns to a boil; reduce to a simmer. Continue to simmer until vegetables are just tender, about 3 minutes.

When vegetables are cooked to taste, very slowly pour the semolina in a thin stream into the pot, stirring constantly. The mixture will bubble up and thicken to creamy smooth. Stir in the butter.

Spoon Curried Summer Semolina into a large warmed bowl. Serve immediately with a mixture of sour cream and yogurt to garnish.

A bowl of roasted cashew nuts and fresh fruit are a tasty complement to this summer curry.

FAMILY BAKED BEANS
Serves 6

Baked beans are traditional summer picnic food. In the mountains, on a cool, rainy August day or evening, the steady warmth from the oven adds a comfortable glow to the house. In the winter anywhere, a pot of baking beans with the heat and aroma filling the kitchen, will also be deliciously welcoming.

1¼ cups dried great northern beans
1¼ cups dried navy or small brown beans
2 cloves garlic, split
2 bay leaves
Salt to taste plus 1 teaspoon salt
Freshly ground black pepper
1 medium onion, chopped
1 cup tomato purée
½ cup chili sauce*

3 tablespoons molasses
2 tablespoons prepared mustard
3 cloves garlic, minced
3 teaspoons chopped fresh thyme leaves
1 tablespoon tamari soy sauce
2 tablespoons oil
1 medium onion, quartered
4 tablespoons butter
¼ cup dry sherry

Soak dried beans in 2 separate pots, with plenty of water to cover, for 6 hours. Drain, rinse, and cover with water again. Set pots over medium heat. Add 1 split garlic clove, 1 bay leaf, and a little salt and pepper to each pot. Cook until beans are tender, but still firm. Cooking time varies between 2 and 4 hours, depending on freshness of beans.

Drain the cooked beans, reserving any cooking liquids. Remove bay leaves, and combine cooked beans in a large pot. Measure out 1 cup of cooking liquid and mix together with chopped onions, tomato purée, chili sauce, molasses, mustard, garlic, thyme, tamari, 1 teaspoon salt, and pepper. Add to bean pot and simmer, partially covered for about 20 minutes. Add the oil.

While the beans are cooking, preheat the oven to 250 degrees F. Place the quartered onion in the bottom of a 2½-quart bean crock or Dutch oven. Pour seasoned beans into pot, and dot the top with butter. Cover and bake for 6 hours. Uncover beans and pour on sherry. Continue baking, uncovered, for 1 more hour.

Serve Family Baked Beans hot, with fresh-picked corn and a leafy green salad. It is also delicious cool for picnics, and spread on bread with mustard.

BAKED KNISHES
Serves 6

These simple country savory pastries are good for every day or special occasions. This recipe makes about 1 dozen knishes, and offers a choice of 2 fillings.

KASHA FILLING:
(makes about 3 cups)
1 egg
1 cup buckwheat groats
2 cups (about) boiling water
2 large onions, coarsely chopped
1 tablespoon butter
2 tablespoons olive or peanut oil
1 teaspoon salt
Pepper

DOUGH:
3 cups cooked, mashed potatoes (about 2½ pounds)
3 eggs
Salt
Freshly ground black pepper
1½ cups whole wheat flour
½–¾ cup unbleached white flour

POTATO FILLING:
(makes 2½ cups)
2½ cups mashed potatoes (about 2 pounds)
2 teaspoons salt
¾ teaspoon freshly ground black pepper
2 tablespoons chopped chives
5 tablespoons melted butter

Stir 1 beaten egg into the groats. Place in a hot skillet to dry-roast, stirring constantly over medium high heat. When dry and slightly browned, pour boiling water over the groats, sufficient to cover. Cover the pot and steam over low heat until groats are tender, about 30 minutes, adding more water if necessary.

Meanwhile, sauté chopped onions in heated butter and oil mixture. When the groats are cooked, add the tender sautéed onions, scraping all the extra cooking liquid out with them. Add salt and pepper, seasoning to taste. This is a basic kasha recipe. Refrigerate unused portion of kasha and add to scrambled eggs, or serve with steamed peas, cabbage, and carrots, or baked potatoes and salad for a main course.

To make knish dough, measure the mashed potatoes into a large bowl. Add 3 beaten eggs and season well with salt and pepper. Stir in the flour slowly, until it is well mixed and a malleable, soft dough has formed.

Potato filling is made by putting mashed potatoes into a mixing bowl, then adding salt, pepper, chives, and butter.

TO ASSEMBLE:

Preheat oven to 375 degrees F. To assemble the knishes, turn dough out onto a well-floured surface. Divide the dough in half for ease of handling, and roll out to about ⅛-inch thickness, using plenty of white flour for dredging the rolling pin and surface. Cut 5-inch squares into the rolled dough. Place about 3 tablespoons of kasha or potato filling on half of each square. Fold over other half and pinch edges together. Lift the filled knish from the table with a spatula and place on an oiled baking sheet. Bake the knishes until lightly browned, about 30 minutes.

Wrap hot baked knishes in a linen towel, set in a basket, wide wooden bowl, or covered crock, and serve with stone-ground mustard. Homemade applesauce with sour cream is a delicious complement for a supper of Baked Knishes, and a crispy tossed green salad is a must.

BAKED BLUEFISH FILLETS
WITH CHERRY TOMATO SAUCE
Serves 6

⅛ cup dry white wine
Dash of tamari soy sauce
Dash of lemon juice
8 small (about 8 ounces) bluefish fillets, or 4 large (1 pound
    each)
Cherry Tomato Sauce (*see recipe below*)
Pinch of crushed fresh thyme leaves
Pinch of cayenne pepper

Combine wine, tamari sauce, and lemon juice in a shallow
pan. Place fish into the mixture, cover, and set in the refrigerator
to marinate for ½ hour. Preheat over to 375 degrees F.

Remove fish and juices to a large, lightly oiled baking dish.
Top with Cherry Tomato Sauce and a sprinkling of thyme and
cayenne. Bake the fish for 10 minutes.

CHERRY TOMATO SAUCE
Yield: about 2 cups
½ onion, chopped
3 cloves garlic, chopped
½ carrot, chopped
½ green pepper, chopped
3 tablespoons olive oil
1 pint cherry tomatoes
Salt and pepper
Chopped fresh basil to taste
Chopped fresh thyme to taste
Chopped fresh parsley to taste

Simmer onion, garlic, carrot, and pepper in olive oil until
onion is transparent. Add tomatoes, cut in half. Raise heat to
medium, add salt and pepper. Cook 5 minutes. Tomatoes should
give off a good deal of liquid. Add herbs to taste, cook 1 minute
more.

This quick Cherry Tomato Sauce is very fresh-tasting with the
exceptionally sweet and juicy taste of cherry tomatoes. It is very
good with any pasta dish, and with fish.

BROILED SOLE WITH BASIL
Serves 4–6

½ cup finely chopped shallots
6 tablespoons butter
1 cup (about) unbleached flour
Salt
Freshly ground black pepper
1½ pounds fillet of sole
½ cup dry white wine
1 egg yolk
½ cup heavy cream
2 tablespoons chopped fresh basil
1 tablespoon lemon juice

FOR GARNISH:
Lemon slices

In a heavy pan over a low heat, sauté shallots in 3 tablespoons butter till translucent (about 5 minutes). Remove shallots with drippings to a medium-sized baking dish.

Preheat broiler. Combine flour, salt, and pepper; toss fish fillets in flour mixture. Adding remaining butter as needed, sauté fish in pan over medium heat till both sides are golden. Place fish in baking dish on top of shallots.

Add wine to frying pan. Reduce, cooking over high heat for 3 minutes. Beat egg yolk and cream in small bowl. Take pan off heat; beat egg and cream mixture into pan juices. Add basil; cook, stirring until slightly thickened, about 2 minutes. Beat in lemon juice. Pour over fish in baking dish. Broil until golden brown on top, about 2 minutes.

Garnish with lemon slices and serve.

This dish can be easily adapted to outdoor grilling for an elegant picnic. Wrap prepared fillets with cream mixture in individual foil wrappers, and place on open fireplace or hibachi, to roast lightly just before serving time.

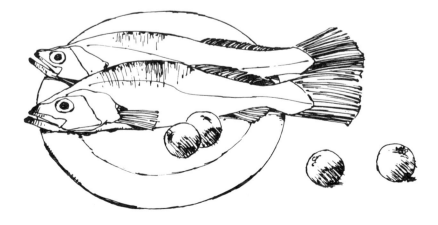

ZUCCHINI BREAKFAST CAKES
Serves 4

1 cup unbleached white flour
½ cup whole wheat flour
3 teaspoons baking powder
¾ teaspoon salt
1¾ cups grated zucchini
2 eggs, beaten
¾ cup light cream
¾ cup yogurt
1 tablespoon honey
2 tablespoons peanut oil

Sift dry ingredients together. Combine zucchini with eggs, cream, yogurt, and honey and mix well. Stir dry ingredients into wet, stirring gently until well blended into a thick batter. Fry at once.

Heat peanut oil in large skillet or griddle. Drop batter by ladleful to make cakes approximately 3 inches in diameter. Brown on 1 side; turn and brown until crispy on the other.

Serve breakfast cakes with fresh strawberry or blackberry jam, or mashed fresh fruit with honey. For supper, serve the cakes with plain tahini spread.

CORN BREAKFAST CAKES:
Substitute 1¾ cups fresh corn kernels (3 to 4 ears) for the zucchini. In the winter, use your home-canned corn (drained) and proceed with the rest of the recipe. In the winter when fresh berries are unavailable, these are delicious with maple syrup.

BREAKFAST SCRAMBLE
Serves 4

3 tablespoons safflower oil
¼ cup chopped onions or scallions
½ cup shelled peas
¼ cup grated zucchini or chopped greens
¾ cup (about 4 ounces) mashed tofu
3 tablespoons sesame seeds
1 teaspoon fresh tarragon or ½ teaspoon dried
1 teaspoon tamari soy sauce
Freshly ground black pepper
3 eggs, beaten

Heat oil in a large skillet. Sauté onions until tender. Add peas, zucchini or greens, tofu, and sesame seeds, and cook until peas are just tender, about 3 minutes. Stir in tarragon, tamari, and a few sprinkles of freshly ground black pepper. Pour in eggs, and gently stir until cooked. Serve hot with fruit and toast.

Breakfast Scramble is good any time of year. In summer, use fresh garden peas with zucchini, chard, or spinach, and fresh tarragon. Fresh dill is also good. In winter, Breakfast Scramble is a substantial start for a cold, busy day. Use your own frozen peas and spinach with dried herbs.

NEW POTATO SKILLET
Serves 4

2½–3 pounds new potatoes
¾ cup water
1½ tablespoons olive oil
¾ teaspoon sesame oil
6 ounces tofu, cut into thin
　squares
3 cups (about 3 pounds)
　shelled peas

2 tablespoons minced fresh
　dill
6 tablespoons chopped
　scallions
¼ cup dry red wine
3 tablespoons tamari soy
　sauce
Freshly ground black pepper

Cube the new potatoes. Place a large heavy skillet over medium heat. Add the water and the oils, and bring to a simmer. Add the potatoes, cover, and cook until just tender, 10 to 15 minutes.

Add tofu, peas, dill, and scallions. Stir to mix well. Add the wine, tamari, and pepper. Cover skillet again, and steam briefly until peas are just tender, 3 minutes. Serve warm, with broiled fish or a simple steamed grain mixture.

PESTO
Yield: 1½ cups

1 cup chopped fresh basil
　leaves
½ cup chopped fresh Italian
　parsley
¼ cup olive oil
2 tablespoons pine nuts or
　walnuts

2 cloves garlic
Good pinch of salt
⅓ cup grated Parmesan and
　Romano cheese
2 tablespoons butter, at room
　temperature (*optional*)

Put all ingredients but cheese and butter in blender and blend until mixed. Pour and scrape into a bowl and mix in cheese and butter by hand for the best texture. It is important to make this immediately before serving. Made too much in advance it can take on an unpleasant bitter taste. This sauce is delicious mixed into any kind of pasta.

To freeze Pesto, prepare as above but leave out the garlic, cheese, and butter. Add them when ready to use. Spread Pesto on wax paper, wrap well, and freeze. It retains a remarkable taste of summer.

PESTO SOUR CREAM DIP:

To the basic Pesto recipe, with or without garlic, add ½ cup sour cream and mix well. The color is beautiful. This goes perfectly with new potatoes boiled in their jackets and cherry tomatoes. Other cut-up, raw or parboiled vegetables are delicious with it too.

TAHINI SAUCE
Yield: 1–1½ cups

Tahini, paste from ground sesame seeds, comes from its native Middle East to flourish in a new Western cuisine. Rich in protein, vitamins and minerals, Tahini is basic to everyday healthy eating. Tahini is easily prepared and complements fresh herbs, fresh fruits and vegetables of summer. This basic recipe can be used as a dip for crisp crudités, or a smooth dressing for a salad, or a sauce for pasta or tofu. Enriched with a little olive oil, chopped fresh herbs, or greens, it is a spread for bread.

½ cup tahini
½–¾ cup water
Juice of ½ lemon
1–2 cloves garlic, minced
¼–½ teaspoon ground cumin

Add water to tahini, a little at a time, mixing thoroughly until very smooth. Add remaining ingredients to taste.

SNAP PEA BUFFET
Serves 4

Enjoy crisp raw snap peas as the center of a cold summer brunch.

2 cups ricotta or farmer cheese
¼ cup minced fresh dill
12 small radishes, finely chopped
1 tablespoon fresh lime juice
1–2 medium cloves garlic, minced
Pinch of salt
Freshly ground black pepper
1 pound snap peas
Tomato wedges

Combine all ingredients except peas and tomatoes in a mixing bowl. Stir well and allow to set for a few minutes in the refrigerator.

Meanwhile, string the peas, and snap off the stem ends. Slice peas in thirds, or leave whole, and arrange in a circle on a platter. Add tomato wedges for more color. Scoop the ricotta mixture into the center of the platter.

At the table, portion out salad into individual salad plates. May be eaten by dipping whole peas into cheese mixture or serve peas sliced with plenty of cheese mixture to cover.

SUMMER SALAD MANDALA
Serves 4–6

This is a bright, appetizing main dish for a hot summer day. It can also be served as a festive first course, or accompany another light main dish.

4 bell peppers
2 heads bibb lettuce
1 bunch watercress
2 hard-boiled eggs, cut in ⅛-inch slices
4 large ripe tomatoes, finely diced
1½ cups cooked chick-peas
2 cucumbers, finely diced in ¼-inch cubes
2 scallions, finely sliced on the diagonal
½ cup black olives
2 teaspoons finely chopped fresh mint
Dressing (*see recipe below*)

Preheat oven to 400 degrees F. Roast peppers for 30 minutes or until they are limp and their skins wrinkle. Wrap in damp towel to cool. When cool, peel and dice in ½-inch chunks, removing seeds and cores.

Arrange bibb lettuce leaves and watercress sprigs on bottom of a large round platter. In center pile hard-boiled egg slices. Circle this with diced tomato. Surround this with chick-peas. Arrange diced roasted peppers around chick-peas; then cubed cucumbers around edge of platter. Scatter scallions, black olives, and chopped mint over platter. Drizzle dressing over salad. Serve with crusty bread.

DRESSING:
Yield: ¾ cup
1 clove garlic
¼ teaspoon salt
1 teaspoon ground cumin
¼ teaspoon ground red pepper
¼ cup red wine vinegar
½ cup oil

Mash 1 clove garlic in mortar with salt. Add cumin, red pepper, and wine vinegar. Gradually add ½ cup of oil. Taste and correct seasoning if necessary.

POTATO HERB SALAD
Serves 8

This is a colorful picnic salad, filled with the cheerfulness of fresh herbs and peas. The scale of the recipe can easily be adjusted to suit any family needs.

8–10 cups (about 4 pounds) diced new potatoes (½–1-inch cubes)
⅔ cup yogurt
⅔ cup mayonnaise
2 tablespoons lemon juice
1 tablespoon tamari soy sauce
2 teaspoons prepared stone ground mustard
1–2 teaspoons salt
Freshly ground black pepper
1½ cups shelled fresh, young peas or snap peas (cut into ¼-inch pieces)
½ cup chopped fresh parsley
6 tablespoons chopped fresh dill
1 teaspoon minced fresh basil
1 teaspoon chopped fresh thyme leaves
½ cup minced chard or celery
6 medium radishes, halved and sliced
⅔ cup chopped scallions
Baby carrots (*optional*)
Other fresh herbs (*optional*)

FOR GARNISH:
Tomato wedges
Fresh parsley sprigs

Drop potatoes into boiling water to cover, and cook until tender but firm, about 15 minutes. Meanwhile combine yogurt, mayonnaise, lemon juice, tamari, and mustard, with salt and pepper to taste. Mix well, and pour over the hot potatoes as soon as they are sufficiently cooked and drained.

Prepare the remaining ingredients, and add to the salad. Refrigerate for 6 to 8 hours to blend flavors.

Serve Potato Herb Salad on a bed of lettuce, garnished with tomato wedges, and sprigs of parsley.

For a delicious young garden potato salad, include bits of tiny carrots and other emerging herbs. Serve with summer fruit and dark bread.

STRAWBERRY ROMAINE SALAD
Serves 6

1 head romaine lettuce
1 pint strawberries, sliced
1 red onion, cut into very finely sliced rings

DRESSING:
5 tablespoons cider vinegar
1 tablespoon honey
1 teaspoon Dijon mustard
½ teaspoon salt
Dash of freshly ground black pepper
1 teaspoon celery seed
¾ cup olive oil

Wash, shake dry, and tear romaine into bite-sized pieces. Arrange sliced strawberries and very finely sliced red onion rings over lettuce. In a jar, combine dressing ingredients. Cover jar and shake well. Drizzle dressing over salad and toss all together. Serve immediately.

MOCK SALMON
Serves 4–6

After making a quart of carrot juice, rescue the nutritious pulp left in the juicerator and turn it into a bright, delicious salad spread.

2 cups carrot pulp
⅔ cup mayonnaise
2½–3 tablespoons lemon
  juice
1 stalk celery, minced
3 scallions, minced
⅔ cup cashew pieces
1½ teaspoons Herba-Mare*

Combine the pulp with all remaining ingredients.

Mock Salmon salad is served in Woodstock, New York, at the Sunflower Deli, stuffed into pita bread with lettuce, tomatoes, sprouts, and tahini, and is the favorite of many local customers. It can also be served as a side dish salad, scooped onto a bed of lettuce, garnished with tomato wedges.

If carrot pulp is unavailable, a fine Carrot Slaw can be made with the same recipe, substituting ground fresh carrots. For deeper color and added nutrition, juice a few beets with the carrots.

* Herba-Mare is a convenient packaged salt, dried vegetable, and sweet-herb blend. It can be found in most health food stores.

YOGURT EGGPLANT SALAD
Serves 4–6

2 medium (1-pound) eggplants
1 large clove garlic
2 teaspoons minced fresh dill
Pinch of cayenne pepper
1½ tablespoons olive oil
3 cups chilled yogurt

Preheat oven to 425 degrees F. Place eggplants on aluminum foil in the oven and roast until they become soft and the skin shrivels. Split and scoop out all the pulp into a large bowl, scraping the skins well. Discard the skins.

With a fork, mash the eggplant to a coarse, uneven texture. Finely dice the garlic, then mash with the back of a spoon, and add to the eggplant. Add the dill and cayenne. Stir in olive oil for extra richness. Fold in the chilled yogurt last.

For an exotic contrast of cold yogurt and warm eggplant, serve this salad immediately. It can also be refrigerated and served chilled at a later time. Very good as an accompaniment for Canary Hill Burgers (*see Index*).

ROASTED PEPPER SALAD
Serves 4–6

6 fresh bell peppers, red and green

DRESSING:
2 cloves garlic
Pinch of salt
Dash of freshly ground black
  pepper
2 tablespoons lemon juice
6 tablespoons olive oil
2 tablespoons finely chopped
  fresh parsley

Preheat oven to 400 degrees F. Coat peppers with a little oil. Bake on a cookie sheet, turning often, till limp and blistered, about ½ hour.

Remove from oven. Place in a bag and let cool. When cool enough to handle, peel and cut into long strips lengthwise, removing core and seeds.

Place peppers in a broad serving bowl.

Prepare dressing. Pound garlic and salt in a mortar until a paste. Remove to mixing bowl and add pepper. Mix in lemon juice, then slowly add olive oil, a tablespoonful at a time. Beat well. Add chopped parsley and pour over peppers in the bowl.

Serve with thick crusty bread.

GARDEN BEAN SALAD
Serves 6

Combine fresh beans from the late garden with fresh herbs and other vegetables and a sparkling salad dressing for a substantial hot-weather dish.

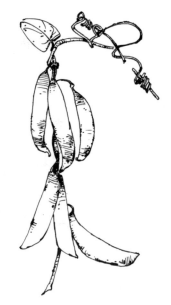

2–3 cloves garlic
1½ teaspoons salt
¾ cup olive oil
⅓ cup wine vinegar
1 tablespoon honey
½ teaspoon freshly ground black pepper
1 cup hot cooked kidney beans
1 cup hot cooked great northern beans
1 cup hot cooked garbanzo beans
2 cups cut-up green snap beans (1-inch pieces)
½ cup chopped scallions
3–4 radishes, sliced
¼ cup diced carrot
¼ cup diced green pepper
1 small red onion, diced
¼ cup chopped fresh parsley
½ cup minced fresh dill

In a mortar mash garlic into salt with pestle. Combine oil, vinegar, honey, mashed and salted garlic, and black pepper in a jar. Cover jar and shake until well blended. Place hot, cooked beans in a bowl, and pour over dressing. Cover the bowl, and set in the refrigerator to marinate for 8 to 12 hours.

Steam the snap beans until tender-crisp, 3 minutes. Stir into the marinated beans, and return bowl to the refrigerator for 2 or 3 more hours.

Add vegetables and herbs; chill again, about 1 hour before serving. With the changing garden crops through the summer, try different crisp vegetable combinations to accent the fresh beans.

GARDEN TOFU-STUFFED TOMATOES
Serves 4

8 ounces tofu (medium-soft, if available)
¼ cup drained, coarsely chopped pimento-stuffed green olives
2 scallions, chopped
¼ cup grated carrot
1 clove garlic, crushed
Dash of tamari soy sauce
3 teaspoons mayonnaise
Lettuce
4 large red ripe tomatoes

FOR GARNISH:
4 small radishes or 4 fresh parsley sprigs.

Mash tofu in a mixing bowl. Add chopped green olives, scallions, carrots, and garlic. Mix lightly, and add the tamari and mayonnaise. Mix well. Set aside, covered, to mellow for about 1 hour.

At serving time, prepare a bed of lettuce on a large platter or on 4 individual salad dishes.

Cut 3 slices through the center-top of each tomato, to about ⅜ inch from the bottom, forming 6 radiating wedges. Set each tomato on the lettuce bed, and stuff with room-temperature tofu mixture. Garnish each with a small, bright radish or a sprig of parsley.

This basic, creamy tofu salad mix is the pride of Woodstock's Health Food Center. The people at the center suggest adding or substituting many garden "crunchies" to vary the taste and texture. Tofu salad is delicious served as an open-faced sandwich on whole wheat toast; children love it. The basic recipe can be easily doubled or tripled. For a colorful buffet, stuff tofu salad in arrangements of shiny green peppers and bright tomatoes, ornamented with a rainbow of garden crudités.

FESTIVE CORN SALAD
Serves 4

Fresh raw corn straight from the garden refreshes a hot summer day in a salad bright with color and spice.

2 cups (4–5 ears) fresh corn kernels
1 clove garlic, minced
½ teaspoon freshly ground black pepper
½ teaspoon sea salt
½ teaspoon Hungarian paprika*
1 tablespoon olive oil
3 scallions, chopped
1 green pepper, chopped
½ red pepper
Dark lettuce leaves

FOR GARNISH:
1½ tablespoons chopped pitted black olives
Fresh parsley sprigs

Place corn kernels in a bowl. Add garlic, pepper, salt, paprika, and oil, and toss. Add scallions and green pepper.

Roast red pepper by skewering over open flame or placing in a 425-degree F. oven until charred. Wrap in a wet towel for a few minutes, then peel and chop, and add to the salad. Toss lightly and set the salad in the refrigerator for 30 to 60 minutes before serving.

When ready to serve, prepare a bed of dark lettuce leaves in a broad serving bowl. Scoop Festive Corn Salad into the center. Garnish top with chopped black olives and a few parsley sprigs.

PARSLEY BANQUET SALAD
Serves 8–10

In a paradise summer when the parsley patch is flourishing thick and green, serve this richly nourishing herb as a sparkling main-dish attraction.

DRESSING:
½ cup olive oil
½ cup lemon juice

---

* If Hungarian paprika is not available, use a pinch of pure chili powder or a dash of Tabasco with regular paprika.

4 medium cloves garlic, minced
¼ teaspoon sea salt
⅛ teaspoon freshly ground black pepper
¼ cup minced fresh mint

2 cups cooked bulgur
4 cups minced fresh parsley
1 cup minced scallions
1 green pepper, finely chopped
1 cucumber, minced
2 large tomatoes, chopped
1 medium carrot, finely chopped
½ red onion, thinly sliced

FOR GARNISH:
Red onion slices

Combine oil, lemon, garlic, salt, pepper, and mint in a jar. Cover and shake well; set aside.

Place cooked bulgur in a large mixing bowl. Add remaining ingredients, except onion for garnish, to the bulgur. Mix to distribute the bulgur throughout the vegetables. Shake the jar of dressing well again, and pour over the salad. Toss lightly.

Cover the salad and set in the refrigerator for 3 to 12 hours to marinate.

Garnish the salad with slices of red onion and serve cold. Parsley Banquet Salad can be served as a light main dish, complemented well by a favorite bread, or fresh steamed corn.

WALNUT CHEESE CRACKERS
Yield: about 3 dozen

¾ cup stone-ground whole wheat flour
½ cup finely ground walnuts
½ teaspoon baking powder
¼ teaspoon salt

Pinch of cayenne pepper
½ cup butter
½ cup grated Cheddar cheese
½ cup grated Swiss cheese
½ well beaten egg

Combine flour, nuts, baking powder, salt, and cayenne in a bowl. Cut in butter with knives, until mixture forms a very coarse meal. Add cheeses and the egg. Blend well until dough is stiff.

Roll dough into a log about 1¼ inches in diameter. Wrap carefully in wax paper and refrigerate several hours.

Preheat oven to 350 degrees F. Slice dough into very thin rounds; place on ungreased baking sheet. Bake 15 to 20 minutes until just lightly browned around the edges. Cool on a rack.

Delicious served with soup and a salad for lunch.

LEMON BROWN BREAD
Yield: three 1-pound loaves

This is a perfect recipe to make on a rainy, cool August afternoon. The steam adds warmth to the kitchen and the warm bread
is a delightful comfort in the evening.

1 cup yellow cornmeal	2 cups buttermilk or sour milk
1 cup rye flour	⅔ cup molasses
1 cup whole wheat flour	¾ cup raisins
2 teaspoons baking soda	1 teaspoon grated lemon rind
¾ teaspoon salt	Juice of ½ lemon

Combine the cornmeal, flours, soda, and salt; mix together
very well.

Combine the milk and remaining ingredients; add to the dry
ingredients. Mix well; do not beat.

Oil three 1-quart molds or three 1-pound coffee cans. Divide
batter equally among the cans and cover tightly with metal lids
or aluminum foil. Set on a rack in a large pot with cover. Add
boiling water to a depth of about 3 inches. Cover the pot and
steam for 3 hours, adding more water if necessary.

Remove cans and set on racks to cool for about 10 minutes.
Unmold the breads and serve warm. Lemon Brown Bread is
very good with corn, beans, a fresh salad, and many fresh garden
combinations. It is delicious for winter eating too.

Lemon Brown Bread can be wrapped when cool and stored
for later. It can then be returned to the mold, and steamed a few
minutes to reheat before serving. It is also good straight from
the bread box, spread with a little cream cheese. For breakfast,
fresh jam can be added, if desired. It also makes a great picnic
or hiker's treat.

ZUCCHINI WALNUT BREAD
Yield: one 9-inch round loaf

Here is a fluffy, light bread with a hint of the garden, and a
delicious, crunchy contrast in the texture and flavor.

1 cup wheat germ
1 cup whole wheat flour
⅓ cup unbleached white flour
1 teaspoon salt
3 teaspoons baking powder
¾ cup chopped walnuts

2 eggs, beaten
½ cup water
¼ cup safflower oil
2 cups grated zucchini
¼ cup honey

Preheat oven to 400 degrees F. Combine wheat germ, flours, salt and baking powder, and stir well to mix. Add ½ cup of the chopped walnuts.

In a separate bowl, beat eggs and add water and oil. Stir in grated zucchini, and add the honey.

Oil a 9 × 3½-inch tube pan. Gently stir the zucchini mixture into the flour mixture, mixing until all moisture is incorporated, but do not beat. Pour into the tube pan. Sprinkle remaining chopped walnuts around the top. Set bread in oven. After 10 minutes, reduce heat to 325 degrees F. and continue baking for 30 to 35 minutes more. Bread is done when cake tester comes out clean, and top is a delicate golden color.

Serve Zucchini Walnut Bread warm or cooled, with butter, sweet cheese, nut butter, or plain. It is a delicious breakfast treat with eggs, or for a summer luncheon with a fresh salad.

BUTTERMILK WHEAT BREAD
Yield: 2 loaves

1 tablespoon yeast
1 tablespoon honey
½ cup warm water
4½–5 cups whole wheat bread flour
2 cups unbleached white flour
1 tablespoon salt
4 tablespoons melted butter
1½ cups buttermilk

Combine yeast, honey, and water in a jar and set aside until foamy, about 5 minutes. Mix 4 cups whole wheat flour, 2 cups white flour, salt, butter, buttermilk, and yeast mixture. Sprinkle dough with ½ cup extra whole wheat flour and turn out onto floured board.

Knead for at least 10 minutes or until dough is smooth and elastic, adding more flour if necessary. Place dough in a buttered bowl, cover with a damp cloth, and let rise in a warm spot until doubled in bulk—about 1½ hours.

Preheat oven to 375 degrees F. Turn dough out onto the floured board, knead for about 2 minutes and let rise for at least

10 minutes while you oil two 8½ × 4½ × 2½-inch bread pans. Form dough into 2 loaves, place in pans, and let rise again until doubled, about 30 minutes. Bake for about 35 to 45 minutes.

Bread is done when light thumping on surfaces with finger produces a hollow sound. Cool 10 minutes; remove from pans to rack to finish cooling before slicing.

RAISIN RYE BAGELS
Yield: 2 dozen

1½ tablespoons active dry yeast
1½ cups warm potato water*
3 eggs, beaten
1 tablespoon molasses
3 tablespoons oil
3 teaspoons salt
¾ cup raisins
2 cups rye flour
1 cup whole wheat bread flour
3½ cups (about) unbleached white flour
3 quarts water
2 tablespoons honey

GLAZE FOR BASTING:
1 egg mixed with 1½ tablespoons water
Caraway seeds or poppy seeds (*optional*)

Dissolve yeast in ½ cup warm potato water. Place remaining water in a large mixing bowl. Add beaten eggs, molasses, oil, and salt. When yeast is bubbly, add it to the mixing bowl with the raisins. Slowly stir in the rye flour. When well blended, add the whole wheat flour. Beat to mix well. Add white flour, 1 cup at a time, until dough pulls away from the sides of the bowl. Turn out onto a well-floured surface. Knead about 10 minutes until smooth and elastic, adding more white flour, as necessary. Place dough into clean, oiled bowl. Turn to oil all surfaces, cover with a towel, and set aside to rise until doubled in volume, about 1½ hours.

Punch the dough down and divide in half. On a flour-dusted surface, knead each half until very smooth. Divide each half into 12 equal parts. Roll each part into a small rope, ¾ × 6½ inches.

* Potato water is the broth from boiled potatoes. Potatoes can be reserved for a later use such as Potato Herb Salad (see Index).

Pinch ends of each rope together with a dab of water. Set aside on an oiled surface to rise slightly, about 15 minutes.

Preheat oven to 425 degrees F. Meanwhile, boil water in a large pot. Add honey. Drop bagels into boiling water, 4 at a time. As soon as they rise to the top, turn them over and continue boiling for 3 minutes. Using a slotted spoon, remove each bagel to an oiled baking sheet. Baste with egg, and sprinkle with caraway or poppy seeds, if desired. Bake 20 to 25 minutes, until golden brown.

TOFU CHEESECAKE
Serves 6–8

CRUST:
2½ cups puffed rice cereal
½ cup finely ground almonds
⅓ cup safflower oil
½ cup honey
½ teaspoon salt
1 teaspoon almond extract

FILLING:
1 pound tofu
3 ounces cream cheese,
　softened
½ cup orange juice
¼ teaspoon salt
1 teaspoon vanilla
⅔ cup honey
5 tablespoons plain yogurt

FOR TOPPING:
Strawberries, blueberries, or blackberries
Honey to taste

Preheat oven to 350 degrees F. Run puffed rice through blender or food processor a half at a time, until a coarse mixture is formed (just a touch will do). Add almonds to puffed rice and toss together. Mix oil, honey, salt, and almond extract together; pour over rice mixture and work in until well coated. Press into a 10-inch pie pan. Bake until lightly browned, 10 to 15 minutes.

Reduce oven temperature to 325 degrees F. With a fork, mash together tofu and cream cheese. Add the rest of the filling ingredients and mix well. Process in blender until smooth, a third at a time. Pour into prepared crust and bake for 35 minutes. Let cool completely, refrigerate until cold. Serve covered with fresh summer berries, sweetened with honey.

PEACH-STRAWBERRY MOUSSE
WITH CRÈME FRAÎCHE
Serves 6

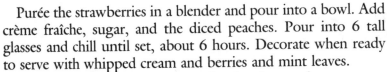

6 cups sliced strawberries
⅓ cup Crème Fraîche (*see recipe below*)
¼ cup sugar (or more if desired)
5 Poached Peaches (*see recipe below*), diced

OPTIONAL GARNISH:
Whipped cream
Whole strawberries
Mint leaves

Purée the strawberries in a blender and pour into a bowl. Add crème fraîche, sugar, and the diced peaches. Pour into 6 tall glasses and chill until set, about 6 hours. Decorate when ready to serve with whipped cream and berries and mint leaves.

This mousse never sets up very firm but is a perfect summery dessert with the best strawberry taste.

CRÈME FRAÎCHE:
Yield: ⅓ cup
⅓ cup heavy cream
1 tablespoon buttermilk

In a blender or a covered jar blend ⅓ cup heavy cream and 1 tablespoon buttermilk and let it sit at room temperature for at least 8 hours. It will be slightly soured and thick (you can easily increase these proportions to have extra because it is just perfect with plain strawberries and keeps for a week in the refrigerator).

If you don't have the time to make the Crème Fraîche, you can substitute a mixture of half sour cream, half whipped cream to make ⅓ cup.

POACHED PEACHES:
Serves 4
¾ cup water
¾ cup sugar
Vanilla bean
5 fresh, whole unpeeled peaches

In a heavy pot, combine water, sugar and a piece (at least 2 inches) of split vanilla bean. Bring to a boil and turn down to a simmer for 10 minutes to make a medium-thick syrup. Add 5 firm ripe peaches and simmer for 10 minutes more. Let them cool in the syrup. Peel and dice them small when ready to use.

BLACKBERRY LIME MOUSSE
Serves 6

2 tablespoons agar-agar*
2 tablespoons cold water
2 pints blackberries
1 lime, juice and grated rind
5 tablespoons honey
2 egg yolks
2 tablespoons crème de cassis or blackberry liqueur
½ pint heavy cream

FOR GARNISH:
Lime zest, julienned
Whole blackberries

Soften agar-agar in cold water in a saucepan. Add blackberries, lime rind and juice, and 1 tablespoon honey. Bring to a boil, mashing the blackberries down and stirring well as the mixture heats. Boil 2 minutes, then remove from heat and cool to room temperature.

Beat egg yolks and 3 tablespoons honey in a warm bowl until pale yellow. Add crème de cassis, beat well, then remove egg yolk-liqueur mixture to the top of a double boiler. Heat carefully over boiling water, stirring until thickened slightly and hot to the touch. Cool to room temperature.

Combine blackberry mixture and egg yolk mixture. Whip cream and remaining 1 tablespoon honey until thick. Gently fold into blackberry mixture. Transfer to a serving dish and chill several hours until set. Garnish with a mound of julienned lime zest and fresh whole blackberries.

* Agar-agar is a gelatinous sea plant, available in flaked form in health food stores. This is the vegetarian equivalent of plain gelatine.

WEDDING CAKE
Serves 50–60

Loving couples pilgrimage to Catskill woodland sanctuaries, lured by June's flower-strewn mountainsides and meadows. Beyond the Buddhist temple, over a threshold of great pines, Magic Meadow blooms lush with daisies and pink mountain laurel. Here, in the lap of Overlook's peak, before the panorama of Indian Head Mountain, lies a natural chapel for an early summer wedding.

Wherever the ceremony, the cutting of an opulent cake by newly joined hands is the crowning moment of the wedding celebration.

Four graduated-size tier cake pans, approximately 8 inches, 12 inches, 18 inches, and 21 inches in diameter, are needed for this Wedding Cake recipe. It is important to use heavy pans. If professional baking pans in these sizes are unavailable, cast-iron skillets can be used. Cast iron is very good because it holds the heat uniformly and allows the cake to bake slowly, retaining moisture. Ovenproof glass is also good.

CAKE:

12 cups unbleached white
    flour
1 tablespoon baking soda
1 tablespoon baking powder
2 teaspoons salt
2 tablespoons cinnamon
4 cups butter
8 cups turbinado sugar
16 eggs, beaten
1 tablespoon vanilla
3 quarts grated carrots
2 cups chopped walnuts or
    pecans

2 cups raisins
2 cups chopped dates
1 quart mashed bananas
2 cups grated coconut
1 quart finely chopped fresh
    pineapple

FILLING:

3–3½ cups peach or apricot
    jam
1 recipe Cream Cheese Icing
    (*see below*)

Preheat oven to 325 degrees F. Sift first 5 ingredients together; set aside. Cream butter until light. Add sugar and continue beating until fluffy and all granules are dissolved. Add eggs slowly, then vanilla, and beat thoroughly.

Mix all fruits and nuts together with grated carrots.

Mix dry ingredients into creamed butter mixture. Add fruit–nut mixture and stir all together to mix well and form a thick batter.

Oil pans and dust with flour. Fill pans ¾ full. Place in oven. Begin watching smaller layers after about 45 minutes of baking. Cakes are done when your tester comes out fairly clean, and top is firm. When testing, be sure to open and close oven door very gently. Larger layers may take up to 1 hour and 30 minutes to bake.

When layers are baked, remove from oven and set on racks to cool thoroughly before attempting to remove from pans.

Assemble the tiers on a giant platter or tapestry-covered board, with peach or apricot jam spread between the layers. Ice top and sides smoothly with the white Cream Cheese Icing.

Pass the beet-colored portion of icing through a cake decorating tube to make rosettes on the center top, with a few more cascading at the edges of the tiers. With star point in the decorating tube, add fluted garlands to border the upper sides of each tier. Finish with a few scattered rose blossoms. Present the cake skirted gracefully with fresh white peonies and sparkling glasses of champagne.

Reduce the Wedding Cake and Cream Cheese Icing recipes to one fourth to make a perfect treat for a smaller occasion. Use a pan about 12 × 9 inches, and bake for about 1 hour.

CREAM CHEESE ICING:
Yields enough to ice one 4-tier cake
2½ pounds cream cheese, softened
¼ cup honey
2 teaspoons vanilla
Juice of ½ lemon
Beet juice for coloring (*optional*)

Whip cream cheese. Slowly add honey. Add vanilla. Add lemon juice to freshen the intense richness. If desired, set aside a portion of icing and color a rosy magenta with beet juice for special decorating use.

PEACH HAZELNUT CAKE
Serves 6–8

½ cup butter
¾ cup sugar
1 egg
2 cups flour (all unbleached white or half white, half whole
  wheat pastry)
2 teaspoons baking powder
½ teaspoon baking soda
½ teaspoon salt
½ teaspoon cinnamon
½ teaspoon freshly grated nutmeg
1¼ cups buttermilk
1 teaspoon vanilla
1 cup chopped peeled peaches, dredged with flour
½ cup ground hazelnuts

Preheat oven to 400 degrees F. Butter an 8-inch round cake pan, an 8½ × 4½ × 2½-inch loaf pan, or a 9-inch tube pan.

Cream together butter and sugar. Add the egg. Sift the dry ingredients together and add them, alternating with the buttermilk (dry ingredients in three additions, buttermilk in two). Add vanilla, peaches, and nuts. Pour into prepared pan and bake until a toothpick inserted in the center comes out clean, about 35 to 45 minutes.

Set on rack to cool about 20 minutes before removing from pan.

BLUEBERRY COFFEE CAKE
Serves 6

TOPPING:
⅓ cup brown rice flour
1 teaspoon cinnamon
½ cup maple syrup
¼ cup wheat germ
¼ cup sunflower seed meal
¼ cup grated coconut
¼ cup butter

BATTER:
1 cup whole wheat pastry
  flour
1¼ cups unbleached white
  flour
½ teaspoon salt

2 teaspoons baking powder
2 cups fresh or frozen
  blueberries
½ cup butter
½ cup maple syrup or honey
1 egg at room temperature,
  beaten
1 teaspoon vanilla
½ cup milk
grated rind of 1 lime
Extra wheat germ for dusting
  pan
½ cup chopped walnuts

Preheat oven to 375 degrees F. To prepare topping, place rice flour, cinnamon, maple syrup, wheat germ, sunflower seed meal, and coconut in a mixing bowl. Work mixture together with the butter. Set topping aside while batter is prepared.

Sift dry ingredients together. In a separate bowl, place blueberries and dredge with a portion of the sifted dry ingredients. Set aside.

Cream butter. Slowly add honey, then egg, and vanilla. Cream until fluffy.

Add creamed ingredients to dry ingredients alternately with milk, incorporating each addition thoroughly. Add grated lime rind, then add the dredged blueberries, stirring very gently, until just mixed.

Butter a round 9-inch cake pan, and dust with a small amount of extra wheat germ. Spread batter into pan, and sprinkle top with chopped walnuts. Spread topping over the nuts. Bake 45 to 50 minutes, until a toothpick inserted into center comes out clean.

Remove from oven and set on a rack to cool for about 30 minutes. Cake can then be depanned and inverted onto a platter for serving.

BLACKBERRY COBBLER
Serves 6

5 cups blackberries
½ cup maple syrup
1½ cups whole wheat pastry flour
½ cup unbleached white flour
3 teaspoons baking powder
½ teaspoon salt
5 tablespoons butter
¾ cup milk or Cashew Milk (*see Index*)
½ pint heavy cream (*optional*)

Preheat oven to 375 degrees F. Place blackberries in a shallow, flameproof baking pan, about 8 × 10 inches. Add maple syrup and stir through the berries gently to mix.

Combine and sift the flours with the baking powder and salt. Cut in the butter until a mealy texture is formed. Add the milk, folding gently until all the mixture is moist.

Place the pan of berries over a medium heat, and bring to a simmer. Remove from heat. Pat the dough to about ¼-inch thickness, and place over the berries. Set the pan into the oven, and bake about 20 minutes, or until golden on top. Serve warm, with cream if desired.

STRAWBERRY SPARKLE
Serves 4

Special, sparkling beverages for summer are easy to whip up with juiced or puréed fresh fruit, combined with ice and seltzer. Everyday thirst-quenching drinks can be made with stored fruit juice mixed with seltzer to taste. This basic combination can easily become an old-fashioned ice-cream soda dessert.

¾ cup sliced strawberries
4 tablespoons fresh lemon juice
½ cup orange juice
½ cup crushed ice
3 tablespoons light honey
1¼ cups mineral water or seltzer
1 pint natural vanilla or honey ice cream

FOR GARNISH:
Whole strawberries

Place strawberries, lemon and orange juices, ice, and honey in the blender. Whip until smooth. Pour equal amounts into 4 tall glasses. Slowly fill each glass with the mineral water. Top each with a scoop of ice cream, and garnish with a few whole strawberries. Serve immediately.

PEACH PRESERVES
Yield: 12 pints

5 pounds peaches, peeled, pitted, and sliced
2½ cups sugar

Combine peaches and sugar in a bowl and refrigerate overnight. By morning there will be a good deal of juice. Pour into a wide pan and simmer for ½ hour, stirring occasionally. If syrup is not yet thick, remove peach slices with a slotted spoon and divide among 12 hot sterilized jars. Raise heat to cook syrup down, stirring carefully to prevent burning. It might take 15 minutes. Pour over peaches in pint or ½-pint jars, to within ¼ inch of top. Fit on hot lids and screw bands. Process for 10 minutes in boiling water bath.

This is a very elegant preserve and works beautifully with white or yellow peaches. It is best to use only perfect peaches for this. Use the less than perfect for a coarser but equally delicious jam where the peaches are cut into chunks, and the jam is made following this same procedure.

STRAWBERRY RHUBARB JAM
Yield: about 4½ half pints

3 cups cut-up strawberries (about 1 quart before being cleaned
  and cut up)
3 cups very finely diced rhubarb
Sugar to taste

Crush some of the berries. Combine all berries with rhubarb
in a large, shallow saucepan. Add sugar to taste.

Bring fruit to a boil and, stirring frequently, cook over me-
dium-high heat until thickened, about 15 minutes to ½ hour.
Skim off foam and ladle into hot, sterilized pint or ½-pint jars
within ¼ inch of top. Put on hot lid. Screw band firmly tight.
Process 10 minutes in a boiling water bath.

RASPBERRY JAM
Yield: about 7 pints

3 quarts red raspberries
½ envelope powdered pectin
3 cups sugar

Put raspberries through a food mill to grind and separate out
the seeds. Discard seeds. You should have about 6 cups fruit
purée. Place in a large pan and add the half envelope of pectin.
Bring to a full boil, stirring frequently. Add sugar all at once.
Stir and bring again to a good strong boil. Boil for about 5
minutes, stirring. Remove from heat and skim off the foam. Pour
into hot, sterilized pint or ½-pint jars, leaving ¼ inch head
space. Put on hot lids, adjust screw bands, and process for 5
minutes in a boiling water bath.

PORT PLUM JAM
Yield: 4 pints

4 pounds dark plums, cut into small chunks
¾ cup honey
½ cup port wine
1 lemon, juice and grated rind

Combine all ingredients in a heavy enameled pot. Cook, stirring frequently to prevent scorching, over medium heat until
mixture begins to thicken—about 30 minutes.

Spoon a little jam onto a chilled saucer and leave to cool a
minute. If it wrinkles when pushed with a finger, it is ready.

Spoon, boiling hot, into hot, sterilized pint or half-pint jars.
Put on hot lids; adjust bands. Process in boiling water bath for
10 minutes.

OLD-FASHIONED CORN RELISH
Yield: 11 pints

Old-fashioned Corn Relish is pungent with spiced vinegar and the nostalgia of great-grandmother's mysterious pantry: From the dark cool room it came with memories of summer tempting golden yellow, bright red and green; a colorful accent for the array of Thanksgiving's harvest treasures.

17–20 ears fresh corn
1 cup chopped onion
1 cup diced sweet red pepper
1 cup diced green pepper
1½ cups finely diced celery
¾ cup honey
3 cups cider vinegar
1 tablespoon yellow mustard seed
¾ teaspoon celery seed
3 teaspoons salt
1 teaspoon turmeric
1 small hot red pepper

Shuck corn and drop ears into boiling water. Boil 5 minutes, then plunge into cold water. Cut kernels from cobs. Measure out 8½ cups.

Chop and combine onions, sweet red and green peppers, celery, honey, vinegar, mustard and celery seed, and salt. Place in a covered pot and bring to boil. Remove cover and simmer the mixture 5 minutes, stirring occasionally.

Blend turmeric with a few spoonfuls of the simmering liquid; return to the pot. Cut the hot red pepper into 1-inch pieces, and sliver. Add to the relish with the corn. Stir, return to boiling, and then simmer 5 minutes, stirring occasionally.

Pack relish into hot, sterilized pint or ½-pint jars, filling to ½ inch from the top. Fit on hot lids, seal, and process 15 minutes in boiling water bath.

Serve Old-Fashioned Corn Relish with appetizers before dinner, or with luncheon sandwiches. It is good mixed with a variety of raw vegetables in salads, too.

PEAR CHUTNEY
Yield: 3 pints

About 2 pounds pears
½ cup raisins
½ cup honey
½ cup apple cider vinegar

½ cup water
4 cloves garlic
1 tablespoon Garam Masala*
1 tablespoon cumin seed
2 tablespoons mustard seed
1 tablespoon peeled, ground fresh gingerroot

Peel, core, and dice pears, and measure 4 cups. Combine pears with remaining ingredients in an enameled saucepot. Simmer gently for 40 minutes. Stir frequently to prevent sticking.

Pour boiling hot into hot, sterilized jars, filling to ⅛ inch from top. Seal with hot, sterilized lids, and adjust screw bands.

BEET PRESERVES
Yield: 4 to 5 pints

This is an old-time recipe to make in the late summer or fall and eat all year round.

3 pounds beets
1⅓ cups honey
2 cups sugar
2 tablespoons freshly ground peeled gingerroot
1½ cups slivered blanched almonds
Peel of 3 lemons, parboiled and julienned

Cook beets in cold water to cover. When they are just tender (not mushy), slip off the skins and julienne.

Bring the honey, sugar, and fresh ginger to a quick boil in a deep pot. Add the beets, turn down the heat, and cook until the syrup is thick, approximately ½ hour. Don't stir while it's cooking, but shake the pot to prevent burning or sticking.

Stir in almonds and lemon peel, turn into hot, sterilized pint or ½-pint jars within ¼ inch of top. Fit with hot lids and screw bands. Process 10 minutes in boiling water bath. Store away from the light.

* Garam Masala: This is an original curry spice blend, based in concept on an East Indian tradition. The spices should be freshly hand-ground for deepest aroma and flavoring. A quantity ground and blended in advance should be sealed in an airtight jar and stored away from light. Garam Masala can be used whenever special flavoring is desired for many foods, or in recipes requiring curry powder. Adjust the proportion of spices according to desired effect and other ingredients used in your recipe. Be most effectively guided by sense of smell. To make Garam Masala yourself, grind the following ingredients together:

4 tablespoons ground cumin	1 tablespoon powdered cinnamon
2 tablespoons turmeric	1 teaspoon cayenne pepper
1 tablespoon ground cloves	¼ teaspoon ground cardamom

PEAR KETCHUP
Yield: 2–3 pints

About 8 pounds pears
2 tablespoons slivered fresh ginger
Sea salt
Powdered cinnamon, to taste
Ground cloves, to taste
Omiboshi plums (*optional*)*

Preheat oven to 300 degrees F. Core and chop pears in blender with just enough water to move blades. Measure 7 cups, and spread in a baking pan, 10 × 14 inches. Bake for about 3 hours, stirring occasionally. The mixture should be thick and brown. Put through a sieve.

Return to casserole, season with fresh ginger slivers and a pinch of sea salt. Add cinnamon and cloves to taste. Continue to bake uncovered for 30 minutes.

For a special, spicy tang, a bit of omiboshi plums may be added to pears at this point, or at serving time.

For storage, pack Pear Ketchup in hot, sterilized pint or ½-pint jars. Fit with hot lids and screw bands. Process 10 minutes in boiling water bath.

PICKLED SNOW PEAS
Yield: 4 pints

Use either sugar snaps or regular snow peas. You can easily do a few small jars at a time as your harvest is ready.

About 1 quart fresh snow peas
4 heads fresh dill
4 1-inch slivers hot pepper
4–8 cloves garlic
2½ cups cider vinegar
2½ cups water
¼ cup salt

Pack raw peapods lengthwise into four hot, sterilized pint-size jars. Add 1 head of dill to each with 1 piece of pepper and 1 to 2 cloves of garlic. Boil vinegar, water, and salt and pour over peas, leaving ¼ inch head space. Cover with hot lids, adjust bands, and process in a boiling water bath for 10 minutes. Store for at least 6 weeks before using.

---

* These can be found in most oriental or health food stores.

Summer Menus

JUNE WEDDING
Summer Fruit Chunks tossed in Wine and Honey
(Peaches, Blueberries, Cherries, Strawberries, Bananas)
*Snap Pea Buffet
*Parsley Banquet Salad
**Easter Bread
Brie
Fresh Chilled Crab Meat with Lemon-Parsley Garnish
*Wedding Cake
Champagne

MOONLIGHT PICNIC
*Strawberry Soup
*Zucchini Walnut Bread
*Pesto Spaghetti
Rosé Wine
*Peach-Strawberry Mousse

MIDSUMMER CELEBRATION COOKOUT
*Tomato Tart
*Broiled Sole with Basil
Herb-roasted Corn
*Garden Bean Salad
*Buttermilk Wheat Bread
*Peach Jam
*Strawberry Sparkle

AUGUST SUPPER
*Corn Chowder
*Walnut Cheese Crackers
*Summer Salad Mandala
Chilled Fruit Juice
*Blackberry Cobbler

LABOR DAY GATHERING
*Roasted Pepper Salad
*Family Baked Beans
Fresh Steamed Corn
Beer or Sparkling Water
*Lemon Brown Bread
Cantaloupe and Raspberries with Mint
*Tofu Cheesecake with Blackberries

* Recipe included in Summer section.
**Recipe from Spring section.

Part Three: Autumn
MOUNTAIN HARVEST

Autumn

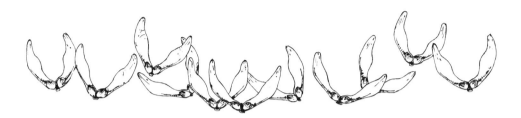

Cold returns to Woodstock on a late summer night. Clouds distill out of the dark mountains and silently condense along creek hollows. Folks rise with early sunlight to see the mountain faces adrift in pools of mist and forests bronzed with the patina of September. Against a cerulean sky brittle, gilded leaves crackle. Deep reds, rusts, and liquid orange ignite over the landscape. Following garlands of gold, explorers join local naturalists to wander the trails. For many, this glorious outing is a long-anticipated annual event.

The morning chill awakens local winter dwellers to sobering thoughts of firewood supplies. On the grapevine winding through Woodstock bars and coffee shops are rumors of woodlots to be shared and deals for seasoned cords. Familiar townspeople, dressed in rugged jackets and comfortable boots, replace the glamour of strangers in suddenly quiet village haunts. There is a prevailing mood of resignation in the wake of carefree summer days, and a plain-spoken greeting, "Ready for winter?" Up in the woods, the sap has receded, leaving the trees ready for prime firewood cutting. Dead and diseased trees are easily spotted for culling in the still leafy canopy. The inexorable roar of a chain saw declares the arrival of early autumn.

Over hills and flats, family vegetable gardens lie full of summer treasures. Gardeners with large investments of love and care set the night watch for settling frost. Excursions set out for the red raspberry farm, and in search of wild apples. The abundance of the local autumn harvest is a communally understood pleasure, like the painted landscape, an essential reminder of why we choose to live here.

Following the October rains, frost settles like silver glitter strewn across vines, mosses, and tender leaves until dawn melts its disguise and reveals the grim face of winter. Leaves whirl in a last windy dance while hills and gardens lie withered and brisk.

In the past, many thought this time beckoned to the Otherworld. As winds howled, spirits seemed to swirl up from dark clouds in figures across the moon. Watchful mortals, enraptured by illusions in every flickering shadow, masqueraded and held high festival as they acknowledged the death of summer.

Thousands of years later, the spirit of Halloween still survives and perhaps flourishes nowhere more than in the Catskills, where howling winds resonate with screeching owls and the distant honks of migrating geese long into the autumn evenings. Smoldering with the essence of dry leaves, ideas materialize with old hats, masks, elaborate face paint, veils, and flowing capes. At twilight an inscrutable masquerade, the magnificent disguise of fading autumn, dances in Woodstock's streets and clubs. At small gatherings, there are cider and delicacies, and somewhere a ritual bonfire, to feed far into the night. At the peak of this Halloween gala, a stream of goblins, clowns, witches, and space creatures reverently passes the haunting one hundred jack-o'-lanterns, a midnight enthronement of mirth and magic, grinning from the dark stands of Sunfrost Farm.

In a procession from the garden, the Halloween masquerade is inspired by the jack-o'-lantern. The ancient custom of vegetable carving gives physical expression to the Spirit of the Garden. Before coming to America, this spirit was kindled in large hollowed turnip lanterns. Later, adapted to the American field pumpkin, the spirit assumed all the identity of harvest pleasure, and Otherworld play.

The occasion of this late harvest rite of carving requires an afternoon gathering of children, a throne of raked leaves, hot mulled cider, and popcorn. With massive pumpkins rolled down from the field, a pen, sharp knife, and willing imagination will release and animate the personality disguised in each pumpkin.

The pumpkin is to become a lantern, requiring a lid to be opened for lighting the candle. Shapes to let patterns of light through can become an expression. A lid or cap is carved out of the top section of the pumpkin and removed. Then the fibrous membrane and seeds can be cleaned out of the inside. A small round depression carved in the inside bottom will support the candle.

With the lid back on, one can find the face on the rounded side and discover the pumpkin's mood, whether menacing or jovial. Some pumpkins are lopsided and knobbed, good for ghoulish crescent eyes; others, round and smooth, suggest surreal, triangular features. These shapes are marked with a black marker line to guide the carving. With the candle lit, the eyes gleaming, nostrils flaring, and the mouth grinning full of teeth, the jack-o'-lantern reflects its fiery spirit in a dance upon a dark wall.

With the dawn of All Saints' Day, the spirits of the Otherworld disappear as if they were never there. Tangible magic of the delirious dark hours has slipped away; the farm stands empty until spring. As deep frost settles into the earth, and as red-clad hunters pass by into the hills, people go out to rescue the last beets and lettuce from their gardens to store for the long, cold winter ahead.

By the end of November, Woodstock's social resource, "Family," recruits prepared foods and home-baked treats from the community, to sponsor a large public benefit Thanksgiving Day dinner. Local people reach out from their own individual family lives to re-create the comfort of old-time gatherings with an extended "family" of friends. Tradition is the enrichment of the experience. A sacrificial bird, the customary centerpiece, dressed with chestnuts and sage, is accompanied by bright squash and cranberries, autumn lettuce, apples, and wild mushrooms. For some folks, the bird might be a local wild turkey. For others, it is a succulent loaf of herbed tofu and nuts. For every table, there is pumpkin or apple pie, and the joyful communion that goes with abundant feasting.

The Apple Orchard

Early settlers coming to the Hudson Valley brought many horticultural favorites from Europe. Among these was the apple.

Colonists discovered that their specimens from Holland, Germany, France, and Britain flourished in this temperate and fertile climate.

Catskill Mountain land barons soon brought apples into their agricultural schemes for the early mountainside tenant farms. While grain and field crops were grown in the broader bottomlands, small orchards could bring production to the narrow fields along hillside slopes between high pasture lands.

Local history teaches us that the famous Jonathan apple was developed on such a farm in Woodstock, just before the Revolution. Originally known as the Rickey, it was adopted and traded with many other varieties by native Americans and traveling settlers to spread across the new world continent, growing wild and abundant.

Today, traces of old pasture trees and small orchards are hidden everywhere in the forested Catskills. Many ancient trees, tall and gnarled, can still be discovered fruiting in good apple years. Along the middle Hudson Valley, in the fertile plains below the eastern rim of the Catskill Mountains, September orchards speckle the groomed landscape. Curious clans of knotty trees stoop with the abundance of yellow ripening pears and late rosy plums, as well as apples. In deep autumn sunlight the orchards are a rainbow of color. Ruby apples drip from twists of drooping branches. Four hundred years have produced succulent descendants from the first hardy colonial Dutch apple trees. The Hudson Valley region now ranks as one of the largest sources in the country for this most highly consumed fruit. Browsing pickers are welcome in many small local orchards.

McIntosh apples are ready for picking in September and account for about a third of all apples grown in the Hudson Valley. Round and red, with a smooth shiny skin, this variety is moderately tart and especially juicy. McIntosh are good for eating fresh, as well as for baking.

The Cortland apple also ripens in the valley at this time. It is round and red, usually larger than the McIntosh. In shorter supply, it is an old favorite among regional people as a delicious general purpose apple. Cortlands are especially good for fresh appetizing salads because they are sweet and firm, and the flesh is slow to brown.

October brings the second major apple crop to the Hudson Valley, the Red Delicious, a crowned, dark red, speckled fruit. Crisp and sweet, it is best for eating raw. Fresh slices are beautiful and tasty with a creamy honey-wine dip.

A scattering of other varieties are also harvested in October, composing another third of the regional crop. Northern Spy is another old favorite variety. Rounded and broad, its traditional uses include juicy raw eating, rich sauce, pies, and cider. Golden Delicious, yellow-green and crowned, is crisp and tangy, a very popular raw-eating apple. It is the gourmet choice for cider making.

The last apple to be harvested in the Hudson Valley area is the rosy Rome Beauty. This large, round, and broad apple is ideal for desserts. Sweet and juicy, it naturally bakes into a very rich consistency. Its rotund size lends itself to baking whole in a pastry wrapping, with a minced dried-fruit-and-nut stuffing.

Cider

Autumn cider pressing is a custom as old as apple growing. On a propitious October day in Woodstock, villagers gather as in homesteading times, with baskets and crates of local apples. There on the village green, amid jugs and bottles, in the spicy fragrance of apples, they share a local wooden press, generously donated for this annual autumn-festival occasion.

This is a time to talk of the discovery of an abandoned orchard, the taste of a forgotten apple variety, woody, crisp, and pollution-free. Apple surpluses are shared to balance and enrich the cider's flavor.

Cider making is an art developed out of days when cider was the predominant all-season beverage. Several apple varieties are pressed together to obtain favorable harmony. A good blend should include a very aromatic variety, another very tart, with another bland and very juicy apple. Apple cider can be used to cook grains. It can be mulled with spices or seasoned for vinegar. Extra cider can be frozen in plastic jugs.

The art of cider making spawned the practice of home distillation and liquor making. There still remain clans of old-timers in the Catskills who share their applejack like a secret social rite. Their practice reflects an interesting way to use extra cider, after the freezer is full.

HARD CIDER

The old process passed on, from *Woodstock: Recollection by Recipe:* "Obtain freshly pressed, unpasteurized cider, made from fully ripe, sound, late apples. These have the highest sugar content. Red skinned, yellow fleshed varieties make the best cider. The better the apples, the better the end product.

"Put cider in a clean wooden barrel in a cool place. A jug may be used for small amounts. The purist works with cider alone, but some like to add honey or brown sugar for a more potent beverage. (This must be invert sugar.) 20 lb. sugar to 50 gallons cider is the usual amount. Some like to add raisins as well. Drill a hole in the bung, and insert a length of rubber tubing, one end in the barrel above the liquid and the other in a jar of water to act as an air lock. This keeps out the 'vinegar bugs'.

"Let the cider work alone until all bubbling in the jar of water has ceased, i.e. from about November to January. Then siphon off the dregs into bottles or a clean keg. Close up tightly, and be tempted with discretion."

BERT VAN KLEEK AND RICHARD CRANE

Of Herbs, Nuts, and Berries

As the northern Catskill forests were consumed by a hungry lumbering industry, early settlers dependent on trees for lumber turned to other sources of cash. One of these was the autumn collection and marketing of ginseng. Indians venerated wild ginseng, employing it as a love charm. They recognized its invigorating power, as did the distant Asians, with whom the new Americans sought trade.

The Catskills remain a principal source of American wild ginseng. The ancestral cunning for ginseng hunting is preserved in a few regional descendants, who hike mountain slopes with the cooling October days, to collect aging specimens of this scarce, potently tonic herb. As a back-to-the-land enterprise, ginseng cultivation has been practiced by the current stock of industrious area people. Cash crops have proved possible in forested mountainside farms.

Among other Catskill Mountain herbs sought by many has been wintergreen. It, too, has been marketed for its distinctive essential oil, distilled for several medicinal and culinary preparations. Like many wild growing regional plants, waxy-green wintergreen leaves and the autumn berries are delicious fresh from the ground.

On northern slopes, under maple and beech trees, nuts drop to the floor of the hardwood forests. Bright cranberries ripen in Yankeetown and other boggy flats. The mountain forager ventures through sprays of color into Indian summer, compelled by autumn's intense display, and the knowledge of special seasonal treasures. Over fields and mountains are many wild flowering and seeding plants, ripe to heal, to charm, or to nourish.

By October, maple trees are glowing radiant with painted boughs, omen for another seasonal cycle. Flaming sumac, platinum grapevines, and yellow wild sunflowers shine in the rim of clearings while meadow carpets bristle with purple and lavender asters.

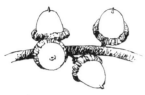

Acorns

ACORNS *Shell and boil nuts in consecutive boiling water baths until water is clear. Grind into meal and mix with other flour for baking bread and pancakes. Mix with cornmeal and water for porridge.*

BLACK WALNUT *A most desirable, appreciated nut for dark, rich, oily flavor. Imparts unique character to cakes, candies, and salads.*

Goldenrod

BUTTERNUT *Collect young, green nuts. Clean and remove outer fuzz. Prepare brine: 1 cup salt to 2 quarts water. Pour over nuts, cover tightly. Change brine every other day for a week. Drain and pat dry. Pierce nuts several times with a needle. Layer in a glass jar, with a sprinkling of powdered ginger, nutmeg, and cloves. Cover with boiling cider vinegar. Seal jars and store for at least 2 weeks.*

CRANBERRIES *Harvest after first frost. Bake in breads, cakes. Chop fine, sweeten, and mix with oranges, apples, and nuts, or cook, sweetened, for a delicious sauce. Freeze extra for Christmas.*

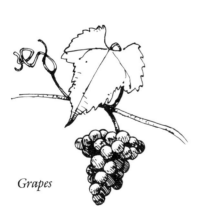

Grapes

GINSENG *Look for 3- or 4-pronged plant with groups of 5-pointed leaves, standing 12 to 20 inches tall. In autumn, the plant appears bright yellow, with a spike of crimson red berries, very vivid on a gray October day. Separate the cluster and replant each berry. Very gently dig the root. Shake off excess soil, and dry slowly in a shady, airy place for long keeping. Eat Ginseng green for its potent rejuvenation power. Chew or brew dried bits of ginseng for an invigorating tonic and health-preserving dietary supplement.*

GOLDENROD   *Collect for dried flower arrangements. Brew for soothing tea in winter. Should not be taken by people with ragweed allergies.*

GRAPES   *Put fresh grapes through juicer; use pulp for rich beverage concentrate mixed with water, seltzer, or other juices. Use for vivid purple dye. For stored juice, put 1 cup clean, stemmed grapes into hot sterilized quart jar. Add 3 to 4 tablespoons honey, and fill jar with boiling water allowing ¼-inch head space. Seal each jar and process 10 minutes in boiling water bath. Store jars 10 weeks before straining and using.*

Jerusalem Artichoke

HICKORY NUT   *Very delicious. Collect and use fresh in cakes, breads, and stir-fries.*

JERUSALEM ARTICHOKE   *Dig for tubers after frost for sweetest flavor. Sauté in butter or steam. Substitute for potatoes.*

RASPBERRY   *Collect leaves of first-year canes. Dry and brew for soothing and medicinal tea, especially for women.*

Hickory Nut

WILD GERANIUM, CRANESBILL   *Small pale green plant with gray-green stem and rose-scented leaves. Pale purple blossom has a narrow, down-curved, pointed petal that looks like a crane's bill, prominent in late summer. Collect fading leaves and rough, knotty root to brew for tea to treat colds that come with the changing season. Bundle whole plants and hang upside down to dry.*

WINTERGREEN   *Collect and use fresh through the fall and winter. For strongest, most flavorful tea, steep a generous amount of leaves in water at least 24 hours.*

Wintergreen

Rain and Mushrooms

Cavernous autumn woods, soaked two days with rain, feed tiny spores. Nurtured in darkness and the warmth of decay, fungus creatures, the colors of mist, unfold out of rotting leaves and niches of crumbling logs. In the play of autumn, they cluster at tree roots, or congregate among the grasses at the edge of woods, like discarded elfin toys.

Through clouds of mist in a shower of painted leaves, the mushroom hunter follows an intuitive sense and subtle dusky odors into dank lowland woods. Out of the gloom, autumn yields this delicious wild game of vegetarian eating.

There are a few prized mushrooms commonly found in the autumn woods and meadows of the Catskills. Different varieties manifest with the particular year's unpredictable seasonal changes. The knowledgeable forager anticipates finding both unpalatable or poisonous and edible mushrooms in equal abundance. It is important to accompany the forage with at least two vividly clear, official mushroom guidebooks for confident, cross-reference identification.

Boletus family mushrooms are often found in sun-dappled grasses of hardwoods, under beeches, or in clearings. They tend to grow in large scattered communities, sometimes clustering in little families of four to six. Boletus are readily recognized by the pores on the underside of the cap. They are usually fleshy and rather thick-stemmed mushrooms. There are many edible Boletus, although cepes are most desirable.

The cepe is a stocky mushroom with a fleshy cap. Soft buff to dark brown in color, the cepe is best when a young, domed specimen, about 3 inches wide, with white pores. It is distinguished by a lighter colored fat stem, widest at the bottom.

Slippery Jack, another edible Boletus, has a slimy, copper-colored dome. The stem is pale yellowish white, covered with specks, deeper in color toward the top. The thick flesh is pale yellow. Slimy skins should be removed before cooking.

Boletus mushrooms have a firm flesh and retain character well in batter frying, stuffing, and roasting, or in a garlic-butter sauté.

The Golden Coral mushroom often appears in abundance among the pine needles of a conifer forest floor. It is part of a family named for its sea-coral shape, with many branchlets forming from ground level out of a thick trunk. Look for the pale beige coral, cream or yellowish white in all parts.

This is a fragile fungus, and must be used soon after harvesting. Dry roast, then brown in butter for a side dish or special sauce.

The Wood Blewit is a common mushroom, found in damp undergrowth of pine woods. It is most characterized by its pale lilac coloring. The convex cap of the young mushroom flattens and darkens with age, growing 2½ to 5 inches in diameter. Under the cap are crowded violet gills. The stem is long, wider at the base and distinctively violet in color. Because of the pervasive purple coloring, Wood Blewits cannot be confused with any poisonous mushrooms.

The Wood Blewit is prized for its subtle aroma. This is enhanced by gently sautéeing in butter. It can be used in most any mushroom recipe.

The Agaricus mushroom family is the wild ancestor of the cultivated mushroom, and is generally similar in appearance. The commonly seen field or horse Agaricus is often found growing in the soft rich soil of the garden, out of manure compost, and in pastures and yards.

They first appear as small round buttons, that quickly grow into dome shapes, spreading out flat, 3 to 4 inches in diameter. Horse and meadow mushrooms are quite firm, but the surface is very soft. The cap varies in tones of yellow-pinkish off-white, with a dark center, and brown patches. The gills are pale yellowish pink, turning purple-gray to purple-brown as the mushroom ages. As the cap grows it leaves a cottony ruffle, which drops off as the dome widens. Stems are plain and fleshy. These mushrooms should not be confused with a similar poisonous mushroom, the Amanita Death Cap or Destroying Angel, which always has all-white gills, and a pronounced heavy ring and volva on the stem.

Meadow or horse mushrooms are delicious eaten raw in salads, or stewed in soups and sauces. They can be basted with Cognac or red wine and sautéed or roasted. They are very good for cooking over an open charcoal fire skewered with other vegetables or basted with oil and set up on the grill.

The Root Cellar

Captured in the swiftness of impelling change, the autumn gardener confronts the harvest, collecting fruit of physical and spiritual labor, preparing the garden for rest, and planning storage of late vegetables and fruits for the long winter ahead.

With the first omens of seasonal change, fruit trees can be pruned of excess draining growth. Bulbs for daffodils, crocus, and narcissus can be planted to cheer the early spring yard. All sensitive perennials should be fed with manure and compost and mulched against the coming cold. It is time to dig up garden herbs and condition them to a pot for a few weeks before placing in sunny kitchen windowsills.

The autumn garden is a welcome nursery for radishes and turnips and a few fast-growing greens. A simple, functioning solar greenhouse, or walk-in cold frame, can be assembled with a few well-planted stakes. Covered with stapled scrap sheets of plastic, stabilized at the bottom edges with rocks, the interior will collect heat and moisture. In this mini-rain forest environment, varieties of lettuce, chives, parsley, and other special herbs will thrive into very cold weather.

With the approach of mid-autumn, the frost vigil begins. Late-ripeners are given every last moment of warm sunny afternoons. Cold nights are followed by days of anxious gathering, cleaning, and putting-by of all remaining garden vegetables. This begins the indoor gardening cycle.

There are simple, basic ways to keep home-grown produce closest to garden-fresh, full of color and vitality, for economical, nutritious, and appetizing cold-weather meals. A root cellar, any insulated underground space such as a stone cellar, will house hardy vegetables in an environment much like the early autumn garden. Bins full of sand and leaves will protect roots and cabbages through the winter. Jars of preserves and pickles keep cool against a dark north-facing wall.

A stone-lined hole in the ground forms a miniature cellar. Inside, a wooden barrel can be stationed diagonally. Lined with leaves, it protects succulent roots buried in light garden soil.

Layers of soil, stones, and leaves heaped over the outside, insulate the vegetables from freezing temperatures, and allow drainage and ventilation. A wooden lid forms the door, easily found through the snow by a positioned postmarker.

An unheated room is good for dried storage; herbs, winter squash, tubers, and mellowing cakes. A well-ventilated attic offers a similar environment with protective darkness and more moderate temperatures. Well-covered glass or metal containers will protect from mice.

An extra refrigerator, running only in the harvest and early winter months, will very conveniently store fresh greens, peppers, snap beans, roots, and fruit for several weeks. Very inexpensive public freezing space can be rented in many communities for crisp broccoli, peas, and sweet green lima beans in January.

As long as the weather remains reasonably dry, other shell beans can be left in the garden to dry on the vine. When they have reached papery crispness, collect pods and spread out on a dry sunny surface. If outside, they must be brought in from the dew. After a few days, the beans can be shelled, spread on baking sheets, and placed in a very low oven for 15 to 20 minutes to ensure thorough drying. Cool and store beans in loosely filled, airtight jars, in the dark. Shake the jars and check periodically for the occurrence of mold. Be sure to return all remnants of bean plants to the compost as they contain important nitrogen-fixing agents.

After red ripe tomatoes have been eaten in every imaginable way, extras should be canned for winter sauces and casseroles. Some of the last green tomatoes should be cooked like eggplant or made into relish.

Just before frost, individually wrap any remaining green tomatoes in newspaper, pack loosely in a box, and set in a dry, shadowed place to ripen. Remove pumpkins and winter squash from the vine very carefully, leaving the stems intact. Bring them into the kitchen, or other moderately warm, dry place, for about ten days. Coming into the warm house from cool garden nights will cure and harden the bark. The squashes can then be shelved in a cool, dry place where many varieties will keep well through February.

All roots can be left in the garden until just before the ground freezes. Parsnips should be left in longer for best flavor. Parsnips and kale can be picked fresh through the winter, with just a light protective hay or plastic covering from the snow.

When all the harvest has been stored in the cellar, pantry, or freezer, and remaining fresh plants have been mulched or covered, it is time to put the garden to rest. All patches of seeding weeds and any diseased or infested vines or stalks should be cleaned out. Vegetable and kitchen scraps, mixed with fresh fallen leaves and pine needles, and any remaining compost can then be spread over the soil surface. Fresh manure should also be added at this time. A good tilling will grind everything together for a fast, nourishing breakdown. The garden can now be tucked in for its long rest under a blanket of rye seed. The rye will sprout and grow a beautiful thick blue-green cover through the early winter. After the thaw, it will continue to grow, until tilled under to further enrich the earth.

COUNTRY TABLE:
Autumn Recipes & Menus

MULLED CIDER
Serves 16

1 gallon cider
4 (3-inch) sticks of cinnamon
1 teaspoon ground allspice
1 teaspoon whole cloves
Sprinkle of freshly grated nutmeg

Put the cider and spices together in a large kettle. Bring to a boil, then simmer. Serve after 15 minutes or so. Spicy aroma and flavors continue to grow with more simmering.

ROASTED SEEDS

While watching the flicker and dance of the Spirit of the Garden, share more hot cider, and the smell of roasting pumpkin seeds.

Preheat oven to 400 degrees F. Separate pumpkin membrane from the seeds. Place seeds in a colander and wash off remaining fiber. Toss seeds in enough safflower oil to coat thoroughly. Lightly salt and spread on cookie sheets. Roast about 20 minutes, until browned. Shake the baking pan occasionally.

Serve pumpkin seeds warm. Store extra seeds in a jar with a lid and snack on them anytime.

AUBERGINE ZINFONIA
Serves 6 to 12

About 2 pounds eggplant (5–6 baby eggplants or 2 medium, sliced crosswise, ½ inch wide)
Salt
⅓ cup olive oil
1 medium onion, cut in rings
1 teaspoon crushed coriander seeds
3 cloves garlic, crushed
2 whole cloves
1 tablespoon chopped fresh basil
1 small bunch seedless purple grapes (about 1 pound)
½ cup dry red wine
Freshly ground black pepper to taste

FOR GARNISH: Chopped fresh parsley

Sprinkle eggplant slices with salt and set in a colander, under a weight. Let drain for ½ hour, then rinse and pat dry.

Heat olive oil in a heavy pan; sauté onion rings over medium heat until transparent; remove. Sauté eggplant slices until brown on both sides, adding more oil if necessary.

Lower heat and add crushed coriander seeds, garlic, cloves, and basil. Return sautéed onion rings to pan. Cover and cook gently 5 minutes.

Add grapes and red wine; cover and simmer very gently for about 15 minutes. Add salt and pepper to taste. Cool, then refrigerate until thoroughly chilled, 1 to 2 hours. Serve cold, sprinkled with chopped parsley, as an appetizer or side dish.

SAVORY PUMPKIN PASTRIES
Yield: 30 pastries

2 cups puréed steamed pumpkin
1 teaspoon ground cumin
¼ teaspoon cayenne
1 teaspoon finely chopped fresh mint
1 tablespoon finely chopped fresh parsley
3 scallions, finely chopped

½ pound feta cheese, finely diced
½ teaspoon salt
½ teaspoon freshly grated black pepper
½ pound phyllo dough
½ cup melted butter
3 teaspoons (about) whole cumin seeds

FOR GARNISH:
Freshly chopped watercress

Preheat oven to 400 degrees F. Combine pumpkin with cumin, cayenne, mint, parsley, scallions, and feta cheese. Add salt and pepper to taste.

Unroll phyllo dough. Remove 1 sheet and brush with melted butter. (Keep rest of dough between dampened towels to prevent drying out.) Cut sheet into 6 pieces, crosswise. Put 1 teaspoon pumpkin filling on bottom of each strip. Fold as a flag: pick up left corner, bring it forward diagonally to meet right side. Pick up the point on the right side and fold it forward and parallel to the same side. Fold right corner diagonally to left side; continue to end of strip. Tuck end of strip over. Make last fold over the tucked end to make a neat package. Place on lightly oiled baking tray. Continue with rest of ingredients until pumpkin filling is used up.

Just before baking, brush each pastry with butter and sprinkle with whole cumin seeds.

Bake 10 to 15 minutes or until golden. Serve immediately, garnished with watercress.

These freeze well.

CARROT TAHINI
Yield: about 2 cups

1 cup (1–2 large) coarsely ground carrots
½ cup tahini
1 tablespoon fresh lemon juice
2 small cloves garlic, minced
¼ cup minced fresh parsley

Place ground carrots in a mixing bowl. Stir in the tahini; add lemon juice, garlic, and parsley.

Serve Carrot Tahini as a spread with alfalfa sprouts and Crusty White Bread (see Index). It is also very good as a dip for raw vegetables.

MUSHROOM-HAZELNUT SOUP
Serves 6–8

¼ cup butter
2 stalks celery, finely chopped
2 cups finely chopped scallions
1½ pounds mushrooms, finely chopped
6 cups Vegetable Broth (*see Index*)
¼ cup uncooked rice
½ teaspoon fresh thyme
Pinch of crushed fresh tarragon leaves
1 cup blanched hazelnuts
1 cup light cream
2 tablespoons tamari soy sauce
½ teaspoon freshly ground black pepper
¼ teaspoon freshly ground nutmeg
Salt to taste
About ⅓ cup dry sherry

Melt butter in large soup pot. Sauté celery and scallions until wilted. Add mushrooms, toss and stew in butter for 5 minutes.

Add 4 cups of the vegetable broth and the rice. Simmer until rice is tender, about 20 minutes, adding herbs toward the end.

Meanwhile combine remaining 2 cups vegetable stock and the nuts and simmer until tender, about 20 minutes.

Purée nut mixture in blender and strain through a fine sieve. Purée vegetable mixture.

Combine both purées in soup pot and heat gently with ¾ cup of the cream, tamari, pepper, nutmeg, and salt if needed. Do not boil. Add dry sherry to taste and serve with a swirl of remaining cream.

CASHEW CARROT SOUP
Serves 4

Cashew Carrot Soup has
gained a reputation as a
favorite around the area, and
is featured presently in
restaurants and
many family kitchens.

¾ cup ground cashews
1½ cups hot water
2 tablespoons safflower oil
1 medium onion, chopped
1 large carrot, grated
2 whole cloves
1 clove garlic, minced
1 teaspoon minced fresh basil
½ teaspoon dried oregano
2 teaspoons tamari soy sauce
½ pint carrot juice

With ground cashews in the blender, slowly add hot water, blending until very smooth. Set creamed cashews aside.*

Heat oil in a heavy 3-quart saucepot. Sauté onion for 1 to 2 minutes. Add grated carrot and stir well to coat with oil. Continue cooking and stirring over low heat until carrots are just tender. Add cloves, garlic, basil, oregano, and tamari. Stir well and then add cashew milk. Heat the soup, and just before serving add the carrot juice. Serve warm.

* This is a basic recipe for "Cashew Milk," which can be substituted for dairy milk in creamed dishes and many baked goods. Cream cashews in enough hot water to achieve desired consistency (from creamy thick to thin) according to use.

SAVORY BORSCHT
Serves 6–8

6 large beets, washed, peeled, and grated
1 potato, grated
1 medium onion, diced
10 cups Vegetable Broth (*see Index*)
3 tablespoons butter or safflower oil
3 tablespoons unbleached white flour
Juice of 1 lemon
2 tablespoons maple syrup
1 tablespoon vinegar
Freshly ground black pepper
Pinch of salt

FOR GARNISH:
Yogurt or sour cream

Place prepared beets, potato, and onion into stock and simmer 10 minutes, until just tender.

Heat butter or oil in a heavy saucepot. Add flour to make a roux. Cook over medium heat 2 minutes, stirring constantly. Slowly add 1 to 2 cups of hot stock, continuing to stir, to form a thick sauce. Add remaining ingredients, except for garnish, to the sauce. Cook and stir 2 or 3 more minutes, until heated through and smooth. Add to main soup pot, stirring to blend well. Chill, and serve topped with dollops of yogurt or sour cream. This soup is also very good hot, garnished as directed for cold. Seasonings may be adjusted according to taste, and sweetness of the herbs.

SQUASH AND APPLE SOUP
Serves 6

¼ cup butter
1 cup chopped onions
½ cup chopped celery
2 apples, peeled and chopped
6 cups Vegetable Broth (*see Index*)
4 cups diced butternut squash
½ teaspoon dried thyme
¼ teaspoon dried rosemary
1 teaspoon salt
Pinch of freshly grated nutmeg
Few grinds of black pepper
1 cup fresh apple cider
½ cup heavy cream

Melt the butter in a heavy soup pot and cook the onions, celery, and apples till soft, about 5 minutes.

Add the vegetable stock and simmer 10 minutes.

Add the butternut squash and seasonings and simmer until tender, about another 15 minutes.

Purée most of the vegetables and broth in a blender; leave a little at the bottom of the pot unpuréed, for texture. Return the puréed mixture to the pot together with the cider and cream. Stir well and cook gently until just heated through.

MISO VEGETABLE SOUP
Serves 4–6

2½ tablespoons safflower oil
1 teaspoon dark sesame oil
1 tablespoon grated peeled fresh gingerroot
2–3 cloves garlic, minced
1 large onion, sliced
1 carrot, sliced thin or julienned
1½ cups shredded cabbage
6 cups boiling water
¼ pound buckwheat spaghetti
3 tablespoons miso
Tamari soy sauce to taste

FOR GARNISH:
3 scallions, chopped

Heat oils in a Dutch oven. Add ginger, garlic, and onion, and sauté 1 minute. Add carrot, stirring and cooking 2 to 3 minutes. Then add cabbage and continue cooking for 2 minutes. Add boiling water and return to a simmer.

Break noodles into the soup and simmer, covered, until they are tender, 10 to 15 minutes.

Remove the soup from the heat. Spoon out a portion into a cup with the miso. Stir until blended and the miso is softened. Add to the pot with tamari. Top the soup or garnish individual bowls with scallions and serve at once.

EGGPLANT SOUP AU GRATIN
Serves 6–8

3 tablespoons olive oil
1 large onion, sliced
4 cloves garlic, crushed
2 medium eggplants (about 2 pounds), julienned
1 teaspoon dried oregano
½ teaspoon dried thyme
4 cups Vegetable Broth (*see Index*)
3 tablespoons dry sherry
Salt and freshly ground black pepper to taste
6–8 thick slices of bread, sautéed in oil and garlic
1½ cups grated Swiss cheese
½ cup grated Parmesan cheese

Heat oil in a heavy soup pot and sauté onion and garlic until transparent.

Add julienned eggplant and herbs and sauté 5 minutes more.

Add stock, bring to a boil, then cover and simmer for about 20 minutes.

Preheat broiler. Add sherry to soup pot and simmer another 5 minutes. Add salt and pepper to taste.

Pour soup into heatproof bowls and top with the garlic bread and cheeses.

Lightly brown under broiler—about 3–5 minutes—and serve immediately.

SCALLOP BISQUE
Serves 4–8

Small scallops from Long Island Sound have long found their way to markets and dining tables along the Mid-Hudson Valley.

8 tablespoons butter
½ cup chopped scallions
½ cup chopped shallots
½ pound mushrooms, thinly sliced
¼ cup chopped fresh parsley
1 teaspoon chopped fresh thyme leaves
1 tablespoon chopped fresh basil leaves
Salt and freshly ground black pepper
2 tablespoons Cognac
4 cups Fish Stock (*see recipe below*) or clam broth
½ cup dry white wine

1 pound bay scallops
4 tablespoons flour
2 eggs
1 cup heavy cream
2–3 tablespoons dry sherry, to taste

FOR GARNISH: Chopped parsley

Melt 4 tablespoons of the butter in large soup pot. Add scallions and shallots and simmer, covered, 15 minutes.

Add mushrooms and cook slowly for 5 minutes: Add chopped herbs, salt and pepper, and Cognac. Increase heat until liquid is almost evaporated.

Add stock and wine; bring to a boil, then simmer 15 minutes to concentrate flavor. Add scallops, cover, cook 2 minutes. Strain broth into a pot and reserve scallop/mushroom solids. Maintain stock at boiling point.

Make the roux: Melt remaining 4 tablespoons butter, add 4 tablespoons flour, cook gently for 5 minutes, stirring constantly to prevent scorching.

Beat the boiling stock into the roux. Simmer for 5 minutes while beating constantly.

Beat eggs and cream together. Add 1 cup hot broth to egg and cream mixture, then whisk eggs and cream into the pot of broth.

Keep soup over low heat; stirring constantly, add dry sherry to taste: It should thicken a little but not boil.

Add scallop/mushroom mixture; heat through. Check seasoning, then serve sprinkled with chopped parsley.

FISH STOCK:
Yield: about 8 cups

2 pounds fish trimmings (use non-oily fish), heads and bones
6 cups water
1 cup dry white wine
1 cup chopped onions
½ cup chopped celery

1 bay leaf
½ teaspoon dried thyme
1 teaspoon salt
6 peppercorns
1 carrot, sliced
1 sprig fresh parsley

Wash fish bones well, then chop into 2-inch pieces. Place in large pot and pour water and wine over them. Add more water if needed to cover.

Bring to simmer over medium heat and cook for 5 minutes. With a slotted spoon, skim off foam as it rises.

Add rest of the ingredients, simmer 30 minutes. Strain stock well and it is ready to use.

APPLE ORCHARD STEW
Serves 3

2 tablespoons olive oil
1 medium onion, diced
½ pound mushrooms, sliced
1 clove garlic, pressed
7 apples, peeled and sliced
½ teaspoon powdered ginger
½ cup raisins
2 cups apple juice
8 ounces egg noodles
2 tablespoons butter
Salt to taste
3 tablespoons cornstarch, dissolved in ½ cup cold water
2 tablespoons Worcestershire sauce
2 tablespoons tamari soy sauce

Heat oil in a cast-iron skillet. Add onions, mushrooms, garlic, and apple slices. Stir in ginger. Sauté until onion is transparent. Add raisins and apple juice. Cover and simmer gently for a few minutes while the noodles are cooked according to package directions.

Drain cooked noodles. Toss in butter and salt, and set aside.

Combine cornstarch and water with Worcestershire and tamari. Stir into the apple mixture. Continue stirring over low heat until thickened. Serve hot over noodles.

PUMPKIN CORNUCOPIA
Serves 6

A beautiful round pumpkin or other sweet winter squash festively celebrates the harvest, overstuffed with delicious surprises in the colors of the season.

1 (3-pound) pumpkin or other round winter squash
2 tablespoons oil
1 cup chopped onions or scallions
1 cup sliced mushrooms
½ cup halved pecan meats
½ teaspoon minced peeled fresh gingerroot
½ cup chopped dates
2 tablespoons dry sherry
1 cup (about 4 ounces dry) steamed wild rice
1 cup sour cream or Soy Cream (*see Index*)

FOR GARNISH:
Escarole, Parsley

Preheat oven to 375 degrees F. Wash the pumpkin and set in preheated oven to prebake about 1 hour, or until tender.

Meanwhile, heat oil in a skillet. Sauté the onions for a minute; add mushrooms. Stir and cook until they are barely tender. Add nuts and ginger. Stir 1 more minute, and add dates and sherry. Remove from heat and set aside.

Remove pumpkin from the oven, leaving oven on. Slice the crown off the top of the pumpkin and reserve. Scoop out seeds and fibrous membranes; set them aside for cleaning and roasting later.

Scrape out about a third of the pumpkin meat and set in a mixing bowl. Mash, and add the wild rice and the onion-mushroom mixture. Gently mix, then fold in the sour cream. Stuff this filling into the pumpkin cavity. Set the crown on the top, and return the pumpkin to the 375-degree F. oven for about 20 minutes, until heated through.

Pumpkin Cornucopia is a beautiful holiday dish, very expressive of the harvest bounty. Set the baked, stuffed pumpkin on a large platter surrounded with crisp leafy escarole and fresh parsley bouquets. Remove the crown, and spoon out a portion of solid, tender pumpkin flesh with each scoop of filling. Complement the Pumpkin Cornucopia with apples and cranberries, dark bread, and a good red wine.

BUCKWHEAT CAKES WITH WILD MUSHROOMS
Serves 6

1 package active dry yeast
1 teaspoon honey
3 cups lukewarm milk
1 cup unbleached white flour
1 cup buckwheat flour
¾ teaspoon salt
3 eggs
6–8 tablespoons butter
1 pound wild mushrooms (if unavailable, soak 1 ounce dried
    mushrooms, e.g., cepes or chanterelles, about 30 minutes,
    drain, and cook with ¾ pound cultivated mushrooms)
1 tablespoon mixed chopped fresh herbs (thyme, parsley, basil,
    etc.)
2 cloves garlic, crushed
¼ cup dry white wine
Freshly ground black pepper
¾ cup (about) sour cream
2 tablespoons chopped scallion tops or chives

To prepare batter for cakes, mix together the yeast, honey, and 1½ cups of the lukewarm milk. Let sit in a warm place 5 minutes, until bubbly, then stir in ½ cup of unbleached flour, ½ cup buckwheat flour, and ½ teaspoon of the salt. Stir 100 times to form a sponge.

Separate eggs, putting the whites aside. Lightly beat the yolks and add to the buckwheat batter. Cover and let rise in a warm place until doubled, about 1 hour.

When the sponge has doubled, add the rest of the flours alternately with the remaining 1½ cups lukewarm milk to make a smooth batter. Cover and let double in bulk again, about another hour.

Meanwhile, sauté the mushrooms, whole or in large pieces, in about 3 tablespoons butter, about 10 minutes. Then add chopped fresh herbs, crushed garlic, wine, remaining salt and pepper to taste. Cook 5 to 10 minutes, until wine has almost evaporated. Keep warm.

Preheat oven to 250 degrees F. Beat the egg whites until stiff and fold into the buckwheat batter. Heat griddle and lightly coat with butter. Pour batter onto hot griddle, enough to make a 6- to 8-inch cake, and cook ½ minute on each side. Keep warm in the oven until they are all cooked.

Drizzle each cake with melted butter, then add some sautéed wild mushrooms, a spoonful of sour cream, and a sprinkling of chopped scallions or chives. Fold over and serve hot.

CREAMY VEGETABLE PIE
Serves 4

FILLING:
4 large potatoes
4 carrots
2 cups peas
1 large onion, finely chopped
½ pound mushrooms, finely chopped

CRUST:
3 cups unbleached white flour
1 teaspoon salt
½ cup vegetable oil
½ cup cold water

CREAM SAUCE:
2 tablespoons butter
2 tablespoons flour
1 cup milk
1 teaspoon salt

Chop potatoes and carrots into bite-size pieces and steam until nearly tender. Drain. Combine in a mixing bowl with remaining vegetables, and set aside.

To prepare pie crust, sift dry ingredients. Then cut in oil with a fork. Mix in cold water. Mix until dough forms a ball; cut in half. Between 2 sheets of wax paper, roll each half into a 9-inch circle. Set aside while preparing the Cream Sauce.

Preheat oven to 350 degrees F.

Melt butter in saucepan, stir in flour. Stir until browned. Add milk slowly, stirring constantly until thickened. Add salt.

To assemble Creamy Vegetable Pie, set one dough circle into pie pan. Fill with the prepared vegetables. Cover with Cream Sauce. Cover with top crust, and pinch edges together. Bake pie until crust is golden, about 45 minutes. Serve hot with crispy green salad.

BAKED BEAN AND APPLE CASSEROLE
Serves 4–6

To fill the kitchen with the spicy aroma of autumn, bake a blend of September produce into a sumptuous main dish.

4 tablespoons oil or butter
1 cup chopped onions
2 tablespoons flour
¾–1 cup Bean-cooking liquid
¼ cup dry red wine
¼ teaspoon chili powder
2 tablespoons tamari soy
   sauce

½ teaspoon dry mustard
⅛ teaspoon freshly ground
   black pepper
1 cup grated sharp Cheddar
   cheese
4 apples
4 medium tomatoes, peeled
2½ cups cooked kidney beans

Preheat oven to 350 degrees F.

Heat 2 tablespoons oil in heavy saucepot. Sauté onions until limp. Add remaining 2 tablespoons oil, and flour. Stir over low heat for a minute. Slowly add bean cooking liquid, stirring constantly. Add wine, chili, tamari, mustard, and pepper. Stir until thickened. Add cheese, and stir until melted. Peel, core, and chop apples. Chop tomatoes and combine with apple and beans. Stir into the cheese sauce and mix well.

Pour into a 2-quart casserole that has a lid. Bake, covered, for 40 minutes. Remove cover and bake 10 minutes more. Let set and cool slightly before serving.

PARSLEY CONFETTI NOODLES
Serves 4

1 pound linguine
6 tablespoons olive oil
2 cups chopped fresh parsley
2 cups crumbled feta cheese
4 cloves garlic
2 tablespoons (about) tamari soy sauce

Cook linguine according to package directions. Meanwhile, combine parsley and crumbled cheese. Press garlic or mince very fine.

Toss hot, freshly cooked linguine noodles in olive oil. Add other ingredients immediately and toss. Stir over low heat to reheat, if necessary. Serve hot.

VITALITY BURGERS
Yield: 6 burgers

¾ cup ground sunflower seeds
¾ cup ground pumpkin seeds
½ cup rolled oats

¾ cup finely chopped onions
1 cup finely grated carrots
2 tablespoons tamari soy sauce

FOR GARNISH:
Pear Ketchup (*see Index*)
Tofu Mayonnaise (*see Index*)
Alfalfa sprouts

Preheat oven to 350 degrees F. Mix all ingredients and form into 6 patties. Bake on oiled cookie tin for 15 minutes. Carefully turn over with spatula and continue baking for 15 more minutes.

Vitality burgers make a nutritious lunch hot or cold. They are excellent in whole wheat pita bread garnished with Pear Ketchup, Tofu Mayonnaise, and alfalfa sprouts.

With the addition of garlic and fresh chopped basil, this mixture may also be used to stuff about 1 pound cooked whole wheat pasta shells. Place in a baking pan, 10 × 14 inches, cover with about 2 cups of a plum tomato sauce of your choice, and bake for 30 minutes at 350 degrees F.

EGGPLANT PARMESAN
Serves 4

1 large or 2 medium
eggplants (about 2 pounds)
2 eggs, separated
¾ cup flour
½ teaspoon salt
½ cup dry white wine
¼ cup water
1 tablespoon olive oil

Oil for frying—a mixture of
olive oil and light vegetable
oil to come up 1 inch in
the skillet
2 cups tomato sauce
2 cups shredded mozzarella
cheese
½ cup grated Parmesan
and/or Romano cheese

Peel eggplant and slice into rounds. Dredge with salt and place in colander, weighted down with a plate for about 30 minutes. Rinse and pat dry.

Preheat oven to 375 degrees F.

Prepare batter: Mix together egg yolks, flour, salt, wine, water, and 1 tablespoon olive oil. Whip whites until they hold a soft shape and fold them into the flour mixture.

Heat oil in skillet. Dip eggplant slices in batter and fry on both sides until golden brown. Drain.

In a 10 × 14 × 2½-inch baking dish, spread a spoonful or two of your favorite tomato sauce, then cover with 1 layer of fried eggplant. Sprinkle heavily with shredded mozzarella and lightly with Parmesan. Pour on another few spoonfuls of sauce, and keep layering until eggplant is used up. Finish with a sprinkle of grated cheeses and place in oven. Bake for 30 minutes or until it's bubbly and the cheese on top is brown.

AUTUMN COUSCOUS
Serves 6–8

Hidden throughout the emerging American cuisine are influences from many cultures. Some foreign traditional styles of cooking have special meaning for well-traveled Americans who return to settle in the Woodstock region. Among these is the ritual preparation of the Moroccan staple couscous. Hurried Westerners who enjoy this dish often accelerate the cooking process, preparing couscous much like other grains. However, nothing compares with the wondrous flavor and texture of traditional couscous, steamed and served smothered in a resulting mysteriously fragrant broth. Here is a recipe incorporating the old tradition with local September produce.

6 tablespoons butter
3 red onions, quartered
1 pound couscous
3 teaspoons ground cumin
½ teaspoon cinnamon
1 teaspoon powdered ginger
2 teaspoons finely ground black pepper
1 teaspoon paprika
¼ teaspoon cayenne pepper
8 cups water or Vegetable Broth (*see Index*)
½ cup finely chopped fresh parsley
1 teaspoon salt
1 cup coarsely chopped tomatoes
1 cup milk
8–10 medium carrots, halved
About 10 turnips, peeled and halved or quartered
5 red potatoes, halved
5 baby eggplants, halved, or 2 regular, quartered (about 1½
    pounds)
1 small pumpkin (about 3 pounds), cut in chunks
1 pound zucchini, cut in large chunks
¼ pound green beans, trimmed
1½ cups cooked chick-peas
½ cup raisins
¼ cup harissa or hot pepper sauce

Over low heat, melt 2 tablespoons of the butter in large, heavy saucepan or, preferably, in the bottom of a *couscoussière,* and toss onions in butter, letting them brown slightly without burning.

Meanwhile, rinse the couscous with about 8 cups water, drain, and spread out to dry in a very large dish or baking pan.

Add the spices to the onions, stir, and then add about 8 cups of water or vegetable broth, the parsley, salt, and tomatoes. Simmer 5 minutes.

To ensure lightness, the couscous needs to be continuously worked, by raking your fingers through the grain to separate any lumps. Once it feels fairly dry, start to sprinkle the cup of milk on it, rubbing the grains between your fingers as you work it in.

Add the carrots, turnips, potatoes, eggplants, and the rest of the butter to the broth.

Set the top of the *couscoussière* onto the bottom part, or use a colander lined with cheesecloth, making sure it is above the level of the broth and that as the steam rises it escapes through the center and not the sides. If necessary, seal the edges with a flour-and-water paste. Sprinkle about a quarter of the couscous into the top section; as it heats up, sprinkle in the remainder. Steam, uncovered, 15 to 20 minutes. Remove pot from heat.

Remove grain to the baking dish, break up lumps with a wooden spoon, and drizzle on a little more milk or water if it looks dry. As it cools, work it again with your fingers and let it dry 10 to 20 minutes.

Return bottom pot to heat. Add pumpkin, zucchini, green beans, and chick-peas, and bring to a boil. Return couscous to the top section and steam a further 20 to 25 minutes, adding raisins to the grain during the last 10 minutes to steam them.

When the couscous is light and fluffy, pour onto a large serving platter, mounding the grain slightly. Arrange some large pieces of vegetables in a well in the center of the mound and drizzle some broth over the grain. Serve the rest of the broth and vegetables in a separate bowl.

Take a few tablespoons of broth and mix with the harissa. Serve in a small bowl on the side so people can season their broth to taste.

Follow Autumn Couscous with a fresh fruit salad perfumed with rose water or almond pastries and mint tea.

LENTIL NUT LOAF
Serves 6–8

⅔ cup chopped onions
2 tablespoons oil
⅔ cup chopped tomatoes
½ buttercup or other winter squash (about 2 pounds),
    steamed
½ cup sunflower seeds
½ cup almonds
½ cup pecans or walnuts
1½ cups cooked lentils
1 tablespoon tamari soy sauce
½ teaspoon paprika
2 tablespoons dried sweet herbs (mixture of savory, marjoram,
    basil, thyme, rosemary)
1 egg, beaten
Salt and pepper
¾ cup Catskill Chili Sauce (*see Index*)

Preheat oven to 350 degrees F. Sauté onions in oil until transparent. Add chopped tomatoes and cook down until slightly thickened and saucy.

Peel and mash the steamed squash. Grind or very finely chop seeds and nuts. Combine lentils with tomato mixture, squash, nuts, tamari, paprika, and herbs. Stir in beaten egg. Mix well. Season to taste with salt and pepper.

Spoon lentil mixture into an oiled 8½ × 4½ × 2½-inch loaf pan. Smooth and spread Catskill Chili Sauce over the top. Bake for 1 hour, until browned and slightly crusty at edges.

Serve Lentil Nut Loaf with baked russet potatoes and extra Catskill Chili Sauce. Add a big leafy green salad to complete the meal.

TOFU TURKEY
Serves 6–8

2 tablespoons oil or butter
1 medium onion, diced
3 stalks celery, diced
½ sweet red pepper, diced
4 medium cloves garlic, minced
2½ cups (½ pound) sliced mushrooms
3 teaspoons crushed fresh thyme leaves, or 1 teaspoon dried
1 teaspoon crushed dried basil
2 tablespoons crushed dried sage
1 teaspoon dried oregano
¼ cup chopped fresh parsley
½ pound whole wheat bread, cubed

½ cup chopped roasted fresh chestnut meats* or walnuts
¼ cup roasted sunflower seeds
½ cup currants
1 tablespoon paprika
⅛ teaspoon freshly ground black pepper
2 eggs, beaten
2 tablespoons tamari soy sauce
¼ cup dry red wine or heavy cream
¼ cup water
1 teaspoon prepared mustard
1–1½ pounds tofu, thinly sliced
½–¾ pound sharp Cheddar cheese, thinly sliced

FOR GARNISH: Wild Mushroom Gravy or thick Cashew Milk (*see index*)

Heat the oil in a large skillet and add the onion. Sauté 1 to 2 minutes, and add the celery. Sauté another 2 minutes. Add red pepper and garlic. Stir a few times; add mushrooms. Stir again and then add the herbs. Stir well to blend and remove from heat.

Place bread cubes, nuts, seeds, and currants in a large mixing bowl. Combine with sautéed vegetables and herbs. Season with paprika and freshly ground pepper.

Beat eggs and combine with tamari, wine, water, and mustard. Pour over bread cube-vegetable mixture. Stir well to blend. Set the mixture aside for 20 minutes.

Preheat oven to 350 degrees F. Oil a 2-quart casserole or loaf pan. Place a third of the bread cube-vegetable mixture in the pan. Cover this with a third of the tofu. Cover the tofu with a third of the cheese. Make 2 more layers in the same way, ending with cheese on the top.

Bake Tofu Turkey for 30 to 45 minutes, until crusty and lightly browned.

Slice the hot Tofu Turkey and serve smothered with Wild Mushroom Gravy (see Index), thick Cashew Milk (see Index), or simple tamari-red wine sauce.

Accompany the Tofu Turkey with baked potatoes or yams, cranberries, a crisp salad, and red table wine.

* For roasting directions, see recipe for Chestnut Roast; consult Index.

BROILED SALMON WITH GARDEN GARNISH
Serves 6

6 tablespoons melted butter
¼ cup lemon juice or dry sherry
½ teaspoon chopped fresh rosemary
½ teaspoon crushed fresh thyme
6 salmon steaks, 1 inch thick
3 large carrots, cut into ½-inch-thick slices
3 large celery stalks, cut into 1-inch diagonal slices
½ pound French-cut string beans
¼ pound snow peas
10 cherry tomatoes
½ pound fresh spinach leaves, washed
Pinch of salt
1 recipe (*see below*) Beurre Rouge Sauce

FOR GARNISH: Chopped fresh parsley or chives

Preheat broiler pan 15 minutes. Combine ¼ cup of the butter, lemon juice or sherry, rosemary, and thyme. Oil broiler pan. Brush salmon steaks all over with butter mixture, and arrange on the pan. Return pan to broiler, with steaks 4 inches from heat source. Broil steaks 10 minutes, turning and basting halfway through the broiling time period.

While fish is broiling, steam vegetables over water, or boiling stock, if available. Steam carrots first, 6 minutes. Add celery and green beans; steam 2 minutes, then add remaining vegetables, and cook 2 additional minutes. Toss with remaining butter and salt.

Transfer broiled fish to warm serving platter. Arrange steamed vegetables around fish. Place a scoop of Beurre Rouge Sauce in center of each steak, and garnish with a bit of chopped parsley or chives. Spoon remaining sauce into a bowl to be served on the side. Serve this colorful dish with steamed red potatoes that have been tossed in butter and parsley.

BEURRE ROUGE SAUCE:
Yield: about 1 cup

⅓ cup cider vinegar
⅓ cup dry white wine
8 scallions, sliced
1 tablespoon chopped fresh
  basil

Salt and pepper to taste
½ cup chilled butter, cubed
2 tablespoons tomato paste

In saucepan, combine vinegar, wine, scallions, and basil. Over medium heat, cook until liquid is reduced to about 1 tablespoon, approximately 15 minutes. Let cool, and season with salt and pepper. (*continued*)

Over very low heat, gradually whisk butter into the prepared liquid, one cube at a time. Whisk continuously to a smooth, shiny paste. Add tomato paste and blend well. Keep sauce warm by setting the pot in a larger pan of warm water until ready to use.

WILD MUSHROOM SAUCE FOR PASTA
Yield: about 3 cups

A bonanza discovery of wild mushrooms can be harvested and dried, threaded along strings, hung in a dark, cool, and dry place. When ready to use, simply soak the dried mushrooms in warm water to reconstitute.

Here is a basic mushroom sauce recommended for serving with pasta as a main dish attraction. Any fresh mushrooms, wild or cultivated, can be used. If your own dried mushrooms are unavailable, dried Italian porcini mushrooms are suggested for their deep flavor and the rich liquor they exude. Porcini are available in most specialty gourmet or health food shops.

¼ ounce dried Italian porcini mushrooms
1 cup water
6 tablespoons olive oil
2 cloves garlic, chopped
2 tablespoons chopped shallots or onions
1-inch sliver of hot pepper
2 tablespoons chopped red sweet peppers
2 cups chopped fresh mushrooms
2 tablespoons fresh chopped basil or 1 teaspoon dried oregano
2 tablespoons chopped fresh parsley
Salt and pepper
½ cup dry red wine

Soak porcini in water for ½ hour. Strain liquid and set aside. Chop porcini.

Put olive oil, garlic, shallots, and hot and sweet peppers in a skillet and cook for 5 minutes over medium heat, stirring frequently. Add chopped porcini and fresh mushrooms. Cook another 10 minutes until mushrooms start to darken. Add reserved soaking liquid, herbs, salt and pepper, and wine and cook until liquid is reduced by half at least.

Serve on cooked pasta, garnished with chopped parsley and grated cheese.

Any extra mushroom mixture is wonderful in omelets.

BAKED VEGETABLES CATALÁN
Serves 6

1 large eggplant (about 1¾ to 2 pounds), halved lengthwise,
   then thinly sliced
Salt
½ cup olive oil
2 onions, thinly sliced
3 large potatoes, peeled and thinly sliced
3 zucchini, thinly sliced
4 tomatoes, sliced
2 peppers, seeded and sliced
4–6 cloves garlic, mashed with ½ teaspoon salt
5 tablespoons chopped fresh basil (or 2½ tablespoons dried)
Freshly ground black pepper
2 cups freshly grated Parmesan cheese

FOR GARNISH:
¼ cup chopped fresh parsley

Dredge eggplant with salt and set in colander. Place a heavy
plate or other weight over the eggplant, and let drain 30 minutes.
Rinse and pat dry.

Preheat oven to 350 degrees F.

In a large frying pan, sauté eggplant in 4 tablespoons oil until
brown. Drain on paper towels.

In a 2–3 quart baking dish, layer a third of each vegetable:
onion, potato, eggplant, zucchini, tomato, and pepper, sprinkling some of the garlic, basil, salt, and pepper, and ¾ cup of
the cheese between each layer. Drizzle with 2 tablespoons olive
oil.

Repeat layering with remaining vegetables, seasoning and oil,
leaving out remaining cheese to be added later.

Cover dish and bake 1 hour. Remove cover, sprinkle with
remaining cheese, and bake another 15 to 20 minutes, until potatoes are tender.

Sprinkle with chopped parsley and serve with a bowl of freshly
grated Parmesan on the side. Add a whole grain bread and tossed
green salad.

COLCANNON
Serves 4

From a tradition as old as tribal masquerades, earth apples stew over the fires of Halloween for a dish tasty with crisp late autumn greens.

6 medium potatoes
2 tablespoons butter
2 tablespoons olive oil
½ cup coarsely chopped onion
3 cups very finely chopped kale
½ cup heavy cream
1 teaspoon salt
½ teaspoon pepper
1 tablespoon chopped fresh parsley
Paprika

Preheat oven to 400 degrees F. Quarter potatoes, and cook in water to cover until tender, 20 to 30 minutes.

While the potatoes cook, heat butter and oil in a Dutch oven and slowly sauté onions until just softened. Add kale to the onions. Stir and cook gently until the kale is tender-crisp, but still green. Remove from heat.

Drain and mash the potatoes and add to the kale and onions. Stir in cream, salt and pepper, and parsley. Turn into an oiled, ovenproof crock or 2-quart casserole. Sprinkle top with paprika, and bake for 10 minutes, or until slightly golden on top.

SWEET POTATOES SUPREME
Serves 4–6

This is a delectable embellishment for a holiday banquet.

Chunks of a sweet winter squash, such as buttercup, could be substituted for the sweet potatoes.

6 medium sweet potatoes
1 cup fresh pineapple chunks
¼ cup sliced almonds
½ cup maple syrup
1 cup sour cream or yogurt
2 egg yolks
Cinnamon
Freshly grated nutmeg

Preheat oven to 400 degrees F. Peel the sweet potatoes, then slice in half. Place in cold water to cover and parboil until just soft, about 15 to 20 minutes. Drain.

In 9 × 12-inch buttered casserole, place potatoes face down. Divide pineapple chunks evenly on top. Sprinkle on sliced almonds.

Blend maple syrup, sour cream, and egg yolks and spread over casserole. Sprinkle with cinnamon and grated nutmeg. Bake for 10 minutes, then lower oven temperature to 350 degrees F. and bake for ½ hour. Serve Sweet Potatoes Supreme hot, with cranberry sauce and a savory casserole, such as Chestnut Roast (see Index).

SAUTÉED PUFFBALLS
Serves 4

Early September brings fascinating puffball fungi appearing along roadsides and forest clearings in abundance. People find puffballs with silvery studs, in groups, small and clustered, or standing alone. Any pure white, meaty, ball-shaped mushroom is safely edible. The taste is bland; its wild nature enjoyed more in texture. For many generations, rural people have commonly fried large puffball slices. Here, herbal embellishment enhances the subtle wild flavor.

3 cloves garlic, minced
2 medium onions, chopped
3 tablespoons butter
1 medium puffball
Salt and pepper to taste
Touch of lemon juice
Fresh crushed thyme, to taste

Sauté garlic and onions in the butter. Wash and cut the puff-ball into about 1-inch cubes. Add to the sauté. Stir until slightly browned. Add seasoning, lemon juice, and thyme to taste. Serve Sautéed Puffballs to accent nut loaves, Squash and Apple Soup, and other harvest dinner dishes, (see Index).

WOODLAND SAUTÉ
Serves 4–6

6 tablespoons olive oil
2 leeks, sliced
3 cloves garlic, crushed
1 pound mushrooms, wild or cultivated
¾ pound fresh chestnuts, baked or boiled until tender*
2 tablespoons tamari soy sauce
1 tablespoon dry sherry (*optional*)
¼ cup chopped fresh parsley
½ cup chopped scallions

Heat olive oil in a heavy sauté pan. Fry leek rings until tender, but not browned, about 5 minutes.

Add crushed garlic. Stir a little and add mushrooms; sauté 5 minutes.

Stir in shelled chestnuts; add tamari and dry sherry. Warm through and sprinkle with chopped parsley and chopped scallions.

This dish is especially enjoyable when served with warm corn muffins, and a mix of lightly sautéed spinach with julienned apples.

EGGPLANT STICKS
Serves 4

1 medium eggplant (about 1½ pounds)
2 eggs, beaten
1 cup cornmeal
1 teaspoon salt
½ cup peanut oil

Peel and slice eggplant into long sticks. Dip in beaten egg until well coated. Combine cornmeal and salt in a small paper bag. Place egg-coated eggplant in the bag and shake to coat with cornmeal. Fry in hot peanut oil until browned, turning with tongs to crisp each side. Drain and serve hot.

* Please refer to recipes for Chestnut Pâté or Chestnut Roast for boiling and roasting directions; *see Index*.

ROASTED BRUSSELS SPROUTS AND CHESTNUTS
Serves 4

1 pound chestnuts	1 teaspoon honey
1 pound small Brussels sprouts	¼ teaspoon paprika
4 tablespoons butter	Salt

Preheat oven to 400 degrees F. Slit shells and oven-roast chestnuts for 30 minutes. Peel and keep warm.

Scrub and trim Brussels sprouts. Place them, still wet, into a heavy saucepot. Add butter, cover the pot, and place over a low heat. Brown the sprouts in this way until golden green, shaking the pot occasionally to prevent sticking.

When sprouts are tender, about 20 minutes, add honey and paprika. Add peeled roasted chestnuts. Toss lightly until they are coated with butter. Sprinkle with a little salt. Serve hot in a covered serving bowl.

BEETS IN ORANGE SAUCE
Serves 4

Beets are a sweet, colorful side dish to complement any summer or autumn eating festivity.

8 medium beets, peeled and cut in half
1 cup fresh orange juice
2 tablespoons maple syrup
¼ teaspoon ground cloves
½ teaspoon cinnamon
1 tablespoon freshly grated orange peel
2 tablespoons arrowroot, dissolved in a little cold water

Steam the beets until tender. Drain, reserving ½ cup of their liquid. Combine ½ cup beet liquid with remaining ingredients except arrowroot and slowly bring to a boil. Add the arrowroot and cook the sweet sauce until thick and clear. Pour sauce over beets and serve at once.

WILD MUSHROOM GRAVY
2 cups

¼ cup dried wild mushrooms
2 cups boiling water or stock
3 tablespoons butter
1 tablespoon minced onion
3 tablespoons whole wheat flour
1 cup stock or water

3 tablespoons tamari soy sauce
½ cup heavy cream or milk
2 tablespoons dark dry sherry
2 tablespoons Catskill Chili Sauce (*see Index*)

Place mushrooms in a mixing bowl. Pour 2 cups boiling water or stock over them, and let stand about 20 minutes. Drain mushrooms, reserving soaking liquid, and mince.

Melt butter in a skillet over a low heat. Add the onion and sauté briefly. Stir in the mushrooms. Brown slightly, then stir in the flour briskly, until a paste is formed. Cook, stirring constantly for 2 minutes. Slowly add the 1 cup stock, together with the reserved mushroom soaking liquid, stirring to keep the mixture smooth. Cook to thicken slightly. Add the tamari, cream, sherry, and chili sauce. Serve hot.

This is an ideal all-purpose savory sauce for fall and winter. It is good served over vegetable loaves, cutlets, and burgers, and especially potatoes.

CHINESE VEGETABLE SALAD
Serves 6–8

This unique and colorful salad is often on the midday menu at Woodstock's Sunflower Deli. It is basically a rice salad, for a main dish, luncheon, or buffet attraction. Featured are the bright, crisp oriental vegetables that flourish in a mid-autumn Catskill garden.

6 cups cooked brown rice
2½ cakes (4 × 2½-inch) pressed seasoned tofu, sliced in thin
    strips
½ head Chinese cabbage (about 1¼ pounds) shredded
½ bunch bok choy, finely sliced
¼ pound mung bean sprouts
1 sweet red pepper, chopped

DRESSING:
¼ cup rice vinegar
¼ cup dark sesame oil
Dash of tamari soy sauce
1 clove garlic, minced
1 teaspoon peeled and minced fresh gingerroot

Combine cooked rice with prepared tofu and vegetables. Combine dressing ingredients, and blend together well. Pour over salad, and toss.

The salad's ingredients may vary to include thin   (*continued*) diagonal slices of celery, fresh snow peas, or bamboo shoots. The unchanging feature in the dish is the special dark, pressed, and tamari-marinated tofu. Prepared in and distributed from New York's Chinatown, it is usually available in health food stores and specialty food shops.

MARINATED BROCCOLI IN TOFU SAUCE
Serves 6

6 tablespoons safflower oil
Dash of dark sesame oil
3 cups broccoli flowerets
3 tablespoons balsamic vinegar*
1 teaspoon salt
1 teaspoon freshly ground black pepper
2 cloves garlic, minced well
1 recipe Tofu Sauce (*see below*)
Butterhead lettuce

Heat 2 tablespoons oil with a dash of dark sesame oil in wok or large skillet. Quickly sauté broccoli until tender-crisp and still bright green. Place in a refrigerator dish.

Combine 4 tablespoons safflower oil with vinegar, salt, pepper, and garlic. Mix well and pour over the sautéed broccoli. Cover and chill, at least one hour.

Meanwhile, prepare Tofu Sauce. Arrange beds of butterhead lettuce on individual plates. Top with marinated broccoli flowerets. Spoon a little marinade over vegetables and lettuce. Top with Tofu Sauce and serve.

This recipe can also be made with an equal amount of snow peas substituted for the broccoli.

TOFU SAUCE:
Yield: 1½ cups
8–12 ounces soft tofu
¼ cup lemon juice
¼ cup tamari soy sauce
Fresh cilantro sprigs
Chopped fresh parsley
Freshly grated black pepper (*optional*)

In food processor or blender, mix all ingredients together until smooth. Add more tamari and black pepper, if desired.

Tofu Sauce is good with many vegetable dishes and salads.

* Balsamic vinegar is a very aromatic, mellow product made from fruited red wine vinegar that has been aged in the Modena section of Italy for at least ten years in special wooden barrels. It is available in specialty food stores. If unobtainable, any vinegar may be used for this recipe.

EQUINOX SALAD
Serves 4–6

3 cups assorted salad greens (lettuce, watercress, beet greens,
  spinach, etc.)
1 cucumber, peeled and thickly sliced
1 sweet green pepper, seeded and cut in chunks
12 young radishes, sliced
3 ripe tomatoes, thickly sliced
¼ pound fresh button mushrooms, sliced
1 tablespoon chopped fresh dill
2 tablespoons chopped fresh parsley
3 scallions, finely sliced
½ cup chopped walnuts

DRESSING:
1 egg yolk
2 teaspoons Dijon mustard
½ teaspoon honey
2 tablespoons cider vinegar
Salt and freshly ground black pepper to taste
¾ cup vegetable oil
½ cup sour cream

Into a large salad bowl, tear the cleaned salad greens. Add the
slices of cucumber, green pepper chunks, radishes, tomatoes, and
mushrooms. Toss with chopped fresh dill, parsley, and scallions.
Scatter the chopped walnuts on top.

In a bowl, whip together the egg yolk, mustard, honey, vinegar, salt, and pepper. Slowly drizzle in the oil, whipping until
thick. Fold in sour cream. Check seasoning and then swirl generously through the salad.

Serve with slices of dark Sesame-Anise Bread (see Index), fresh
rye bread and butter.

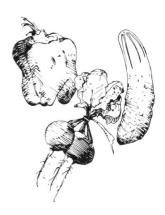

APPLE-NUT SALAD
Serves 4

2 cups diced fennel (anise)
   stalks
2 Macintosh apples, diced
¾ cup walnut pieces

DRESSING:
½ cup mayonnaise
2½ tablespoons chopped
   fennel tops
1 teaspoon poppy seeds
1 teaspoon honey
1 tablespoon lime juice

    Place diced fennel, apples, and walnuts together in a small salad bowl.
    Combine mayonnaise with remaining ingredients. Stir to mix well. Pour mixture over fennel and apples. Toss and serve.

OCTOBER BEET SALAD
Serves 4–6

4 cups cooked beets cubed, peeled
½ red onion, sliced

DRESSING:
¼ cup sesame oil
¼ cup tamari soy sauce

¼ cup lemon juice
2 tablespoons apple cider
   vinegar

FOR GARNISH:
¼ cup sunflower seeds

    Combine cooked, cubed beets and onion slices in salad bowl.
    Mix oil, tamari, lemon juice, and vinegar. Pour over the beets. Toss, and sprinkle with sunflower seeds. Serve.
    These beets are delicious embellished with tart autumn greens, fresh from the garden. Add tangy bok choy and succulent spinach leaves, chopped, about 1 to 2 cups, to add color and crunch.

PARSNIP SALAD
Serves 4

1 pound parsnips
6 scallions
3 stalks celery
8 radishes

12 stuffed olives
1 apple
1 recipe Carrot Mayonnaise
   (_see below_)

    Cut parsnips into strips, then dice. Place in pot and just cover with cold water. Bring to boil, refresh, and drain. Chop scallions; slice celery, radishes, and olives; dice apple. Combine vegetables with Carrot Mayonnaise and serve in a chilled salad bowl.

CARROT MAYONNAISE
Yield: 1 cup

2 teaspoons chopped fresh parsley
2 teaspoons chopped fresh mint
1 clove garlic
2 carrots, steamed until tender
1 egg yolk
⅔ cup vegetable oil
3 teaspoons lemon juice
Salt and pepper
Freshly grated nutmeg

In blender or food processor, purée parsley, mint, garlic, and carrots. Add egg yolk. With motor running, trickle in oil. Add lemon juice, salt, pepper, and nutmeg, to finish.

RIVERBY HOUSEWARMING SALAD
Serves 25

2 heads iceberg lettuce, cut in bite-size chunks
1 medium head red cabbage, shredded
1 medium head cauliflower, cut in flowerets
1 bunch celery, diced
2–3 apples, diced
½ pound raisins
½–1 pound walnuts
Dressing (*see below*)

Place vegetables, fruits, and nuts in a salad bowl and toss with dressing just before setting out.

This is a good salad to use for a party, but it may be adapted for a smaller number of people.

DRESSING:
Yield: a little over 1 pint
½ cup cider vinegar (may be part fresh lemon juice)
2 teaspoons molasses
2 teaspoons tamari soy sauce
¾ teaspoon dry mustard
1 large clove garlic, crushed
1½ cups oil (half olive, half safflower)

Combine vinegar, molasses, tamari, mustard, and garlic in a quart jar; cover and shake vigorously. Add the oil and shake again. Allow the dressing to stand awhile to develop flavor.

SOY CREAM
Yield: 2 cups

Soy Cream is a rich, thick, tangy cream to be used anywhere sour cream is used. It is delicious and very similar in taste and texture, without the solid fats.

1 tablespoon soy flour
1 tablespoon unbleached white flour
1 cup water
1 cup safflower oil
Salt
1½ tablespoons lemon juice or vinegar

Mix flours with water in a small saucepot. Set over a medium heat, and bring to a simmer. Continue to cook about 7 minutes, until thickened, stirring to prevent sticking.

Pour the thickened sauce into the blender. Slowly drizzle in the oil as the blender is running. Add salt to taste, and lemon juice. Store Soy Cream in a clean covered jar in the refrigerator. Keeps well for about one week.

Enjoy Soy Cream in spreads and dips, or mixed with steamed or mashed vegetables, such as baked potatoes, or a chilled mixture of mashed avocado and tofu. Season with scallions, savory herbs, or curry spices.

TOFU MAYONNAISE
Yield: 1½ cups

4 to 6 ounces soft tofu
1 tablespoon fresh lemon juice
1 tablespoon brown rice or apple cider vinegar
1½ teaspoons miso
3 tablespoons water
3 tablespoons olive or safflower oil

Mix all ingredients except oil in blender. Then add oil slowly while blender is running, until mixture is smooth. More oil may be added if thinner texture is desired.

Mix Tofu Mayonnaise into cabbage salads or sandwich spreads—anywhere that traditional egg mayonnaise is used.

PUMPKIN BISCUITS
Yield: 4 large biscuits

¼ cup butter
½ cup hot cooked squash or pumpkin pulp

1 cup whole wheat pastry flour
½ cup unbleached white flour
½ cup yellow cornmeal
3 teaspoons baking powder
½ teaspoon salt
½ cup heavy cream or milk or nut milk

Preheat oven to 425 degrees F. Stir butter into hot squash or pumpkin pulp until melted and blended. Combine flours, cornmeal, baking powder, and salt. Cut in the butter-pumpkin mixture. When blended, gently stir in enough cream or milk to make a soft dough. Do not overwork the dough.

With the hands, press dough into 4- or 5-inch rounds, about ½ inch thick. Place on an oiled baking sheet.

Set the biscuits in the oven and bake for about 12 minutes, until golden brown. Serve hot. Delicious for breakfast with jam or maple syrup, or for dinner with soup.

CHALLAH
Yield: 1 large braided loaf

In many ancestral traditions, autumn has been perceived as the end of the annual cycle. Challah, traditional bread to inaugurate the Jewish sabbath, is also the symbol for Rosh Hashanah. Served at the New Year dinner ritual, Challah weaves the harvest grain into a golden braid, with hope for happiness and prosperity in the year to come.

1 tablespoon yeast
⅔ cup warm water
1 tablespoon honey
Pinch of powdered ginger
5 whole eggs
3 egg yolks
1 tablespoon salt
¼ cup light oil (sunflower is good)
½ cup wheat germ
5–6 cups unbleached white flour or 4 cups unbleached white,
    1–2 cups whole wheat bread flour

GLAZE:
1 egg, beaten
Poppy seeds

Dissolve yeast in water with honey and ginger. In a large bowl, place yeast mixture, eggs, egg yolks, salt, oil, and wheat germ. Add enough flour to form a kneadable dough. Knead on a floured board for about 10 minutes until smooth and elastic. Place in an oiled bowl and turn to oil top. Cover and let rise until doubled in bulk, about 1½ hours.

Punch down. Turn out on floured board, knead for 2 minutes, and divide dough into 3 pieces. Roll each piece into a rope and braid the 3 together. Pinch ends and turn under to seal. Place on an oiled cookie sheet. Brush with beaten egg and sprinkle with poppy seeds. Let rise about 45 minutes.

Preheat oven to 375 degrees F. Bake dough for about 40 minutes. Thump top with finger to test. Bread is done when this makes a hollow sound.

Serve Challah with apple slices dipped in honey, and celebrate a new year with the ancients.

SESAME-ANISE BREAD
2 loaves (8-inch round)

1½ cups lukewarm water
½ cup lukewarm milk
1 tablespoon active dry yeast
1 teaspoon honey
2½ cups whole wheat bread flour
2½ cups unbleached flour
2 teaspoons salt
2 tablespoons oil
1 teaspoon sesame seeds
2 teaspoons anise seeds
Cornmeal

GLAZE:
2 tablespoons melted butter
1 tablespoon sesame seeds

In a large mixing bowl, combine lukewarm liquids, yeast, honey, and the 2½ cups whole wheat flour. Beat until smooth, about 150 to 200 strokes. Cover and allow to rise in a warm place until doubled in bulk, about 45 minutes.

Punch down and add the 2½ cups unbleached flour, salt, oil, 1 teaspoon sesame seeds, and 2 teaspoons anise seeds. Turn dough out onto a lightly floured surface and knead about 10 minutes, pushing dough down and forward with the heel of your hand. Add more water if necessary. Knead until dough is smooth and elastic.

Turn dough into a greased bowl, turning over once so the greased side is up. Cover with a damp cloth. Set in a warm place and let double in bulk, 1 to 1½ hours.

Punch down the dough, turn onto a lightly floured surface.

Knead lightly and divide into 2 equal balls. Let sit 5 minutes.

Sprinkle a baking sheet lightly with cornmeal. Turning one of the balls between your hands, form into a cone shape and place on the prepared baking sheet. Flatten the cone with the palm of your hand. Repeat with second ball. Cover lightly with a damp towel and let rise until doubled in bulk (about 2 hours).

Preheat oven to 400 degrees F. Slash edges of bread slightly. This allows steam to escape and lets bread rise a little more. Bake 10 minutes, reduce heat to 350 degrees F. and cook a further 25 minutes, until golden brown and hollow-sounding when tapped on the top.

Remove from oven. Brush lightly with melted butter and sprinkle with sesame seeds. Bake further 10 minutes, or until bread sounds hollow when tapped underneath. Cool on a rack.

Serve in wedges. Delicious with butter and a dark buckwheat honey for breakfast or to mop up sauces for dinner.

CRUSTY WHITE BREAD
Yield: Two 10-inch loaves

2½ cups warm water
2 tablespoons yeast
1 tablespoon vinegar
1 tablespoon salt
2 tablespoons olive oil
¾ cup bran
¾ cup wheat germ
8 cups (about) unbleached white flour
Sesame seeds
Dry white wine

Place ½ cup warm water in a large bowl. Add yeast, stir to dissolve, and set aside 10 minutes to proof. Add the remaining water and stir in vinegar, salt, and oil. Add bran, wheat germ, and 2 cups flour. Beat about 100 strokes. Stir in 4 more cups flour, 1 at a time, mixing until smooth with each addition. Add remaining flour slowly until dough leaves sides of bowl. Turn out onto floured surface, and knead 10 minutes. Place in an oiled bowl in a warm place. Cover and allow to rise about 1½ hours, or until doubled in bulk.

Punch down and shape into 2 tapered loaves. Place on an oiled baking sheet that has been sprinkled with sesame seeds. Cover with a light towel. Let rise until doubled, about ½ hour. Gently slash the loaves end to end, about ½ inch deep. Let loaves rise 10 minutes, then brush surfaces with wine.

Meanwhile, preheat oven to 400 degrees F., and place a pan of hot water on the oven floor. *(continued)*

Put the loaves into the oven. For extra crustiness, spray the loaves lightly with water about 3 times, allowing ample water to hit the oven walls to create lots of steam. Do this quickly to avoid oven heat loss. The loaves are done when browned, and bread sounds hollow when top is thumped lightly, about 20 minutes. Cool on rack.

CURRANT BREAD
Yield: 2 large or 3 small loaves

1½ cups milk
3 tablespoons honey
1 tablespoon salt
7 tablespoons butter
1 tablespoon yeast
1 cup warm water
Pinch of powdered ginger
2 teaspoons cinnamon
6 cups unbleached white flour
2 cups whole wheat bread flour
1 cup currants soaked for ½ hour in ¼ cup water, orange
    juice, or dry sherry and then drained
3 tablespoons sugar

OPTIONAL GLAZE:
1 beaten egg, or melted butter
Cinnamon sugar

Heat the milk with the honey, salt, and 4 tablespoons butter, until the butter is melted, then let cool to tepid. Dissolve yeast in water with ginger and add to milk. Stir in cinnamon and enough flour to form a kneadable dough.

Turn onto a floured board and knead, adding flour as necessary, until smooth and elastic—around 10 minutes. Put the dough in a buttered bowl, turn to coat top also with butter, cover, and let rise until doubled in bulk—about 1½ hours.

Punch dough down, turn onto floured board, dredge the currants in a little flour. Knead in the currants, 3 tablespoons butter and 3 tablespoons sugar. Let rest for 10 minutes.

Butter 2 or 3 8½ × 4½ × 2½-inch bread pans and form dough into loaves. Place in pans and let rise for about 1 hour.

Preheat oven to 400 degrees F. Bake loaves for about 30 minutes until golden brown.

OPTIONAL: Before baking, brush tops of loaves with an egg wash or melted butter and sprinkle with cinnamon sugar (see Index).

PUMPKIN CUSTARD PIE
Serves 6–8

PASTRY:
½ cup whole wheat pastry flour
½ cup unbleached white flour
¼ teaspoon salt
5½ tablespoons butter
About 4 tablespoons ice water

FILLING:
1¾ cups puréed baked or
    steamed pumpkin
½ cup heavy cream
1 cup milk
½ cup honey
¼ cup molasses
¼ teaspoon salt
1½ teaspoons cinnamon
1 teaspoon powdered ginger
¼ teaspoon ground cloves
2 eggs, separated
3 tablespoons chopped walnuts or pecans

OPTIONAL GARNISH:
Whipped cream

Preheat oven to 425 degrees F. Mix flours and salt together in a bowl. Cut in butter with pastry blender until the mixture resembles the texture of peas. Cut in just enough ice water to hold dough together, being careful to handle it as little as possible. Turn out onto a sheet of floured wax paper. Dust lightly with more flour, cover with another sheet of wax paper, and roll out into a thin 9-inch circular sheet. Fit into a 9-inch pie pan and flute the edges.

Mix puréed pumpkin with ½ cup cream, milk, honey, molasses, salt, and spices, until very smooth. Blend in egg yolks.

Beat egg whites separately until soft peaks form. Fold into the pumpkin mixture. Pour filling into pie shell. Sprinkle with nuts.

Set pie into preheated oven. After 15 minutes reduce heat to 350 degrees F., and continue to bake for about 45 minutes, or until tester comes out clean.

Allow the pie to cool for at least 20 minutes before serving. Garnish with whipped cream, if desired.

PUMPKIN-RUM PUDDING
Serves 6

1 tablespoon agar-agar
4 tablespoons dark rum, plus 1 tablespoon (optional)
4 egg yolks
6 tablespoons maple syrup, plus 1 tablespoon (optional)
1 cup puréed baked pumpkin
½ teaspoon cinnamon
¼ teaspoon allspice
⅛ teaspoon freshly grated nutmeg
1 cup heavy cream

OPTIONAL GARNISH: 4 macaroons

In a small bowl, sprinkle agar-agar over rum and let soften. Place bowl over gently simmering water and stir about 2 minutes.

Beat egg yolks and maple syrup until thick and lemon-colored. Fold in puréed pumpkin and spices. Fold in agar-agar and rum.

Whip cream until stiff, adding an extra tablespoon of maple syrup and rum if desired, and then fold gently into pumpkin purée. Turn into an attractive serving dish and chill well. This is delicious served with macaroons crumbled coarsely over the top.

PLUM TART
Serves 6–8

PASTRY:
1½ cups whole wheat pastry flour
½ cup cake flour
½ teaspoon cinnamon
1 teaspoon ground cardamom
Grated peel of 1 lemon
3 tablespoons finely ground walnuts
12 ounces (1½ sticks) ice cold butter, cut in ½-inch chunks
3 tablespoons light honey
2 tablespoons ice water
1 egg yolk

PLUMS:
2 tablespoons butter
2 tablespoons honey
1 lemon, juice and grated rind
1½ pounds red or purple plums, halved

FILLING:
1½ cups heavy cream
2 eggs plus 2 egg yolks
3 tablespoons honey
3 tablespoons almond liqueur

To make pastry: In a large bowl, combine flours, cinnamon, cardamom, grated lemon peel, and ground walnuts. With fingertips blend in chunks of butter until mixture resembles coarse meal.

Combine honey and ice water and egg yolk and quickly work into dough until it will form a ball. Use a little more ice water if necessary. Wrap and refrigerate 30 minutes to 1 hour.

Place 2 sheets of wax paper on a table. Place dough in center and sprinkle with a little flour. Cover with 2 more sheets of wax paper. Roll out dough to a 14-inch circle.

Remove top layers of wax paper. Place a 10-inch tart pan nearby. Lifting bottom sheet, invert dough over the pan, carefully peel off paper, and press dough into the pan. Wrap pan and refrigerate dough another 30 minutes.

Preheat oven to 375 degrees F.

To prepare plums: Combine butter, honey, and grated lemon rind and juice in a pan. Melt over low heat, then add halved plums. Poach very gently 10 minutes; cool.

For filling: Combine cream, eggs and egg yolks, honey, and almond liqueur. Beat well to combine.

Line dough in tart pan with foil and fill with beans. Bake 10 minutes, remove foil and beans, bake another 5 minutes.

Pour about half the cream mixture into the tart shell. Arrange plum halves on top, rounded side up. Pour rest of the cream around plums. Bake about 30 to 35 minutes or until filling is firm. Delicious hot or cold.

MAPLE NUT COOKIES
Yield: 2 dozen

1 cup unsweetened butter, softened
¾ cup maple syrup
1 egg
2 teaspoons vanilla
1 cup whole wheat pastry flour

1 teaspoon baking powder
1 cup wheat germ
2 cups rolled oats
1 cup raisins
1 cup chopped walnuts

GLAZE: 2 egg yolks, 2 tablespoons water

Preheat oven to 375 degrees F. Cream butter. Slowly add maple syrup, then egg and vanilla. In a separate bowl, stir together whole wheat flour, baking powder, wheat germ, rolled oats, raisins, and walnuts. Blend wet and dry ingredients.

With floured hands, make small patties and place on a greased cookie sheet. Brush with egg yolk glaze. Bake for 10 minutes or until browned.

APPLE NUT STRUDEL
Serves 6–8

4–6 medium cooking apples
½ cup chopped walnuts or pecans
¼ cup raisins
2 tablespoons honey or maple syrup
1 tablespoon oil
1 tablespoon flour
6 sheets of phyllo dough
5 tablespoons melted butter
Poppy seeds

Preheat oven to 350 degrees F. Peel apples, if desired. Core and thinly slice. Combine slices with nuts, raisins, honey, oil, and flour. Stir together.

Unroll phyllo dough. Remove 1 sheet and lay it on a smooth surface. (Keep rest of dough between dampened towels to prevent drying.) Brush with melted butter. Cover with another sheet of pastry, butter, and repeat process with remaining 4 sheets.

Spread apple filling over the last pastry, leaving wide margins at ends and sides. Fold margin of long sides over on the filling. Roll the pastry from one end. Gently lifting, with the help of spatula, place the pastry on an oiled cookie sheet. Slit the top in 2 diagonal slashes, and brush with a bit more butter. Sprinkle with poppy seeds.

Bake for 30 minutes, or until golden. Apple Nut Strudel is delicious served warm, topped with yogurt or honey ice cream.

WALNUT SPICE CAKE
Serves 6–8

This is a traditional-style autumn dessert, created especially for black walnuts. They will infuse the whole fluffy cake with an incomparable rich, dusky flavor. If black walnuts are unavailable, English walnuts or wild hickory nuts are also delicious.

¼ pound butter, softened
1 cup honey
2 eggs, room temperature
1 cup unbleached white flour
1 cup whole wheat pastry flour
1 teaspoon baking soda
¼ teaspoon salt
1 teaspoon cinnamon
¼ teaspoon ground cardamom
½ teaspoon ground cloves
⅛ teaspoon freshly grated nutmeg
1 cup chopped black walnuts
1 teaspoon vanilla
⅔ cup buttermilk or sour milk

FOR GARNISH:
½ pint heavy cream, whipped
Maple syrup to taste

Preheat oven to 350 degrees F. Cream butter. When very light and fluffy, slowly add the honey. Beat until well blended. Beat eggs, and add to the butter mixture very slowly, beating until the mixture is light and creamy.

Sift the flours together with soda, salt, and spices. Measure ⅔ cup walnuts into a small bowl, and dredge with a small amount of the dry ingredients. Set aside.

Combine the vanilla with the buttermilk. Add the buttermilk and dry ingredients alternately to the creamed mixture, blending each addition thoroughly. Fold in the dredged walnuts.

Place the batter into an oiled 9-inch tube pan. Sprinkle the top with the remaining nuts. Bake for about 40 minutes, or until the tester comes out clean.

Set the cake on a rack to cool. After about 20 to 30 minutes, it can be removed from the pan and set on a round platter. Fill the center with a mound of whipped cream sweetened with maple syrup, and serve with hot coffee or chickory roast tea, with cream.

DARK TOMATO PRESERVE
Yield: 5 pints

Collect wild blue Concord grapes in mid-September to cook with the garden's last ripe tomatoes. The result is a very rich, musky jam, dark as the mysteries of autumn.

3 quarts chopped peeled
  tomatoes
1 quart halved, seeded
  unpeeled Concord grapes
5 cups honey

3½ cups fresh lemon juice
1½ tablespoons whole cloves
2 teaspoons whole allspice
6 2-inch cinnamon sticks

Combine tomatoes and grapes in an enameled pot with honey and lemon juice. Vinegar may be substituted for about a third of the lemon juice, if necessary.

Tie whole spices in a cheesecloth bundle, and place in the tomato mixture. Simmer slowly for 3 hours, stirring occasionally. During the last 45 minutes, stir frequently to prevent sticking. Fill 5 pint-size hot sterilized jars to ¼ inch from top and seal with sterilized dome lids; adjust bands. Process 10 minutes in boiling water bath.

SEPTEMBER SOUP STOCK
Yield: 7 quarts

After the pantry is filled with jars of tomatoes and corn, and the freezer with peas and beans and broccoli, prepare September Soup Stock with the last of garden surplus. Produce ripening too abundantly for eating, but not the best choice for ordinary canning will add wonderful flavor to this stock.

½ cup safflower oil
2 cups chopped onions
¼ cup minced garlic
½ cup chopped fresh parsley
¼ cup chopped fresh dill
¼ cup chopped fresh basil
2 tablespoons crushed fresh
  thyme leaves
2 bay leaves
2 teaspoons celery seed
2 teaspoons salt

1 teaspoon freshly ground
  black pepper
¼ cup tamari soy sauce
1½ quarts boiling water
1½ quarts cubed mixed
  summer squash
1½ quarts diced carrots
1½ quarts cut-up stemmed
  green beans (1-inch lengths)
1 quart diced peeled potatoes
1 quart chopped tomatoes

In a large heavy pot, heat oil. Add onions and sauté until golden. Add garlic, herbs, and seasonings. (Choose whatever fresh herbs are available, from the garden or market, totaling 1 to 1½ cups.)

Stir well and add the boiling water. Soup may be transferred to a larger pot at this point, if necessary. Add all the prepared vegetables, and cook about 5 minutes.

Ladle simmering soup stock into 7 hot, sterilized quart jars. Adjust lids and screw tops. Process in pressure canner at 10 pounds pressure for 40 minutes.

Here long-cooked vegetables merge all their nutrients into a mineral-rich broth. This is a ready, convenient soup base, to be taken from the shelf in winter and embellished with available fresh vegetables, and beans, noodles, tofu, or rice, with more water, wine, or cream. Seasonings can be adjusted to taste at this time. The stock can be used as is or puréed for a creamy soup.

Choice of garden vegetables may be altered for making a basic soup stock, but the processing time in the canner must be equal to that needed for the vegetable requiring longest processing.

CATSKILL CHILI SAUCE
Yield: 10 pints

With the bloom of fresh autumn apples and ripe tomatoes, this rich, spicy relish is a year-round delight. Unique in flavor, extra jars on hand make homey gift surprises for favorite dinner hostesses.

4 quarts (about 2 dozen large) chopped, peeled ripe tomatoes	1 tablespoon minced garlic
	2½ cups honey
	1 tablespoon salt
5 cups chopped red apples	1 tablespoon ground allspice
1 quart chopped onions	1 tablespoon yellow mustard
1 quart (4 large) finely chopped green peppers	seed
	1 teaspoon cinnamon
1 hot red pepper, minced	2¾ cups apple cider vinegar

In a large enameled pot, combine tomatoes, apples, onions, pepper, garlic, and honey. Cook slowly, until thickened, stirring occasionally, about 1½ hours. Watch carefully during the last 30 minutes, stirring to prevent scorching.

As the mixture thickens, add the salt, spices, and vinegar. Cook to desired thickness, 1 to 1½ hours. Pour boiling hot into 10 hot sterilized pint jars, leaving ⅛ inch at the top. Adjust hot sterilized lids with screw bands.

Serve Catskill Chili Sauce with any grain or nut burgers. Spoon over vegetable loaves before baking. Catskill Chili Sauce can be processed in the blender to obtain a smooth ketchup consistency, for an interesting variation.

Autumn Menus

SEPTEMBER HARVEST
*Squash and Apple Soup
*Equinox Salad
*Challah
Sweet Butter
*Vitality Burgers
**Pear Ketchup
*Marinated Broccoli in Tofu Sauce
Fresh Cider
Apple Slices with Honey and Poppy Seeds
*Maple Nut Cookies

LOGGERS' LUNCH
*Scallop Bisque
*Aubergine Zinfonia
Beer
*Crusty White Bread
*Carrot Tahini
Escarole and Chickory
*Plum Tart

HALLOWEEN
FEAST OF THE JACK-o'-LANTERN
*Savory Borscht
Apples
*Sesame-Anise Bread
Butter
**Pear Chutney
*Woodland Sauté
*Colcannon
*Mulled Cider
*Walnut Spice Cake with Whipped Cream

NOVEMBER FOREST DINNER
*Mushroom Hazelnut Soup
*Sweet Potatoes Supreme
Red Wine
*Tofu Turkey with *Cashew Milk
**Old-fashioned Corn Relish
*Chinese Vegetable Salad
***Cranberry Relish
*Savory Pumpkin Pastries
Coffee

THANKSGIVING FEAST
*Mushroom Hazelnut Soup
*Currant Bread
*Dark Tomato Preserve
**Old-fashioned Corn Relish
*Roasted Brussels Sprouts and Chestnuts
Chilled Chablis
*Broiled Salmon with Garden Garnish
*Riverby Housewarming Salad (¼ recipe)
*Pumpkin Custard Pie
Coffee

* Recipe included in Autumn section.
** Recipe included in Summer section.
*** Recipe included in Winter section.

Part Four : Winter

SNOWFALL & EVERGREENS

Winter

Within days of harvest feasting, the bane of winter haunts the barren hills surrounding Woodstock. Frost descends the ridges, consuming craggy trees and mosses, and sinks quietly into rocks and soil. Crystalline gardens lie still as the frozen waterfalls, waiting for the first snow. Local winter dwellers retreat with the comforts of a full pantry, carrots and cabbages in the root cellar, and a fragrant pot simmering on the wood stove. Savored are visions of gingerbread people and plum pudding, candles, and a glowing Christmas tree.

For many regional people, December is vibrant with the anticipation of holiday pleasure. Artists, inspired by the stark beauty of a mountain winter, fill their Christmas orders, then present choices from the year's vintage at craft fairs and holiday exhibitions. Woodstock's shops, studios, and craft galleries glimmer with treasures. Decked with hemlock sprays and graced with pine garlands, Tinker Street windows are enchanted with globes of blown glass, silver rings, wooden rocking horses under porcelain moons, rainbows, and lace. Out of a flurry of ribbon, yarn, paper, and paints, personal handmade cards, ornaments, and tokens are exchanged among friends, a gracious popular custom in this artists' community.

Holiday spirits climb with the towering illuminated spruce on the village green. At dusk on Christmas Eve, excitement peaks as Woodstock families and friends, skiers, and Christmas shoppers gather for a community festival in the middle of town. As every local child knows, Woodstock is a rollicking pause for Santa on the first leg of his great world journey. Into the frosty evening, an old-time brass chorus in top hats warms the crowd with Christmas carols, while boots of all sizes dance in the slush. Above the echo of singing voices, searchlights scan the skies from village rooftops, soon to discover the cunning old elf himself climbing down from the Old Dutch Church steeple, or inching through the crowd in an antique wagon behind a draft horse. Down the street clangs a big fire truck ushering in an entourage, with dancing elves waving balloon greetings for Santa. In the crunching exhilaration of the crowd, somehow every child manages to get a private audience and a stocking full of surprises.

Pervading interest in preserving an old tradition brings people into the snowy pine woods for decorative mountain greenery, cones, berries, and a family holiday tree. Evergreens, in dominion over the winter forest, climb the mountainsides, graceful white pines, and great hemlocks with feathery sprays of tiny cones. Verdant ground-cedar patches the forest floor; mountain laurel rustles bright green in the sleeping silvery hardwoods. Rugged spruce trees mount the highest elevations, where gnarled cedars with thick clusters of icy blue berries cling to the crags. An effort to climb out onto the cedar's wizened, sharply bristled branches to prune a sprig of its beauty conjures the legendary vision of the spirit of a chained sorceress said to be imprisoned there. In lower ledges, barberry obligingly yields bright red berries for shining Christmas accents.

Layered varieties of evergreens, contrasting silvery blues with dark rust greens, silky and brisk needles bound into an opulent wreath, are a visual feast. In some traditions the pine spray is regarded as a living symbol for the humble straw that cradled the Christ Child. For many in the cold northeast, the wreath decorates the entranceway until the first green of spring is revealed.

The Hearth

Community fires in the winter solstice night were probably a comforting custom with Indians, as with ancestors of many early settlers from Europe. Fire was still the center of the home for the first Dutch-Americans. Some stone dwellings, such as Woodstock's prerevolutionary farmhouses, were constructed out from a hearth wall, where the fireplace was built deep enough for the whole family to gather and watch for Kriss Kringle. On long winter evenings the family would huddle near the hearth, sing songs, drink cider, and play finger shadow games, while vibrant imaginations were kindled with the spit and glow of the fire.

The use of a cookstove is very recent in the history of human civilization. Until its advent around one hundred years ago, cooking was done in clay or iron pots suspended over the open fire. Baking was done in similar, covered vessels, placed in or near the coals.

Open-fire cookery creates a warmth for the appetite, and a unique woody seasoning of its own. The tradition is well preserved in the backyard barbecue; but the increasingly popular wood stove heater makes a great indoor supplementary cooking facility. Once the fire is moderately burning, the stove top is good for simmering soups, chunky stews, or a rich tomato sauce.

On a cold winter night, everyone gets warm hands and glowing faces reaching tongs into the fire to get the coals just right for roasting. Take a variety of vegetables out from winter storage—russet potatoes, beets, carrots, or parsnips—to bake in the wood stove.

After scrubbing vegetables, wrap them securely in heavy aluminum foil. With long-handled tongs or fork, place them into a bank of coals, between or under walls of simmering logs. Reach in with tongs and turn the vegetables once or twice during baking, testing for tenderness. Baking in the coals takes about 30 minutes, depending on the size of the vegetables and the intensity of the heat.

When tender, unwrap the vegetables and serve in a cloth-covered, warmed crockery bowl to keep hot. Roasted vegetables are delicious with fish or bean burgers, and garnished with butter, sour cream, salt, and pepper.

Gifts From the Kitchen

The mountains became settled with many ways of greeting the winter in ritual and custom, as in other phases of the seasonal cycle. Sleigh rides through crystal nights celebrated the holiday spirit a century ago, although there was little time for play. Back in the warm kitchen, candlemaking, a major winter chore, was an occasion to gather friends and good food. As personal Christmas greetings became more outwardly displayed, families made small ornaments from gourds and bits of cloth, or bound corn husks, and hard-baked kitchen dough, and set them in the boughs of the Christmas tree.

Nothing is closer to the old spirit of winter holidays and the garden harvest than homemade gifts from the kitchen. Packaged in imaginative containers, garnished with ribbons and paper, they are most personal and loving offerings.

The bundles of wild herbs that came into the kitchen through summer and fall are now medicinal, culinary, and decorative delights. A bouquet of tansy, barberry, and everlasting, tied with ribbon and bits of pine, attach magic to Christmas packages. Make a "tea" of an herbal mixture such as yarrow and red clover, for a tonic to stand up to the winter. Blend basil, oregano, and parsley for an instant pizza garnish.

Herbs that were carefully dried and promptly stored in airtight containers will have retained their color, medicinal value, and fresh aroma. Present an herbal mixture in an antique canning jar, sealed with rubber and bailing wire. Cut a square of brown paper for a label. Pen a simple border trim with a colored marker. Add a descriptive name for your tea or herbal blend, with a suggestion for its use. Attach the label with a bit of glue to the jar, and trim with a gingham bow to complete a gift with a warm, rustic feeling.

For special soup garnish bouquets, assemble bunches of dried parsley, rosemary, thyme, and basil from the garden, with peppercorns, bay leaf, and whole seeds of celery and caraway. Mix generous pieces of the whole herbs with the seeds in snipped, layered cheesecloth squares. Gather up with a bright ribbon.

Cluster the herb garnishes in a small trimmed basket with bundled cinnamon sticks and vanilla beans; or assemble a few of the bundles with heads of fresh garlic in a new cooking pot for an extravagant surprise. Add a recipe card for a winter vegetable stew.

Fragrant from your kitchen, homemade Maple Granola Supreme (see Index) is a great treat for a nutty snack or breakfast lover. Make a pound or two to fill a new casserole crock or vintage novelty kitchen container.

Shiny jars of homemade relish, chutney, or brandied fruit make cheerful, distinctively welcoming gifts. Jams, freshly made, or stored from the autumn, are traditional favorites. A circle of bright calico makes a decorative ruffle cap. Center the circle (5 to 6 inches wide) over the undisturbed jar lid. Secure with the metal band, or a length of matching ribbon, and fluff up the ruffle. Add a label made from contrasting colored paper.

A basket arrangement of Currant Bread, encircled with ribbons, or a Saffron Wreath bread, with a pint each of Raspberry Jam and Carrot Marmalade, makes a gift lavish enough to please an entire family (see Index for recipes). This combination will package well, too, for mailing. Wrap the bread airtight with plastic wrap; or use clear cellophane touched with a hot iron to seal. Use plenty of packing material embellished with pot holders or tea towels to protect the glass jars.

Whimsical creations and many classical fantasy creatures emerged from the kitchen of a Woodstock craftswoman to delight the Christmases of her two growing children, and adorn the holidays at the local rainbow store. Her kitchen clay has since evolved to porcelain, but the simple flour and water formula is established as a medium to delight anyone, very responsive and quick, for spontaneous artistic expression.

Mix 2 parts flour with 1 part salt. Add 1 tablespoon oil and 1 cup water for every 3 cups of the dry mixture. Add liquid very slowly, until a unified, malleable dough is formed. Knead for a few minutes, until pliable. This kitchen play dough has the best texture when used fresh. However, it will keep well in a plastic container in the refrigerator.

Simple ornaments can be made by rolling out the dough and cutting shapes with cookie cutters. Make ducks, Santas, gingerbread people, or reindeer, and engrave an outline or texture with a sharp tool, such as a nut pick.

Unique figures for the tree, tiny elves, owls, or angels, and scenic reliefs for wall hangings can be made from dough, according to your imagination. Press a quantity of dough into ¼- to ½-inch thickness, and mold, with your fingers, slicing and texturing with a small steel paring knife or X-acto blade. Interesting textures can be made from many household items, pressed into the surface. A favorite gimmick is to pass a small quantity of dough through a garlic press to create little tangled ropes that make a great illusion of hair. Join all the extra parts or layers to the original surface with additional moisture.

Keep the dough ornament on a good-size piece of aluminum foil to allow for easy transfer. Cover the dough carefully with a piece of plastic to avoid drying out between work sessions.

When creations have been completed, cut and trim edges if necessary. Insert a small piece of U-shaped wire into the center back for hanging. Set the ornament aside to dry slightly at room temperature (about 12 to 24 hours). Transfer to a baking sheet and bake in a 200-degree F. oven to complete drying (6 to 10 hours). The back of the ornament should feel dry and firm when sufficiently baked.

Paint ornament cookies or wall hangings with acrylic paints. Dilute colors to get a tinted quality, and allow some natural cookie color to come through. Apply a thin coat of varnish to all surfaces when the paint is dry. Varnishing can be repeated for additional protection. Dough creations keep best if wrapped and stored airtight between holiday seasons.

Portions of unbaked craft dough can be colored for delightful everyday play of young children. Add food coloring to the water at the initial mixing, or knead color into small portions of pre-pared dough. Children like their own store of different-colored dough to build monsters, roads and bridges, or animals, and then tear them down to blobs again. When dough ages and becomes oozy, get more play hours by kneading in a little more flour.

Winter Garden

Fragrances of fellowship and food flash across dark December chill and settle in warm memory. Christmas comes and passes, a diamond in the snow.

In an evening's transformation, the old year is buried. Snow falls through dusky, thickening silence. Filling crevices of bark and rock, drifts pile gently over standing dried weeds and trees, and warmly against the house. In an enchanted morning, ponderous black tree figures march obliquely with narrow shadows, rigid against endless rising, falling white.

In the ghostly garden, the clumsy cold frame, once walled splendidly with thick layers of leaves and fat red tomatoes, now stands shabbily deserted. Weather-worn corn stalks shiver over clumps of dead marigolds in a forlorn landscape. Bits of wire from pea supports lie woven in the white blanket where they yielded to summer's eager vines. Under layers of leaves and ice, the garden sleeps in a dream of nimble hands stirring worms and warm air in the soft nursing soil.

One hopeful, sunny January morning, your feet propped near the fire, the brightly colored seed catalogues are opened. A comfortable pleasure to start the year anew with a basket of last year's leftover seed packets, a pencil, bit of graph paper, and notebook, to plan a new garden again.

The mastery of cold compels discipline and personal reflection. On a dark afternoon, we draw the toboggan full of firewood in a gentle slush across the snow. The wind turns in the evergreens. The still air hangs an icy veil across the deep of winter. We watch, cloistered around the fire, from bright inner worlds. Feed the fire; nurture the inside garden, the family and home.

The natives who lived in the Hudson Valley plains for hundreds of generations must have regarded the mountains with greatest awe in winter. In shadows of darkening days, the craggy mountain peaks and dark gorges speak with fierce squalls, unceasing, thick snowfalls, and in solemn ice forests, a terrifying hush.

Catskill winters have historically been a time of scarcity and hardship. Early settlers faced death with minimal or no provisions in their first winters among the craggy rocks and knotted forests. As fierce winds shook the trees, and thick ice covered all berries, roots, and water, people were forced to trust the strange, but resourceful natives for help. Many Americans were birthed into the fleece of borrowed fur pelts in makeshift shelters, as anxious newcomers appealed to the Indians for the secrets of rocks, streams, seeds, herbs, and animals.

Success in survival evolved through years of shifting industry and high land values in the Catskills. In our time there are still year-round local residents who struggle. Land-poor old stock families, displaced merchants, laborers, and settlements of aspiring musicians and artists face hardship with every winter. Farm animals and old cars need attention in ice-bound mornings. Snowbanks and steep hills are still economic obstacles. There are always sleeping children to keep warm, and water supplies to keep from freezing. There is firewood to saw, chop, and carry. Winter's sparkling severity sculpts an economy of mind, and burns the inner fires stronger.

In the spirit of survival, an effort to preserve a bit of summer's greenery in a simple kitchen garden will enliven any difficult winter. Pots of basil, parsley, chives, and thyme grace a sunny window, and freshly flavor winter vegetables, stews, and salads all season, while feasters delight in the resourcefulness of the cook. Fresh herbs do as well as any house plant, requiring sunlight, regular waterings, and occasional drops of fish or seaweed emulsion for healthy growth.

A steady supply of sprouting beans and seeds completes a winter kitchen garden. Any dried garden beans can be sprouted for salad or stir-frying. Soak the dried beans (lentils, too) in water to cover for about 36 hours, changing the water 3 or 4 times during that period. Drain and place beans in a canning jar with layers of cheesecloth fitted across the top and secured under the screw-on band. Allow plenty of space for beans to grow; they increase their volume as much as 7 times.

Place the jar in a dark, cool place. Rinse larger beans frequently, at least 4 to 5 times daily, pouring fresh water through the cheesecloth, shaking to circulate well, and then draining back out. Continue this process for 4 to 5 days, until beans show healthy, fat sprouts. Refrigerate until ready to use. Tiny alfalfa sprouts require less initial soaking, about 12 hours, and less frequent rinsing to sprout easily.

As descendants of early settlers became shrewd, obtaining dominion over the wilderness, they could begin to regard winter as Master in a grand scheme of the seasons. Freezing noticeably invigorated the vegetation, and pruned the spirit, to encourage a flourishing spring. Farmers came to recognize snow as a poor man's nitrogen; its natural insulation protection for soil and perennials. Homesteaders discovered that often in the most severe February, yielding soil waited under the deep snow, ready for an early garden nursery.

In these last days of winter, many gardeners look forward to starting garden plants indoors. With a simple indoor nursery scheme, you can anticipate a longer garden season, enjoying lettuce and tomato salads and herbed steamed zucchini at midsummer. Zinnias and asters will be ready to beautify garden borders, and the scent of blooming marigolds to discourage pests in the ripening brassicas. As soon as the ground thaws, rich garden soil can be dug and brought inside. A quantity of vermiculite mixed into the soil will allow good drainage and oxygen circulation for the new seedlings. The soil mixture can be scooped into paper cups or cartons for individual plants, or spread into flats, large basins, or shallow wooden boxes for sowing in rows. Once seeds have been deposited, the soil must be kept moist. Daily waterings will help ensure germination. A light plastic cover will hold moisture, but covered flats must be watched carefully for any sign of mold. Removing the plastic for short periods to allow circulation of air will keep a healthy environment. With the first sign of green, the flats should be placed in southern windows, where full sunlight will encourage vigorous growth.

Many vegetable varieties actually thrive on transplanting. Seedlings in the brassica family, such as broccoli, cauliflower, and cabbage, which enjoy the cold weather, can be set out in the garden about 6 weeks after germination. Other seedlings can be set into the cold frame for 2 or 3 additional weeks of extra protection, to harden off.

Once the ground has warmed in the spring, these last seedlings can be transplanted, along with the sowing of a full choice of garden seeds, as nature unfolds the pleasures of a new annual cycle.

WINTER ROAST:
Winter Recipes & Menus

CHESTNUT PÂTÉ
Yield: Approximately 2 cups

1½ pounds fresh chestnuts
1½ cups diced celery
1 small carrot, chopped
1 small onion, chopped
1 small potato, chopped
3 cups boiling water
¼ cup chopped fresh parsley
1 teaspoon dried thyme
1 teaspoon dried basil
Salt and pepper to taste
½ cup sweet butter, softened
½ cup heavy cream

Slash chestnuts with an X on their flat sides. Place chestnuts in a saucepan, and cover with water. Bring to a boil, reduce heat, and simmer for about 10 minutes, covered. Drain and cool. Peel and skin the chestnuts. Set aside.

To 3 cups boiling water, add the celery, carrot, onion, and potato. Reduce heat and simmer for 20 minutes. Add the herbs and simmer for 15 minutes more. Season to taste. Strain the stock through a colander, pressing out as much liquid as possible. Measure 2 cups of stock into a saucepot. If necessary, supplement stock with water.

Put chestnuts into the pot of vegetable stock. Simmer slowly for about 45 minutes, until chestnuts are very tender. Drain, and grind the chestnuts as fine as possible in a food mill or processor. (Remaining vegetable stock can be reserved for future use in a soup or stew.)

Place the ground chestnuts in a deep mixing bowl with the butter. Work together with a spoon, then whip with beater until fluffy; season to taste.

Just before serving, stir in the cream. Mound pâté on a platter, and surround with bits of ground-cedar, holly, or pine. Serve Chestnut Pâté with thin, crisp rye crackers or Crusty White Bread (see Index), and a special brightly colored display of raw salad vegetables, radishes, carrot and celery sticks, scallions, etc.

CRANBERRY BROTH
Serves 4

1½ cups chopped prunes
2 large apples, cored and
  grated
3 pears, cored and grated
½ cup cranberries, ground

2 cups hot cider
¼ cup orange juice
¼ cup water
¾ tablespoon chopped
  cranberries

FOR GARNISH: Sour cream, cranberry pieces, 1 scallion,
  slivered

Combine the prunes, apples, pears, and cranberries in a
3-quart enameled saucepot. Add the cider, stir well, and heat.
Cover partially. Simmer 5 minutes, then gently add the orange
juice and water. Simmer 15 minutes over low heat.

Strain and purée the cooked fruit mixture through a food mill
into another pot or bowl, reserving all liquids. Discard pulp.
Add the chopped cranberries (reserving a few for garnish) and
gently heat, about 3 minutes.

Spoon into individual bowls. Add a dollop of sour cream, a
few fresh red cranberry pieces, and slivers of green scallion. Serve
warm.

HEARTY POTATO SOUP
Serves 8

3½ pounds potatoes
2 cups powdered milk
4 tablespoons butter
2 tablespoons salt
Pepper to taste
¾ pound cottage cheese

About 2 cups milk
3 teaspoons minced fresh or
  frozen basil, or 1 teaspoon
  dried, crushed
¾ cup sour cream

Leave potatoes unpeeled if they are clean and smooth. Wash
and cut up potatoes to equal at least 2 quarts. Place cut potatoes
in a large kettle; cover with ample water and cook until tender,
about 20 minutes.

Partially mash the undrained cooked potatoes in the cooking
water, leaving some small chunks. Add powdered milk and butter to achieve desired richness. Add salt, and pepper to taste.

Place cottage cheese in the blender. Process with a little soup
liquid and some of the milk until very smooth, then add to the
kettle. Add basil. Add more of the milk to thin the soup to
desired consistency. Correct seasoning. Gently reheat: do not
boil. Add sour cream just before serving. Serve with a pot of
hot greens and warm corn bread with thick maple syrup.

CREAM OF TOMATO SOUP
Serves 4–6

4 cups peeled, chopped tomatoes
1 tablespoon chopped onion
¼ teaspoon celery seed
1 small bay leaf
2 cloves
4 tablespoons butter
4 tablespoons flour
1½ teaspoons salt
Dash of pepper
3 cups milk
3 tablespoons Cognac (*optional*)
⅓ cup cream (*optional*)

FOR GARNISH: Chopped fresh parsley, chives, or watercress

Cook tomatoes and onions with seasonings for about 15 minutes, in their own juices, over low heat. Press through a sieve.

Meanwhile, heat butter in a heavy saucepot, stir in flour, salt, and pepper, and cook for a minute, stirring constantly. Remove from heat and add milk, stirring until well blended. Add Cognac, if desired. Return to low heat, and cook until thick and smooth, stirring constantly.

Reheat tomato pulp and add to hot white sauce very slowly to avoid separation. Add cream, if desired, but do not reheat after this addition. Serve immediately, with a garnish of chopped parsley, chives, or watercress.

SPICY SPLIT-PEA SOUP
Serves 4

This is a very aromatic, appetizing pot of soup to have simmering on the wood stove.

1 pound green or yellow split peas
1 quart water
3 large garlic cloves, chopped
1 cup chopped carrots
1 cup chopped onion
½ cup chopped celery
½–1 dried hot pepper (depending on hotness), chopped, or ½
  teaspoon cayenne pepper
3 tablespoons olive oil
About 3 tablespoons tamari soy sauce or to taste
2–3 quarts water
1 teaspoon salt
Chopped fresh parsley
Freshly ground black pepper

Both yellow and green peas offer interesting options for the taste and color of Spicy Split-Pea Soup. Soak the peas for a few hours or overnight to shorten cooking time. For an even faster preparation, instead of soaking, bring the peas and 1 quart water to a boil in a covered pot; remove from heat after a minute or so and let sit for an hour.

Drain peas and set aside. In a large Dutch oven or pot with cover, sauté the rest of the vegetables with the oil. When onion is transparent, about 10 minutes, add the peas. Stir them until they are coated with oil. Add the tamari, 2 quarts water, and salt. Bring to a boil, reduce heat, and simmer for about an hour. Check on the liquid, adding more if necessary.

When peas are soft, add parsley and pepper. Check other seasonings: salt, cayenne, tamari. The soup can be puréed in the blender at this point, or served with the appealing thick texture of the plumped peas.

WINTER GARDEN BARLEY SOUP
Serves 6

STOCK:
4 tablespoons oil
3 stalks celery, diced
1 large carrot, diced
3 medium potatoes, diced
2 medium onions, diced
1 bay leaf
1 teaspoon celery seed
3½ quarts boiling water
4 tablespoons dried split peas
Salt to taste
Freshly ground black pepper
1 tablespoon tamari soy sauce

SOUP:
¼ cup dried wild mushroom
   pieces
2 tablespoons oil
2 tablespoons butter
1 onion, chopped
1 medium carrot, finely
   chopped
1 large stalk celery, finely
   chopped
¾ cup barley
4 ounces fresh mushrooms,
   sliced
1 cup frozen lima beans
2 tablespoons whole wheat
   flour
Tamari soy sauce
Salt
Freshly ground black pepper

FOR GARNISH: Chopped fresh parsley and dill

TO MAKE STOCK: Place oil in a large heavy soup pot. Drop in the diced vegetables and sauté gently about 3 minutes. Add bay leaf and celery seed. Stir around, then pour in the boiling water. Add the split peas and gently simmer, partially covered for 45 minutes to 1 hour. Season with salt, pepper, and tamari. Mash the vegetables into the stock. Strain into another large pot through a coarse sieve or colander, lightly pressing to get all possible liquid. Return to a simmer.

Place dried mushrooms in a small bowl. Pour 2 cups of hot stock over them. Leave to soak for 20 minutes. Remove and chop the mushrooms very fine, reserving liquid.

Heat 1 tablespoon oil and 1 tablespoon butter together in large heavy pot. Add the chopped onion, carrot, and celery. Gently cook together for about 10 minutes. Pour simmering stock over the sautéed vegetables. Add the dried mushrooms, their soaking liquid, and the barley. Gently simmer, partially covered, about 45 minutes.

Heat remaining oil and butter in a pan. Add the fresh mushrooms and sauté very slowly, until they are just tender. Remove the mushrooms from the pan with a slotted spoon, reserving the cooking oil. Add the mushrooms and lima beans to the simmering soup.

Stir flour into the remaining mushroom cooking oil. Heat

2 minutes, stirring briskly. Ladle some stock slowly into the roux, stirring constantly, to make a thick sauce, then stir this mixture back into the large soup pot. Simmer 20 minutes. Season with a little tamari and salt and with freshly ground black pepper. Serve garnished with parsley and dill, and warm, fresh bread.

ONION SOUP
Serves 4

1 tablespoon olive oil
3 tablespoons butter
5–6 cups thinly sliced Spanish
    onions
1 teaspoon salt
4 tablespoons tamari soy
    sauce
1 tablespoon flour
2 quarts water or Vegetable
    Stock (*see Index*)

1 cup dry wine, red or white
1 bay leaf
1 teaspoon chopped fresh
    thyme, or ½ teaspoon
    dried
Freshly grated black pepper
Chopped fresh parsley
French bread
½ cup grated Swiss cheese
1 cup grated Parmesan cheese

In a heavy Dutch oven heat oil and butter; add onions and stir to coat them with fat. Cover and cook very slowly on a very low heat for 30 minutes. They will exude a lot of liquid and get very sweet.

When onions are transparent and very soft, remove cover, raise heat, and, stirring frequently, allow the onions to take on a golden-brown color, about 30 more minutes. The liquid will be cooked down.

Add salt, tamari, and flour. Cook for about 5 minutes and add water or stock, 1 cup at a time, stirring with a wire whisk. Then add the wine, bay leaf, and thyme. Simmer for at least 30 minutes, or up to 1 hour. Add pepper and parsley, and remove bay leaf.

Onion Soup can be served like this, sprinkled with some grated Parmesan cheese.

To serve Onion Soup as a main dish to warm a cold winter evening, preheat oven to 350 degrees F. Place the prepared soup in a heatproof 3-quart casserole. Slice the French bread about ¾ inch thick, brush both sides with oil and sprinkle with freshly ground black pepper. Place slices on a baking sheet in oven. Bake for about 15 minutes on each side, or until lightly browned. Arrange the bread over the soup and cover all with the grated cheeses. Bake at 350 degrees F. for about 30 minutes, until cheese has melted and soup is bubbly.

TOFU STEW WITH DUMPLINGS
Serves 6

STEW:
1½ pounds tofu cakes
4 large potatoes
4 large carrots
1 large onion
½ cup olive oil
1 teaspoon curry powder
2 cups frozen or fresh peas
½ cup flour
¾ cup cold water
Tamari soy sauce to taste
Salt and pepper to taste
Dumplings (*see recipe below*)

Chop tofu, potatoes, carrots, and onion into large chunks.

Heat oil in a large Dutch oven, or a heavy pot with a tight-fitting lid.

Stir curry powder into hot oil, then add tofu and vegetables, except for peas. Stir until coated with oil and curry, then add water to cover. Simmer covered until potatoes and carrots are nearly tender, about 15 minutes.

Mix flour into cold water to make paste; add to vegetables, stirring constantly until stew becomes thickened. Add salt and pepper and tamari to taste.

Add peas, and drop the dumplings on top. Cover and simmer until dumplings are cooked, about 15 minutes.

DUMPLINGS:
Yield: about 6 small
1 cup flour (half unbleached white, half whole wheat)
2 teaspoons baking powder
½ teaspoon salt
2 tablespoons butter or oil
1 egg, well beaten
⅓ cup milk
1 tablespoon finely chopped fresh parsley (*optional*)

Sift together dry ingredients; then mix in butter or oil with a fork. Add egg and milk. Parsley is optional but very good. Mix well.

Drop mixture by spoonfuls into hot vegetable stew. Cover tightly and simmer until dumplings are done, about 15 minutes. They will rise to the top and puff up. To make sure they are done, pierce one with a knife to see if it is cooked all the way through.

CHESTNUT ROAST
Serves 6

2 pounds fresh chestnuts
¼ cup pecans
2 tablespoons butter
3 tablespoons olive oil
1 medium onion, chopped
3 cups chopped mushrooms
½ cup minced celery
3 teaspoons minced garlic
¼ cup minced fresh parsley
1 teaspoon dried thyme
Freshly ground black pepper
6 ounces tofu, mashed
4 eggs, slightly beaten
1 cup milk

1 cup heavy cream
⅓ cup sour cream
¼ cup Madeira
Salt to taste
2 tablespoons tamari soy
 sauce
Wild Mushroom Gravy
 (*optional, see Index*)

FOR GARNISH:
About 3 cups mashed
 potatoes
Paprika

Preheat oven to 400 degrees F. Deeply slash each chestnut with an X. Place them in a large roasting pan or on a baking sheet. Roast until the peels open, about 30 minutes. Set aside until cool enough to handle. Lower oven temperature to 375 degrees F.

Peel chestnuts with a sharp knife. Grind the chestnut meats in a food mill or processor to a coarse meal. Measure out 4 cups and place in a large mixing bowl.

Grind the pecans and add to the chestnuts.

Heat butter and olive oil. Add onions, stir to coat. Add mushrooms and celery, and sauté gently until just tender. Stir in garlic and herbs. Remove from heat, and season with pepper. Set aside.

Combine mashed tofu with the eggs, and next 4 ingredients. Season lightly with salt. Add tofu mixture to the bowl of ground nuts. Stir to combine well. Add the sautéed vegetables. Stir and season with tamari. Place mixture in a well-oiled 9 × 3½-inch tube pan. If desired, spoon a coating of Wild Mushroom Gravy over the top. Bake at 375 degrees F. for 30 to 40 minutes. The roast should appear browned and crusty around edges.

Remove the roast from the oven and place on a rack to cool slightly. Gently remove from pan to a large plate. Fill center with mashed potatoes, sprinkled with paprika. Serve with a pitcher of Wild Mushroom Gravy.

TOFU CAKES IN MAPLE SAUCE
Serves 4

This recipe for tofu is delicious served with Winter Vegetable Stir-fry. Vegetables for the Stir-fry should be prepared while salted tofu is standing.

18 ounces tofu
Sea salt
2 large eggs
4 tablespoons unbleached
   white flour
2 tablespoons water
2 tablespoons peanut oil
2 tablespoons dark sesame oil

1 tablespoon diced fresh
   peeled gingerroot
2 scallions, chopped
1 tablespoon maple syrup
2 tablespoons tamari soy
   sauce
2 tablespoons arrowroot,
   dissolved in ½ cup cold
   water

Cut tofu cakes in half, then slice laterally, sprinkle with sea salt, and set aside on paper towels for 10 minutes.

Using a wire whisk, beat together the 2 eggs, flour, and water to make a smooth batter. Dip tofu pieces in batter until thoroughly covered.

Place a frying pan over medium heat until hot, then add the peanut oil and fry tofu until browned on both sides. Drain on paper towels.

In same skillet, heat the dark sesame oil and stir-fry fresh gingerroot and scallions for a minute.

Add mixture of maple syrup, tamari, and arrowroot and water. Simmer sauce over low heat for a few minutes. Return tofu to pan, shake the pan, and turn tofu, spreading the sauce around on both sides. Serve at once with Winter Vegetable Stir-fry (see recipe below).

WINTER VEGETABLE STIR-FRY
Serves 4

Clean and prepare all vegetables and spices in advance, placing each ingredient in a separate bowl.

2 tablespoons sesame oil
3 cloves garlic
2 tablespoons minced peeled fresh gingerroot
¼–½ teaspoon cayenne pepper
1 cup chopped onions
1 cup thinly sliced carrots
1 cup chopped broccoli
½ pound snow peas

1 cup diced green beans
1 cup chopped sweet red pepper
½ pound mushrooms, sliced
1½ cups Vegetable Broth (*see Index*) or water
3 tablespoons arrowroot dissolved in ½ cup cold water
2 tablespoons tamari soy sauce

Heat large skillet or wok until hot. Add oil and garlic, ginger, and cayenne. Drop in onions, carrots, and broccoli and stir-fry 4 minutes. Add snow peas, green beans, and red pepper, and continue stir-frying 3 minutes. Add mushrooms and cook another 2 minutes.

Add vegetable broth and bring to boil.

Add arrowroot dissolved in cold water and tamari to vegetables. Simmer until sauce thickens and vegetables are cooked tender-crisp. Serve immediately over steamed brown rice, with Tofu Cakes in Maple Sauce.

ALMOND CHILI
Serves 4–6

2 tablespoons oil (cold-pressed olive, safflower, or soy)
2–4 cloves garlic
½ teaspoon cayenne pepper
1 tablespoon ground cumin
1½ tablespoons chili powder
1 cup each, chopped onion, celery, carrots
1 cup whole almonds
1 cup chopped green peppers
4 medium-large tomatoes, peeled
2½ cups cooked kidney beans (reserve ½ cup liquid)
4 tablespoons tomato paste
3 tablespoons dry red wine
2 tablespoons tamari soy sauce

Heat oil and sauté garlic until browned, then add spices.

After a minute add onions, then celery and carrots. Cook until tender, about 7 to 10 minutes.

Meanwhile, dry-roast almonds in skillet over medium heat until lightly browned, shaking pan to turn almonds and prevent burning. Add to vegetable mixture, along with green pepper.

Cut tomatoes into chunks and add to sauté. Add drained beans, tomato paste, wine, and tamari.

Mix thoroughly, cover, and cook over lowest possible heat for 40 minutes, stirring frequently and adding some of the reserved bean liquid as needed for desired thickness.

Serve with hot buttered corn bread.

BLACK BEANS AND YELLOW RICE
Serves 4–6

BLACK BEANS:
1½ cups dried black beans
½ teaspoon salt
1 bay leaf
2 tablespoons olive oil
1 medium onion, chopped
¼ teaspoon chili powder
1 teaspoon ground cumin
4–5 cloves garlic, minced
⅛ teaspoon freshly ground black pepper
Juice of ½ lemon

FOR GARNISH: 1 green pepper, minced, Half slices of lemon

YELLOW RICE: (*see recipe below*)

Soak the beans in water to cover for about 6 hours. Rinse, drain, and place in a large pot with enough water to cover. Add salt and bay leaf and simmer until the beans are tender, about 3 hours.

Heat olive oil in a heavy skillet. Add the chopped onions and sauté until tender. Add chili powder, cumin, and garlic, and stir over low heat about 1 minute. Add this mixture to the cooked beans. Return to low heat, and simmer until the beans are cooked down and thickened, about 40 minutes. Season with pepper and lemon juice.

Serve black beans very hot, over a bed of Yellow Rice. Garnish the top with minced green pepper, and half slices of fresh lemon.

YELLOW RICE:
Yield: 4 cups
2 cups dry short-grain brown rice
4 cups water
Pinch of salt
¼ teaspoon Spanish saffron (1 teaspoon turmeric can be
  substituted)

Place the brown rice with water, salt, and saffron in a 2- to 3-quart pot. Set over medium heat, cover, and bring to a boil. Reduce heat immediately and simmer, very slowly, for 45 minutes. It is best not to remove the cover and lose any steam before this time. When the rice is tender, fluff with a fork.

DINNER OMELET
Serves 2

¼ cup butter
⅓ cup chopped onion
1 teaspoon crushed dried sage
2 cups cubed firm whole wheat bread
4 eggs
1 cup grated sharp Cheddar cheese
Fresh Mushroom Sauce (*see recipe below*)

Melt butter in a large skillet, and sauté onions. Add sage, stir, and add bread cubes. Stir until bread is coated with butter. Set aside.

Make each omelet individually.

Heat separate omelet pan or small skillet. Beat 2 eggs well. Coat skillet with oil, and pour in eggs. Sprinkle ½ cup grated cheese onto the eggs; then add the bread mixture. Cover the pan tightly and reduce heat to very low, or remove from heat altogether. If the lid fits the pan well, the omelet will continue to cook. When the cheese has melted, and the eggs are firm, fold the omelet and slide onto a plate. Cover with Fresh Mushroom Sauce and serve immediately.

For second omelet, repeat procedure with 2 more eggs and remaining ingredients.

FRESH MUSHROOM SAUCE:
Yield: about 1½ cups
¼ cup butter
1 cup chopped mushrooms
2 tablespoons flour
1 cup water
2 teaspoons salt
1 tablespoon tamari soy sauce

In a skillet, melt butter and sauté mushrooms. Add flour to mushrooms; stir with wooden spoon until mushrooms are coated. Over low heat slowly stir in water and continue stirring until thickened. Add salt and tamari.

COUNTRY CABBAGE PIE
Serves 6

DOUGH:
¾ cup unbleached white flour
¾ cup whole wheat pastry flour
¼ teaspoon salt
¼ pound butter
½ cup (about) buttermilk

Blend flours and salt in a mixing bowl. Cut in butter coarsely, until mixture resembles small peas. Add buttermilk, a little at a time, gathering mixture into a ball. Chill, while making the filling and sauce.

FILLING:
1 tablespoon olive oil
3 tablespoons butter
½ cup sliced onion
1¾ cups diced cabbage
1¾ cups sliced mushrooms
1 scallion, minced
2 tablespoons minced fresh
   parsley

1 teaspoon dried tarragon
½ teaspoon dried marjoram
½ teaspoon crumbled dried
   basil
½ teaspoon salt
5 hard-boiled eggs

Heat the oil and butter in a large skillet. Add the vegetables and stir 2 to 3 minutes over moderate heat. Add herbs and salt. Stir around about 30 seconds and remove from heat. Chop the hard-boiled eggs and add to the vegetable mixture.

SAUCE:
3 tablespoons butter
2 tablespoons whole wheat flour
2½ tablespoons unbleached white flour
Salt and pepper
1 cup warm milk
3 tablespoons heavy cream

In a saucepan, melt 2 tablespoons of the butter, then rapidly stir in the flour. Add salt and pepper. Cook over medium heat about 1 minute. Slowly stir in milk, forming a smooth, thick sauce. Remove from heat and stir in the cream.

TO ASSEMBLE:
Preheat the oven to 450 degrees F. Pour the cream sauce over the vegetables. Gently fold together.

Roll out slightly less than two thirds of the chilled dough. Place it in a large, 10-inch pie plate or cast-iron skillet.

Pour the creamed vegetable filling into the pie plate, spread evenly, and dot with remaining butter. Roll out remaining dough into a 10-inch circle and place over the top of the filling, pinching edges together.

Bake for 25 minutes or until crust is golden brown and crispy.

SAVORY CORN BREAD LOAF
Yield: 1 loaf, 9 × 5 × 2½ inches

6 cups corn bread crumbs
¼ pound butter
1 large onion, finely chopped
½ pound mushrooms, chopped
2 teaspoons dried sage, crushed
2 tablespoons chopped fresh parsley
3 eggs
½ cup milk
1 teaspoon salt
Pepper
Tofu Gravy (*see recipe below*)

Preheat oven to 350 degrees F. Place crumbs in a large mixing bowl. In a skillet, melt butter and sauté onion and mushrooms with sage and parsley. Add to crumbs. Then stir in beaten eggs and milk. Add salt and pepper.

Press into large oiled 9 × 5 × 2½-inch loaf pan and bake for 30 to 35 minutes. Serve immediately with Tofu Gravy.

TOFU GRAVY:
Yield: about 3 cups
18 ounces firm tofu
½ cup olive oil
4 tablespoons flour
2–3 cups water or Vegetable Broth (*see Index*)
1 teaspoon salt
¼ cup tamari soy sauce
Pepper to taste

Chop tofu into small chunks. Heat oil in skillet and stir-fry tofu over medium heat until golden. Reduce heat and add flour. Stir until tofu is coated. Add 2 cups water or broth, stirring until thickened. If it seems too thick, stir in additional liquid. Add salt, tamari, and pepper to taste.

This gravy is also very good on mashed potatoes, rice, or toast and is popular with children.

SHEPHERD'S PIE
Serves 4–6

2–3 cloves garlic
1 tablespoon ground cumin
1 cup chopped onion
2 tablespoons oil
½ pound mushrooms, sliced
1 cup fresh or frozen peas
3 cups cooked Kasha (*see Index*)
¼ cup tahini
1 egg, beaten
2 tablespoons tamari soy sauce
4 medium potatoes, cooked with skins
¾ cup milk
6 tablespoons butter
2 tablespoons chopped fresh parsley
Freshly ground black pepper
Paprika

FOR GARNISH:
Sour cream

Preheat oven to 400 degrees F. In a skillet, sauté garlic, cumin, and onion in oil until onion is transparent. Add mushrooms, and after a minute, remove from heat.

Combine onion mixture with peas, cooked kasha, tahini, egg, and tamari. Spread into buttered 2-quart casserole.

Mash cooked potatoes with skins with milk, 4 tablespoons of the butter, parsley, and pepper. Spread evenly over kasha mixture, dot with remaining butter, and sprinkle with paprika. Bake until browned, 20 to 25 minutes. Serve with sour cream garnish.

CORN SCALLOP
Serves 4

1 pint home-canned corn (or fresh, lightly steamed corn)
½–1 cup light cream or milk
4 tablespoons butter
2 tablespoons whole wheat flour
½ teaspoon salt
⅛ teaspoon pepper
2 eggs, beaten
1 cup bread or cracker crumbs, whole wheat or rye
Paprika

Preheat oven to 350 degrees F. Drain liquid from canned corn into measuring cup. Add enough milk or cream to measure 1 cup. (For fresh, lightly steamed corn, use 1 cup cream.) In a heavy saucepot, heat 2 tablespoons butter; add flour, salt, and pepper. Stir briskly until thick roux forms. Cook 2 minutes, and slowly add corn liquid-milk mixture. Cook, stirring constantly, until thickened.

Remove from heat, and add drained corn. Slowly add beaten eggs, stirring to blend. Pour into greased 2-quart casserole.

Heat remaining butter in a skillet. Add bread crumbs and stir until all the butter is evenly distributed. Continue to brown 1 minute. Sprinkle the crumbs over the corn mixture in the casserole. Sprinkle with paprika. Place in a shallow pan of water. Bake 45 to 50 minutes.

Corn Scallop is delicious as a main dish, with soup and salad.

LIMA BEAN CASSEROLE
Serves 4

1 tablespoon oil
4½ tablespoons butter
4 scallions, chopped (about 4 tablespoons)
2 tablespoons chopped fresh dill
2 tablespoons sesame seeds
2 cups fine whole wheat bread crumbs
Salt and pepper
3 cups frozen lima beans
1½ tablespoons whole wheat flour
2 teaspoons dry mustard
1 tablespoon dried savory
¾ cup Vegetable Stock (*see Index*) or water
1 tablespoon tamari soy sauce
1 tablespoon honey
3 teaspoons lemon juice
½ cup grated Romano cheese

Preheat oven to 375 degrees F. In a skillet, heat oil; add 2 tablespoons of the butter. When the butter has melted, stir in the scallions, dill, and sesame seeds. Add bread crumbs and brown slightly. Season to taste, Set aside.

Meanwhile, in a covered pot, steam lima beans until tender. Toss with 1 tablespoon butter. Set aside.

In a heavy pot, melt remaining 1½ tablespoons butter. Add flour and stir to make a thick roux; brown gently and season. Add mustard and savory; then slowly add the stock, stirring until thick and smooth. Add tamari, honey, and lemon juice.

Place lima beans in a lightly oiled shallow 2-quart casserole. Pour the prepared sauce over the beans. Sprinkle top with bread crumb mixture and grated cheese. Bake 25 to 30 minutes, until golden and crusty on top.

FESTIVE LASAGNA
Serves 8

1 pound cream cheese
1 pound mozzarella cheese, grated
1 pound ricotta cheese
1 quart Winter Tomato Sauce (*see recipe below*)
1 pound lasagna noodles, cooked
1 pound mushrooms, sliced
½ pound pitted black olives, halved or sliced
1 cup grated Parmesan cheese

Preheat oven to 350 degrees F. Combine cream cheese, mozzarella, and ricotta in a mixing bowl.

Oil a large 14 × 10 × 2-inch baking dish. Layer all ingredients, starting with a little tomato sauce spread over the bottom of the pan. Add a layer of lasagna noodles, then a little more sauce, followed by the mixture of the cheeses spread evenly over all. Mushrooms and olives may then be added in alternating layers, followed by a layer of some of the Parmesan cheese. Repeat layers until all ingredients are used. Top with remaining tomato sauce, and sprinkle Parmesan over all.

Bake about 1 hour until golden and bubbly. After baking, let stand for ½ hour before cutting and serving.

WINTER TOMATO SAUCE:
Yield: about 1 quart
2 large cloves garlic
1 teaspoon salt
3 tablespoons olive oil
1 cup chopped onions
½ cup chopped carrots
½ cup chopped green peppers
1 quart home-canned tomatoes
¼ teaspoon cayenne pepper
Freshly ground black pepper
Fresh or dried basil or thyme to taste
¼ cup chopped fresh parsley

Chop garlic with salt and place with oil in a large skillet. Sauté briefly and add onions, carrots, and peppers. Sauté until onions are transparent. Add tomatoes, cayenne, and black pepper. Bring to a simmer. Cook until the liquid is reduced by half, about 10 minutes. Add basil or thyme and cook for 5 more minutes. Check for seasoning, add parsley, and serve.

This recipe can be successfully enlarged. In the summer use fresh tomatoes, and freeze the sauce. If home-canned tomatoes are not available, substitute good quality imported Italian plum tomatoes.

MOUSSAKA
Serves 6

2 large eggplants (about 2½ pounds)
1 cup unbleached white flour (or half unbleached white, half
   whole wheat; or half unbleached white, half cornmeal)
1–2 cups olive oil
½ cup dry white wine
1 pint Tomato Sauce (*see Index*)
1 cup grated mozzarella cheese
2 cups Medium White Sauce (*see recipe below*)
1 cup cottage cheese
2 eggs
1 teaspoon freshly grated nutmeg

Preheat oven to 400 degrees F. Cut unpeeled eggplants into
½-inch slices. Dredge slices with salt. Set in colander under a
weight to drain, about 30 minutes. Rinse and pat dry. Coat slices
with unbleached white flour, or a combination of whole wheat
flour or cornmeal with white. Heat olive oil in a heavy skillet,
and fry the coated eggplant slices until browned. Drain on paper
towels.

Add wine to tomato sauce. In a 4-quart casserole, layer eggplant
with tomato sauce and mozzarella.

Prepare a medium white sauce. Cool slightly, and add cottage
cheese, beaten eggs, and nutmeg. Pour the sauce over the layered
eggplant, and sprinkle with a few grains of freshly grated nutmeg.

Bake until lightly browned on top, 30 to 45 minutes. Serve
Moussaka hot, with a fresh green salad.

MEDIUM WHITE SAUCE:
Yield: 2 cups
4 tablespoons butter or oil
4 tablespoons flour (half whole wheat, half unbleached white)
½ teaspoon salt
Dash freshly ground black pepper
2 cups milk

Melt butter over low heat. Add flour, salt, and pepper. Whisk
until well blended. Brown for 1 minute and remove from heat.
Gradually stir in milk and return to medium heat. Cook, stirring
constantly, until thick and smooth.

STUFFED FLOUNDER ROLLS
WITH MUSTARD SAUCE
Serves 4

6 tablespoons butter
1 onion, finely chopped
1 teaspoon dried sage
3 cups corn bread crumbs
2 eggs, beaten
4 large fillets of flounder (about ¾ to 1 pound each)
Mustard Sauce (*see recipe below*)
Paprika

Preheat oven to 350 degrees F. Melt butter, add onion and sage, and sauté. Pour this over corn bread crumbs. Stir in eggs. Spread stuffing on each fillet, and roll the fillet, end to end, over the stuffing. Place fillets in a buttered baking dish. Cover with Mustard Sauce, and sprinkle with paprika. Bake for 20 to 25 minutes, until fish flakes easily.

MUSTARD SAUCE:
Yield: 1 cup
2 tablespoons butter
2 tablespoons flour
1 cup milk
1 teaspoon dry mustard
½ teaspoon salt
Pepper to taste

Melt butter. Blend in flour. Add 1 cup milk, stirring constantly until thickened. Add mustard and salt and pepper.

WINTER CABBAGE
Serves 4–5

1 onion, chopped
4 tablespoons butter
1 small head cabbage (about 2½ pounds) chopped and
    shredded
1 clove garlic, chopped
4 tablespoons Hungarian paprika*
1 cup drained sauerkraut

FOR GARNISH: ¼ cup chopped fresh parsley

* If Hungarian paprika is unavailable, use a pinch of chili powder or dash of Tabasco with regular paprika.

Sauté onion in butter. Add cabbage and garlic. Cook 10 minutes until cabbage is soft and translucent. Add paprika. Cook over low heat for 10 more minutes. Mix in sauerkraut and heat thoroughly. Remove to serving platter and garnish with parsley.

Serve this winter dish with sour cream and boiled potatoes or noodles.

CABBAGE AU GRATIN
Serves 6

1 head red or white cabbage (about 3 pounds)
4 tablespoons butter
4 tablespoons flour
2 cups milk
1 cup grated sharp Cheddar cheese
1 teaspoon salt
Pepper to taste
½ cup grated Parmesan cheese

Preheat oven to 350 degrees F. Grate or finely slice cabbage and pack loosely in a buttered 3-quart casserole.

Melt butter over low heat. Blend in flour. Add milk slowly, stirring constantly. When mixture begins to thicken, add Cheddar and stir until melted. Add salt and pepper to taste. Pour mixture over cabbage. Sprinkle top with Parmesan. Bake for about 45 minutes, until browned and bubbly.

SESAME CARROTS
Serves 4–6

2–3 large carrots
4 tablespoons butter
2 tablespoons sesame seeds
½ teaspoon honey
Freshly grated nutmeg
Few drops of lemon juice

Diagonally slice carrots. They should measure about 3½ to 4 cups. Steam until just tender, about 15 minutes.

Meanwhile, melt butter in saucepot or deep skillet over medium heat. Drop the sesame seeds into the pan and stir for about 30 seconds, just until they begin to pop. Stir in the honey. Add the steamed carrots and mix to coat them well. Lower the heat, and sprinkle the carrots with freshly grated nutmeg, and a few drops of lemon juice for accent. Remove from heat and serve.

CASHEW CAULIFLOWER
Serves 4–6

1 medium head (about 2 pounds) cauliflower or equivalent
    frozen flowerets
¼ cup raw cashew nuts
6 tablespoons butter
Freshy squeezed lemon juice

FOR GARNISH:
Fresh parsley sprigs

Preheat oven to 375 degrees F. Clean and trim fresh cauliflower. Place in a steamer or large pot with about 1 inch of
water, and steam until barely tender, about 15 minutes. If frozen
cauliflower is used, steam until thawed and just tender.

Finely chop the cashew nuts. Melt butter in a skillet over low
to medium heat, and add the cashews. Sauté gently for about
45 seconds. Sprinkle with a few drops of lemon juice.

Place steamed cauliflower head in a 10-inch skillet or baking
dish. Pour the cashew butter over the top, spreading around
well. Place the dish in the oven and bake until just lightly browned,
about 15 to 20 minutes.

Remove the baked cauliflower to a platter. Serve hot, garnished with small bunches of parsley around the edges.

KITCHEN GARDEN SALAD
Serves 4

Here is a pretty medley of vital protein-rich sprouts from the
winter kitchen garden—garnished with color from the root cellar.

1 cup mung bean sprouts
½ cup pinto bean sprouts
½ cup alfalfa sprouts
2 large radishes, diced
1 carrot, diced
2 scallions, sliced

DRESSING:
2 tablespoons dark sesame oil
¼ cup olive oil
¼ cup rice vinegar
1 tablespoon tamari soy sauce
¼ teaspoon grated peeled
    fresh gingerroot

Mix sprouts together and arrange in a small bowl, garnished
with radishes, carrots, and scallions.

Combine oils, vinegar, tamari, and fresh gingerroot. Shake or
whisk to mix well. Pour this dressing over sprouts mixture. Cover,
refrigerate, and allow to marinate at least 5 minutes before serving.

AVOCADO BANANA SALAD
Serves 4

½ head iceberg lettuce
A few chicory leaves
1 avocado
Juice of ½ lemon
1 large banana
Mayonnaise Dressing (*see recipe below*)

On a platter or in a shallow wooden bowl, prepare a bed of thinly sliced lettuce hearts and bits of dark chicory. Peel and slice an avocado and place over the lettuce. Sprinkle with lemon juice. Peel and diagonally slice a large banana and place across the avocado slices. Top with a few spoonfuls of Mayonnaise Dressing.

MAYONNAISE DRESSING
Yield: 1 cup

1 cup mayonnaise
4 tablespoons fresh lemon juice

1 teaspoon honey
Pinch of salt

Combine all ingredients and stir vigorously.

CRANBERRY RELISH
Serves 4

2 cups cranberries
¼ cup light honey
½ cup chopped walnuts
1 large Delicious apple, cored and chopped
1 navel orange, peeled, seeded, and chopped
Romaine lettuce leaves
Curly endive or chicory leaves

Coarsely grind the cranberries and place in a small bowl. Cover with honey, stir, and set aside for about 10 minutes.

Toss cranberries with chopped walnuts, apple, and orange. Arrange lettuce leaves on a small platter. Serve Cranberry Relish piled on the bed of lettuce.

BRUSSELS SPROUTS AND WALNUT SALAD
Serves 6

30 Brussels sprouts (about 1 quart)
2–3 heads soft leaf (butterhead) lettuce
½ cup walnut pieces

DRESSING:

3 tablespoons wine vinegar   ⅓ teaspoon Dijon mustard
½ cup safflower oil   3 cloves garlic, crushed
¼ cup olive oil   ⅓ cup walnut pieces
¼ teaspoon sea salt

   Trim Brussels sprouts, and steam until just tender, about 10 minutes. Wash lettuce heads, and shake dry.
   Assemble sprouts, lettuce, torn into pieces, and ½ cup walnuts.
   Combine vinegar, oils, salt, mustard, garlic, and ⅓ cup walnuts in blender jar. Blend well. Toss salad well with dressing.

WINTER GREEN SALAD
Serves 6–8

½ head romaine lettuce   1 large carrot peeled and
½ small head escarole   sliced
½ small head curly endive   1 avocado, peeled and
   or chicory   chunked
1–2 stalks celery, sliced   About ¼ cup Dark Garlic
                                   Salad Dressing (*see recipe*
FOR GARNISH: *below*)
½ red onion, thinly sliced
¼ cup chopped fresh parsley

   Clean and wash heads of lettuce, and shake or spin out excess moisture. Tear lettuce into large salad bowl. Add prepared celery, carrots, and avocados. Toss in a small amount of Dark Garlic Salad Dressing, just enough to lightly coat the lettuce. Top salad with onion slices and chopped parsley. Serve immediately.

DARK GARLIC SALAD DRESSING
Yield: 1 cup

¾ cup olive oil
4 tablespoons fresh lemon juice
1½ tablespoons tamari soy sauce

2 tablespoons sesame seeds, roasted*
1 large clove garlic, minced (about 2½ teaspoons)
Freshly ground black pepper
Minced fresh parsley, chives, or scallions (*optional*)

Combine ingredients in a jar. Cover and shake vigorously, until mixture is thick and creamy. Pour over salad and toss. Make sure the dressing is well mixed each time it is used.

CRACKED-WHEAT BREAD
Yield: 4 loaves, 8½ × 4½ inches

1 cup bulgur
2 cups boiling water
1 tablespoon yeast
½ cup warm water
2 tablespoons salt
¼ cup honey
1½ cups milk (can be sour)
½ cup soft butter or light oil
6 cups whole wheat bread flour
5 cups unbleached white flour

Put bulgur in a bowl, pour boiling water on it, and let sit for ½ hour or more. The wheat will swell as it absorbs the water.

Mix yeast and ½ cup water in a jar and let proof. Add salt, honey, milk, butter, and yeast mixture to cracked wheat.

Add flours, stirring between additions when dough seems workable. Knead on floured board, adding more flour as necessary. It will be sticky and take a while—at least 12 minutes. When it is smooth and elastic, place in a buttered bowl and allow to rise, covered, in a warm spot for 1½ to 2 hours, until doubled in bulk.

Punch down and knead for 2 minutes and let rest for 10 minutes while you oil 4 8½ × 4½ × 2½-inch loaf pans. Form bread into loaves and let rise again until doubled, about 1 hour. Preheat oven to 375 degrees F. Bake loaves for 35 to 45 minutes, until golden and hollow-sounding when thumped on the top surface. Set on rack to cool for 15 minutes before removing from pan.

---

* To roast sesame seeds, simply spread over bottom of a small, heavy skillet; place over medium heat and shake the skillet to keep the seeds moving as they roast. Remove from heat when a dark aroma begins rising from the pan, or as they begin to pop. Pour immediately into the other dressing ingredients, as the heat from the seeds spreads the flavor.

DARK HERB BREAD
2 small loaves or 1 large

2 tablespoons dry yeast
2 cups warm water
1 teaspoon honey
2½ cups whole wheat bread flour
2½ cups rye flour
1½ cups unbleached white flour
¼ cup olive oil
1 tablespoon salt
1 teaspoon ground pepper
¼ teaspoon cayenne pepper
2 large cloves garlic
½ medium onion
1 teaspoon dried rosemary or thyme
3 tablespoons chopped fresh parsley

Dissolve the yeast in ½ cup warm water, with the honey, and allow to proof.

Combine all flours and add yeast mixture, the rest of the water, the oil, salt, pepper, and cayenne. Mix well. Add more flour if necessary to make a firm sticky dough.

Chop garlic, onion, rosemary, and parsley as fine as you can and add to dough. Turn onto a board and knead until firm, about 15 minutes, adding more unbleached white flour as necessary.

When the dough is firm and elastic, place in a bowl oiled with olive oil and turn to coat top. Cover with a damp cloth and let rise in a warm place until doubled in bulk, about 2 hours.

Punch down, turn out onto floured board, and knead for about 5 minutes. Let dough rest for 10 minutes while you oil two 8½ × 4½ × 2½ inch or one large 2-quart bread pan or casserole. Form into loaves, cover with a cloth, and let rise until almost doubled, about 1 hour. Preheat oven to 375 degrees F.

Bake for about 40 minutes for the smaller, and 50 minutes for the larger loaf. When they are done, they will be brown all over and sound hollow when tapped on the bottom. Cool on racks.

SKUNK HOLLOW PUMPERNICKEL
Yield: 3 8-inch round loaves

From the kitchen of a rugged cabin on the dark bottomland, deep in the hollow below Cooper Lake comes an old-fashioned, slow-rising bread. Its steamy dark aroma survives now as a comforting memory of times and people gone from us.

2½ tablespoons yeast
3 cups warm potato water,
  refer to Raisin Rye Bagels
  (*see Index*)
⅓ cup molasses
3 tablespoons oil
4 tablespoons cocoa
4–6 cups whole wheat bread
  flour
1 tablespoon salt

2 tablespoons caraway seeds
3 cups rye flour
¾ cup raisins
Cornmeal

GLAZE:
Egg white

Dissolve yeast in warm potato water. Add the next 3 ingredients. Slowly stir in 3 cups of whole wheat flour, mixing well. Beat 200 times with a wooden spoon. Add another cup; beat 300 times. Stir in the salt and seeds. Add the rye flour. Turn the dough out on a floured board; let rest 5 minutes. Knead the dough for about 10 minutes, adding more flour until it is no longer sticky, but smooth and elastic. Set the dough in a large oiled bowl, and cover with a clean towel. Allow the dough to rise 40 minutes in a warm, draft-free place, or until it is doubled in bulk.

Punch down, and divide into 3 loaves. Knead ¼ cup raisins into each. Knead until smooth, and shape each loaf into a smooth round. Place loaves on an oiled cookie sheet that has been sprinkled with cornmeal. Oil tops lightly and sprinkle with flour to prevent loss of moisture. Let rise slowly in a cool spot for about 2 hours. (Loaves can be placed in the bottom of the refrigerator to rise up to 24 hours at this point.)

Preheat oven to 400 degrees F. Slash a shallow X on each loaf top. Allow the loaves to sit for 10 minutes at normal room temperature. Baste with slightly beaten egg white. Bake 35 minutes, or until loaves sound hollow when gently thumped.

SAFFRON WREATH

A very festive bread as a wreath or braid or rounds.

⅓ cup boiling water
½ teaspoon saffron threads
1 tablespoon dry yeast
½ cup warm water
1 teaspoon honey plus ⅓ cup
1 cup milk
¼ cup butter
1 teaspoon salt
2 eggs
2 teaspoons cinnamon
1 teaspoon freshly grated nutmeg
1 teaspoon ground cloves
1 cup mixed currants and golden raisins
7 cups (about) unbleached white flour, or 3 cups unbleached
    white, 3 cups whole wheat bread flour

GLAZE: Melted butter

Pour boiling water over saffron and steep for 5 minutes.

Dissolve yeast in warm water with teaspoon of honey and let proof.

Scald milk, add butter, ⅓ cup honey and salt and let cool. When mixture is about body temperature, combine with yeast mixture and add eggs, spices, and currants and raisins. Add flour, 1 cup at a time, and mix well to make a stiff dough.

Turn dough onto a floured surface and knead until smooth and elastic, about 7 minutes.

Place dough in a buttered bowl and turn to coat top with butter. Cover with a damp cloth and place in a warm spot to rise until doubled in bulk—about 1 hour.

Punch dough down and knead on a floured board for about a minute.

Cut dough into 3 equal portions and let rest for a few minutes.

Roll dough pieces into long slender ropes, about 36 inches long, as equal in length and thickness as possible. Form the 3 ropes into a braid, pinching them together and entwining them. (To even them out you may have to cut bits of dough off at the top and bottom; these can be rolled, coiled, and baked for a mini snack for yourself.) Join the ends of the braid together to form a circle. Place the wreath on a very large greased baking sheet. You can put a jar or glass into the center (well buttered, please), so the wreath will hold its form, for another rising. Let rise until almost doubled (about 20 minutes) and brush with melted butter. Remove jar just before baking.

Preheat oven to 425 degrees F. Bake wreath for 10 minutes, lower temperature to 350 degrees F. and bake for 20 to 30 minutes until golden brown.

Cool completely on a rack. Decorate with holly or other greenery and set out with candles.

For safe shipping, wrap the fresh, cooled bread securely in 2 layers of self-sealing plastic wrap. This can then be wrapped in heavy aluminum foil to ensure freshness. Then place the loaf in a shipping carton of slightly larger size and surround it with thick bunches of tissue paper to hold it in place. A fresh linen tablecloth or set of dishtowels as a bonus gift can be rolled and placed around the loaf in the shipping carton to add to the packing material. Sealed in brown paper and addressed, your beautiful bread is ready to send anywhere to delight someone during the holidays.

NUTTY CHRISTMAS STOLLEN
1 large loaf

A fancy, filled, and folded sweet bread from an old Dutch tradition. Some say stollen represents a sweet new Baby Jesus, wrapped in his blanket.

1 tablespoon yeast
¼ cup warm water
6 tablespoons honey
¼ teaspoon salt
½ cup milk, scalded and cooled
6 tablespoons butter, melted and cooled
3 egg yolks
2 teaspoons grated lemon peel
1 cup whole wheat flour
2 cups unbleached white flour, plus extra, if needed
1 recipe Nut Filling for Stollen (*see recipe below*)

GLAZE:
1 egg white, slightly beaten

FOR GARNISH:
Whole pecans

Combine yeast and water in large mixing bowl. Let stand 5 minutes. Stir in honey, salt, milk, butter, egg yolks, and lemon peel. Blend well.

Add whole wheat flour and beat thoroughly. Slowly add white flour until a stiff dough forms. Turn out onto a well-floured surface and knead 10 minutes, adding more white flour as necessary. Place dough in an oiled bowl, turn to coat with oil, cover with a cloth, and set aside to rise 1½ hours.

Punch down and knead again to remove all bubbles from the dough. Roll out into a 10- to 12-inch oval. Place on an oiled baking sheet. Mound Nut Filling for Stollen lengthwise on half the dough, within 1½ inches of edge. Fold other half over the mound. Pat edge gently into place with heel of hand.

Cover with a cloth and let rise for 30 minutes. Preheat oven to 325 degrees F.

Gently brush dough with beaten egg white, and decorate edge with a few whole pecans. Bake 45 minutes, until well browned. Set on a rack to cool.

For a special holiday morning, serve Nutty Christmas Stollen warm, with a little shiny icing and a bottle of champagne. Set the stollen on an oval platter and surround with small red candles.

Icing can be made by whipping butter until very light, then sweetening it slightly with honey.

The soft, moist texture of Nutty Christmas Stollen lends itself to being made ahead of the holidays and successfully frozen. Its long, flat shape is convenient for secure packaging and sending through the mail.

For mailing, wrap stollen as described for Saffron Wreath. Add a small antique linen napkin and a few red candles to the package for an elegant, choice gift.

NUT FILLING FOR STOLLEN:
to fill 1 large loaf
1½ tablespoons butter
1 cup whole almonds
¼ cup walnuts
¼ cup plus 1 tablespoon honey
¼ teaspoon cinnamon
½ teaspoon almond extract
½ teaspoon vanilla
1 tablespoon dry sherry
3 large dried apricots
1 teaspoon lemon juice

Melt butter in large, heavy skillet. Add nuts and sauté over medium heat for about a minute. Add ¼ cup honey and cinnamon. Stir a few seconds, then add extracts and sherry and remove from heat.

Place nut mixture in a grinder or food processor. Grind to a coarse texture. Set aside. Grind apricots, 1 tablespoon honey, and lemon into a smooth paste. Stir into the nut mixture to mix well, but not thoroughly.

Spread mixture over dough as directed.

PLUM PUDDING
Serves 18

1 cup dry whole wheat bread crumbs
1 cup hot milk
½ cup honey (orange, wildflower)
5 egg yolks, well beaten
½ pound dark raisins, chopped
¼ cup chopped black figs
2 ounces dried apricots, chopped
¾ cup chopped Brazil nuts

¾ cup chopped pecans
2–3 tablespoons flour
½ pound butter
¼ cup dry red wine
¾ teaspoon freshly grated nutmeg
1 teaspoon cinnamon
¼ teaspoon ground cloves
¼ teaspoon ground mace
1 teaspoon salt
4 egg whites, stiffly whipped

FOR GLAZE:
Honey, about ¾ cup
Kirsch, about ¾ cup

Place bread crumbs in a large mixing bowl. Pour hot milk over the crumbs, mix and allow to stand until cool. Stir in the honey and egg yolks.

In another bowl, place the dried fruits and nut meats. Stir in just enough flour to coat everything lightly, and then toss into the bread crumb mixture.

Work in the butter, then add the wine, spices, and salt. When all ingredients are well mixed, fold in the whipped egg whites.

Lightly oil 2 large or 3 small plum pudding molds. If these are not available, coffee cans with plastic lids may be substituted: three 1-pound cans, or two 2-pound cans. Evenly divide the batter into selected molds. Cover, and set on a rack in a large pot. Pour boiling water into the large pot, up to about halfway on the molds. Cover the large pot, and set over medium heat to steam for 6 hours. A standard canning pot works well for this process. Check the supply of boiling water periodically, adding more if necessary.

Remove molds from steamer; set on racks to cool. When completely cool, unmold carefully, baste on all sides with honey. Pierce slits into the tops with cake tester or slender knife. Slowly spoon about 3 to 5 tablespoons kirsch over each top, allowing each spoonful to soak down. Wrap each pudding in a kirsch-soaked napkin, then tightly in foil. Place in a box in an unheated room, about 50 degrees F., and allow to age for two weeks.

When the holidays arrive, remove the pudding, unwrap, and place on a small platter. Slice thinly, and serve with cups of creamy, thick, brandied eggnog. Plum Pudding may also be served warm, with traditional brandied hard sauce, made with honey.

MAPLE RUM CAKE
Serves 8

2 cups raisins
2 cups chopped dried apricots
2 cups chopped dried pineapple
1¼ cups dark rum
1¾ cups maple syrup
1 teaspoon lemon extract
3 cups walnuts
1 cup butter
4 eggs
2 cups unbleached white flour
1 teaspoon cinnamon
½ teaspoon ground mace
½ teaspoon ground cloves
¼ teaspoon salt
½ teaspoon baking soda

Mix fruit in a large bowl, add ½ cup rum and enough hot water to just cover fruit. Let sit for at least ½ hour, though overnight is best.

Preheat oven to 275 degrees F.

Add maple syrup, lemon extract, and nuts to fruit mixture.

Cream butter; incorporate eggs.

Sift dry ingredients together. Combine with the butter mixture, and stir into the fruits and nuts.

Butter and line loaf pans with wax paper. Use three 8 × 4 × 2-inch or two 9 × 5 × 2½-inch pans.

Fill pans and bake, with a pan of water in bottom of the oven, for 2½ hours, until a cake tester when inserted comes out clean. Cool slightly. Remove from pans and set on racks to cool completely.

Take 3 squares of unbleached muslin or plain white cotton and soak in remaining dark rum. Wrap cakes in cloths and place in closed container for two weeks. Serve well aged, with holiday eggnog.

CHOCOLATE-RASPBERRY FANTASIA
Serves 12

6 ounces dark semisweet
   chocolate
6 tablespoons coffee essence
   (1 tablespoon instant coffee
   in 6 tablespoons water)
6 eggs, separated
1 cup fructose*
1 tablespoon flour
4 teaspoons butter, softened

1½ cups whipping cream
Honey
1 tablespoon framboise
   (*optional*)
Confectioners' sugar
Raspberry preserves,
   about 1 cup

FOR GARNISH:
Whole fresh raspberries or strawberries
Long-stemmed dark red rose

Combine chocolate with coffee essence in top of double boiler and cook over hot water, stirring until smooth. Remove from heat and cool slightly. Beat egg yolks with electric mixer until pale yellow. Gradually add ¾ cup of the fructose, beating constantly until mixture is nearly white and forms a ribbon when dropped from beater. Beat in cooled coffee-chocolate mixture; add flour.

Position rack in center of oven and preheat to 350 degrees F. Coat bottom of 12 × 18-inch jelly roll pan with 2 teaspoons butter. Line with wax paper cut long enough to extend over edges. Coat paper with rest of butter, dust with flour. Shake out excess.

Beat egg whites in large bowl until stiff peaks form. Gradually add remaining ¼ cup fructose, beating constantly until stiff and glossy. Stir a quarter of the egg whites into the chocolate mixture. Fold in rest of whites.

Spread evenly in jelly roll pan and bake until it is lightly crusted and will spring back when pressed, 18 to 20 minutes. Remove from the oven, cover with a lightly dampened towel, and let rest 15 minutes.

Whip cream; sweeten with a little honey and flavor with 1 tablespoon framboise, if desired.

Dust 2 long sheets of wax paper lightly with confectioners' sugar. Loosen edges of cake with dull knife and turn out onto the paper. Spread with raspberry preserves, then whipped cream. Lay a line of raspberries (or sliced strawberries) along one edge. Gently roll up, and set on a long oval white platter. Lay a full, dark red rose along length of cake. Serve.

* Fructose, the essential fruit sugar, is available packaged or bottled in the supermarket dietetic section.

FIG-FILLED COOKIES
Yield: 2½ dozen

Here is a classic children's favorite.

PASTRY:
1½ cups whole wheat pastry flour
½ cup unbleached white flour
3 teaspoons baking powder
¼ teaspoon salt
½ cup butter
2 eggs
½ cup (about) milk or heavy cream
Fig Filling (*see recipe below*)

Preheat oven to 425 degrees F. Sift flours, baking powder, and salt together. Cut in butter with pastry blender, until mix is like coarse cornmeal.

Slightly beat eggs. Remove 2 tablespoons to set aside for glazing. Add enough milk or cream to larger quantity of eggs to make ¾ cup. Add just enough of the liquid mixture to dry ingredients to make a soft dough.

Divide dough in half. Turn a half at a time out on a lightly floured wax paper. Dust top lightly with flour, and cover with another sheet of wax paper. Roll out to a rectangle 16 × 9 inches. Trim to uniform shape.

Spread Fig Filling gently lengthwise over half the rectangle, leaving ¼ inch border.

Fold other half over the filled side. Seal by gently pinching edge to border. Brush tops with reserved egg.

Place on an oiled baking sheet, and bake 12 to 15 minutes, until golden. Remove rolls from oven and set on a rack to cool. Slice each roll horizontally into about 15 bars.

FIG FILLING:
to fill 2½ dozen cookies
30 dried Turkish figs
3 tablespoons honey
3 tablespoons lemon juice

Grind figs in food mill or processor, and mix with honey and lemon juice.

JAM TARTS
Yield: 1½ dozen

Enchanting little cookie tarts, with a special use for your autumn jams. Use a 2-inch fluted cookie cutter or any variety of other shapes.

½ cup sugar
1 cup (½ pound) butter
5 cups sifted flour
½ teaspoon salt
1 teaspoon baking powder
1 teaspoon vanilla
1 teaspoon lemon extract
2 eggs
Various jams, for filling

CINNAMON-SUGAR GARNISH:
1 tablespoon cinnamon mixed with 3 tablespoons sugar

Combine first 8 ingredients with your hands, form into balls, wrap in wax paper, and chill an hour in the freezer or at least 2 hours in the refrigerator or overnight.

Preheat oven to 375 degrees F. when you are ready to form cookies.

Using a lightly floured rolling pin, roll out dough about ¼ inch thick on a floured surface. Cut out shapes with selected cookie cutter—2 per tart. All dough trimmings can be rerolled until the dough is used up.

On half the rounds put a small spoonful of jam near the center. Dip your index finger in water and run it around the inner edge; this will help seal the cookie. Put another round on top and pinch edge tight with your forefinger. Place on an oiled baking sheet. Mix cinnamon and sugar and sprinkle with cinnamon-sugar. Bake until lightly browned, about 15 minutes. Cool on racks.

Jam Tarts are very suitable for shipping. Individually wrap in plastic wrap. Layer in a box or covered cookie tin with wax paper and tissue for extra security.

CARROT MARMALADE
Yield: 5 pints

4 cups diced carrots
2 lemons
2 oranges
1¾ cups honey
¼ cup liquid pectin

Steam diced carrots until tender.

Meanwhile, thinly peel the lemons and oranges with a sharp knife. Slice the peels into ¹⁄₁₆-inch-wide strips; cut the strips to 1- to 2-inch lengths.

Thinly slice the peeled oranges and lemons. Then cut into quarters, being careful to reserve all juices.

Place the prepared fruit with its juices and rinds in a 3-quart enameled pot with the steamed carrots. Bring to a boil and cook 15 minutes, stirring frequently to avoid scorching the bottom.

Add the honey to the carrot-fruit mixture. Stir well and simmer for 30 minutes.

Remove marmalade from the heat. Stir in the pectin. Continue stirring for 5 minutes. Pour into hot sterilized jars to ¼ inch from top. Seal with hot lids and screw bands.

STRAWBERRY SNOW
Serves 6

Celebrate the year's late winter fleecy snowfall with a treat that brings a bit of the enchanted landscape into the snug kitchen.

½ pint heavy cream
8 ounces whole (sugarless) frozen strawberries
½ cup maple syrup
½ teaspoon vanilla
1–1¼ quarts fresh snow

Pour heavy cream into blender. Add strawberries, maple syrup, and vanilla. Whip until thick, smooth, and creamy.

Gather a heaping quart of fresh, soft snow into a large mixing bowl, avoiding any hardened crust particles.

Pour strawberry cream mixture over the fresh snow, and stir in a folding motion with a large wooden spoon until all the cream and snow are mixed into a sherbet consistency. Serve immediately, in individual bowls. Delighted children will return for seconds.

VALENTINE CANDY
Yield: 8 dozen

CENTERS:
¼ cup chunky peanut butter
1 cup powdered maple sugar
1 cup chopped mixed nuts (pecans, walnuts, almonds, Brazils)
¼ cup chopped dates
¼ cup raisins, chopped
6 tablespoons butter, softened
1 teaspoon vanilla
¼ cup maple syrup

FOR COATING:
Lightly toasted grated coconut
Chocolate (*see Chocolate Dipping recipe below*)

Combine all ingredients and mix well. Chill slightly. Form into ¾-inch balls. Roll the balls in lightly toasted grated coconut, or dip in chocolate. Place the finished candies in individual candy paper or foil wrappers, and package in little boxes wrapped in red paper. A sweet surprise for someone you love.

CHOCOLATE DIPPING:
1½–2 pounds dark sweet chocolate
8 dozen Valentine Candy centers
Extra whole nuts

Chocolate dipping demands special attention to get a most attractive result. Dark sweet chocolate, actually semisweet to taste, is first choice and pretempered. It must be handled little, in cool dry conditions, and carefully kept at a constant temperature during melting and dipping. Candies resulting will be glossy and tempting, with fancy chocolate swirls on top.

Choose a dry winter day, in a cool kitchen, for candy making. Select a double boiler. Insert a small food thermometer, with readings between 80 degrees F. and 130 degrees F., into water of bottom pan, with face over the side for easy reading. Arrange top pan securely so that no water will splash out of bottom and into the chocolate.

Grate the chocolate over wax paper, by holding the block with another doubled piece of wax paper. Melt ½ cup of grated chocolate at a time in the top of the double boiler, over a constant water temperature of 88 degrees F. to 90 degrees F. When all the chocolate has melted over a carefully maintained temperature, Valentine Candy centers can be dropped one at a time into the pot. Slip a fork under the coated center and lift it out, drawing fork along edge of pan to drain off excess chocolate. Invert coated center on wax paper. Draw fork up over the top side of the candy to form a little swirl with the extra chocolate.

Keep water temperature under the melting chocolate constant, and stir the chocolate frequently during dipping. If the temperature should exceed 92 degrees F., retemper the chocolate by raising the temperature to 120 degrees F. Then place the pan of chocolate into a basin of water at room temperature. Stir the chocolate constantly until it cools to 85 degrees F. Return to double boiler over water temperature of 88 to 90 degrees F.

Keep your chocolate-dipped candies at normal to cool room temperature, away from drafts, until set, 15 to 30 minutes.

When most of the melted chocolate has been used, and the remains are too shallow for even, uniform dipping, drop extra nuts into the pot. Stir and remove by spoonfuls as chocolate nut clusters, placing in little improvised foil cups to cool.

Winter Menus

FIRESIDE SUPPER
*Cream of Tomato Soup
*Dark Herb Bread
*Black Beans and Yellow Rice
*Avocado Banana Salad
Pineapple Juice
*Fig-filled Cookies

CHRISTMAS BREAKFAST
Grapefruit and Orange Sections
Scrambled Eggs with Avocado
*Nutty Christmas Stollen
*Chestnut Pâté
Champagne

SNOW TRAIL LUNCH
*Winter Garden Barley Soup
*Skunk Hollow Pumpernickel
Butter and Assorted Cheeses
Mixed Vegetable Juice
Apples and Oranges

HOLIDAY FEAST
*Cranberry Broth
*Saffron Wreath Bread
*Chestnut Roast
**Wild Mushroom Gravy
*Sesame Carrots
*Cashew Cauliflower
Baked Russet Potatoes
Light Red Wine
*Winter Green Salad with
*Dark Garlic Salad Dressing
*Plum Pudding
Brandied Eggnog

* Recipe included in Winter section.
** Recipe included in Autumn section.

Index